Violence and Social Justice

Violence and Social Justice

Vittorio Bufacchi
University College, Cork

First published 2007 by
PALGRAVE MACMILLAN
Houndmills, Basingstoke, Hampshire RG21 6XS and
175 Fifth Avenue, New York, N.Y. 10010
Companies and representatives throughout the world

PALGRAVE MACMILLAN is the global academic imprint of the Palgrave Macmillan division of St. Martin's Press, LLC and of Palgrave Macmillan Ltd. Macmillan® is a registered trademark in the United States, United Kingdom and other countries. Palgrave is a registered trademark in the European Union and other countries.

ISBN-13: 978–0–230–55295–1 hardback
ISBN-10: 0–230–55295–1 hardback

This book is printed on paper suitable for recycling and made from fully managed and sustained forest sources. Logging, pulping and manufacturing processes are expected to conform to the environmental regulations of the country of origin.

A catalogue record for this book is available from the British Library.

A catalog record for this book is available from the Library of Congress.

10   9   8   7   6   5   4   3   2   1
16   15   14   13   12   11   10   09   08   07

Printed and bound in Great Britain by
Antony Rowe Ltd, Chippenham and Eastbourne

For Brian Barry,
Who taught me everything I know about political theory

Table of Contents

Preface   viii

Introduction   1
1 The Concept of Violence   11
2 Violence and Integrity   29
3 Violence by Omission   48
4 Violence and Intentionality   66
5 Four Faces of Violence   88
6 Why is Violence Bad?   110
7 Violence and Social Justice   128
8 Exploitation, Injustice and Violence   145
9 Violence for Justice   164
Conclusion   187

Bibliography   200
Index   212

Preface

I first became aware of violence as a philosophical problem on 11th September 2001. At the time of the fatal attack I was working in my office making minor changes to my undergraduate course syllabus 'Introduction to Political Philosophy', a course I had been teaching for many years, and which I was going to teach again within a few weeks. There was nothing unique about my introductory course in political philosophy, being the standard mix-bag of key concepts and thinkers: utilitarianism; JS Mill; Rawls; Nozick; feminism; communitarianism; Marxism, and to finish it off, a large serving of democratic theory. By the end of the day, everything had changed. I soon came to the conclusion that I would be doing a disservice to my discipline, and to my students, if my course in political philosophy did not at least try to make sense of the tragic events of that day.

In the end, I scrapped my course syllabus, and in 2001–2002 my 'Introduction to Political Philosophy' was transformed overnight into a course on the ethics of violence. For better of worse, this is how I got involved in philosophical questions of violence. In preparing my new course syllabus I soon realised, to my surprise, that there was very little on violence written by philosophers in the last 30 years, and even less by political philosophers. Sociologists, psychologists, anthropologists, political scientists have all been writing about violence, for generations, but contemporary political philosophers seemed to be almost universally uninterested in the concept of violence.

The aim of this book is to do my bit to counter this trend, and trigger some interest amongst political philosophers to questions of violence. I firmly believe that the two most pressing problems in political philosophy today are injustice and violence, furthermore that the concepts of social justice and violence have more in common than one may think. This book sets out to explore the common grounds between social justice and violence.

Over the years I have incurred a number of debts to people and institutions who have generously given me their time and support. In 2004–2005 I was awarded a prestigious research fellowship from the

Irish Research Council for Humanities and Social Science (IRCHSS), which gave me the opportunity to focus on my research for a year without having to do any teaching. Also, between 2002 and 2005 I was the beneficiary of two awards by the Research Fund of the College of Arts, Celtic Studies and Social Sciences at University College Cork. I'm very thankful to both of these institutions, without their support this book would still be 'work-in-progress'.

Over the last 4 years I have tried out my ideas on violence and social justice on many unsuspecting undergraduate students at my university in Cork, who duly responded by highlighting the many shortcomings in my work. There are too many of them to mention individually, but I'm very grateful to all of them for their patience while I was struggling to make sense of this difficult topic. In 2004–2005, thanks to the IRCHSS, I was able to spend two semesters as a Visiting Professor at two outstanding American universities: the University of Colorado in Boulder (August – December 2005), and Dartmouth College (March – May 2006). My colleagues and students at these two universities provided me with the ideal environment to conduct my research, a perfect mix of intellectual stimulation and sincere friendship. No one could ask for more. At Boulder I learned a great deal from Lisa Bates, Alison Jaggar, Claudia Mills, while at Dartmouth College Susan Brison, Anne Sa'adah, Allan Stam, Ben Valentino, made the process of writing this book as enjoyable as it could possibly be.

In the last 6 years I was also invited to present my ideas on violence at a number of universities. I am grateful to all the people who attended my talks at University College Dublin; National University of Ireland at Galway; London School of Economics; University of Colorado at Boulder; Dartmouth College; University of Kent; Williams College; University of Manchester. For constructive comments on earlier versions of some parts of this book, I wish to thank Federico Varese, Eve Garrard, Iseult Honohan, John Baker, Attracta Ingram, Norman Geras, Paul Kelly, Simon Kirchin, Felix Ó Murchadha.

On a more personal level, there are a few individuals who must be singled out for their support over the years. This book is dedicated to Brian Barry, who I have known since 1988. He has been a model for me ever since I embarked in this profession, not only in terms of his scholarship (which I know I will never be able to equal), but also for his commitment to political philosophy. For Brian, political philosophy has always been much more than an academic subject. What I have learned from him is that writing political philosophy can be a form of political activism. I have still much to learn about political philosophy, but the little I know, I owe to him.

Anyone who knows Brian Barry will know that he is only one-half of the Brian-and-Anni team. As a graduate student, while struggling to keep up with Brian's outstanding intellect, Anni was always there to give me support, and to make me feel special. Over the years I have become as fond of Anni as I am of Brian, and what they have given me, in their different ways, cannot be put into words. I am grateful that they are part of my life.

When I moved to Boulder for five months in 2004, my only contact in the city was an old friend of my wife, who lives in Boulder with her husband and three kids. Although I had only met them once before, I was welcomed in their family as a long-lost sibling. During my time in Boulder I ended up spending more time with this family than in my own flat. Their humanity and generosity is contagious, and they made my stay in Boulder a memorable and special experience. Beth Osnes is an incredible woman, being an outstanding mother, scholar, political activist and friend. Her husband, JP, and their three children (Peter, Melisande and Lerato) made me feel part of a family at a time when I was away from my own. If I have achieved as much as I did while in Colorado, it is in large part due to them.

In the 6 years that it has taken me to write this book, I have benefited from the constant encouragement and love of my wife, Jools Gilson-Ellis, who gave me as much time and space and support as I needed to bring this project to conclusion. I know she will be glad to see this book in print, also because it may finally bring an end to what has been an obsession for me. My tendency to raise awkward issues about violence at breakfast (and lunch and dinner), on a daily basis, week after week, month after month, for 6 years, will not be missed in our home. The fact that she was prepared to put up with it for as long as she did suggests that love can be a powerful antidote against violence. Our daughter Natalie Maya came into our world less than 2 years ago, at a time when my book manuscript was at the make-it-or-break-it point. The desire to spend more time playing with her was the strongest incentive to bring this project to closure.

I can only hope that my little girl will never experience the sort of injustice and violence that fills the pages of this book.

Different chapters of this book draw in small part on the following publications:

'Violence by Omission', in F. Ó Murchadha (ed.) *Violence, Victims, Justifications*, London: Peter Lang, 2006, pp.95–114.

'Two Concepts of Violence', *Political Studies Review*, Vol. 3, April 2005, pp. 193–204.

'Why is Violence Bad?' *American Philosophical Quarterly*, Vol. 41, No. 2, April 2004, pp. 169–180.

'The Injustice of Exploitation', *Critical Review of International Social and Political Philosophy*, Vol.5, No.1, 2002, pp.1–15.

I wish to thank the editors and publishers of these journals and books for permission to use the relevant material in substantially modified forms here.

Introduction

Violence and social justice

As we enter the twenty-first century, two major problems face humanity: the perpetual predicament of global social injustice, and the escalating level of violence around the world. Under the heading of global social injustice we find all the issues that have engaged political philosophers for the last fifty years or so, from perpetual human rights abuses to rising levels of social, political and economic inequalities to impending environmental disasters. The only difference is that while fifty years ago these subject matters were of mere philosophical interest, today the same issues have become a matter of unprecedented urgency. Violence in general, and political violence in particular, is also intolerably high, in all its forms, from sexual and racial violence to suicide bombers to state terrorism. Furthermore one's impression is that things are only going to get worse, at least in the immediate future.[1]

The aim of this book is to argue that the issues of social justice and violence are not unrelated, and that much more work needs to be done in political philosophy on the vast area where these two spheres overlap. In particular, this book will attempt to argue that a comprehensive study of the concept of violence can helps us to make sense of the meaning of injustice, while on the other hand engendering a more extensive commitment to social justice is the best (and arguably only) antidote against the rising level of violence.

The first task of a theory of justice is to suggest ways of overcoming or even eradicating injustice. And yet, contemporary political

1

philosophy seems to have forgotten about the concept of injustice. Considering the vast and increasingly technical literature on every aspect of distributive justice, from measuring liberty to picking out the just equalisandum, it is surprising how little has been written on the concept of injustice since Rawls's *A Theory of Justice* revolutionized political philosophy in 1971. One of the aims of this book is to re-instate the concept of injustice at the centre of our theorizing about social justice.

Judith Shklar gives a useful insight into injustice when, in *The Faces of Injustice*, she reminds us that victims of injustice often choose not to recognize the injustice of the situation, principally because of the degrading nature of being a victim. This is a precious insight. Injustice creates victims, and being a victim of injustice is degrading because it exposes one's vulnerability, which is indicative of a person's powerlessness. This suggests that injustice is the manifestation of certain power relations within society between dominant and subordinate forces, where the latter are vulnerable and powerless to the former.[2]

What is most interesting about the ideas of powerlessness and vulnerability is that these two concepts define not only the essence of injustice, but also the experience of victims of violence. Powerlessness and vulnerability are the common denominators shared by our dual concerns for social injustice and violence. And although injustice and violence are distinct concepts, their similarity on this issue can be revealing. In particular, what appears nebulous in terms of injustice becomes lucid when rephrased in terms of violence. Violence being a more extreme phenomenon than injustice, it is possible to see more clearly what is bad (and wrong) about injustice by exploring the phenomenon of violence. For this reason, the first five chapters of this book will be devoted exclusively to a philosophical analysis of violence.

Understanding violence helps us to recognize the true nature of injustice, as well as define the aims of a just society. Like violence, injustice can also be considered the disempowerment of persons. Like injustice, violence is also *prima facie* bad and wrong. This does not mean that the terms 'violence' and 'injustice' are interchangeable, or that the term 'violence' ought to be used polemically when describing an injustice – as suggested by those who champion the thesis of structural violence. Yet, since both injustice and violence can be defined from the point of view of the victim, understanding violence can help us to understand injustice.

There are two possible ways of explaining what is bad and wrong about an injustice. The first is to say that an injustice is bad because of the detrimental material impact the injustice will have on the injured party. This explanation, which echoes the great deal of attention economic justice has attracted in the literature on distributive justice, has some merits, but it is ultimately unsatisfactory. To account for the badness of injustice in terms of the unjustified loss of material goods that were rightly due to someone is not simply to misunderstand the tragedy of an injustice, but also to trivialize it. The alternative explanation is to say that injustice is bad and wrong because victims of injustice are humiliated into feeling powerless and vulnerable, just like the victims of violence. This is why the literature on violence in general, and accounts of why violence is bad in particular, is not only enlightening, but potentially highly beneficial to any theorist of social justice. If the aim of a theory of justice is to overcome or eradicate injustice, it is crucial to understand exactly what injustice is, and why injustice is bad. A better understanding of violence can facilitate theorists of justice to understand the true nature of injustice. A theory of violence is therefore a necessary component of any theory of justice.

The irony about political violence and social justice is that violence is one method of resolving political conflict, but conflict resolution is also the prerogative of social justice.[3] This suggests that the relationship between political violence and social justice is more convoluted than may be assumed, the two not always being mutually exclusive. Political violence and social justice interact on at least three different levels.

First of all, from an evaluative and perhaps normative point of view, the term 'violence' has a negative connotation, while 'justice' has a positive connotation. Violence is prima facie wrong, whereas social justice defines the priority of the right. This is why we usually associate political violence with the negation of social justice, as the history of imperialist wars and recurring genocides remind us. But it would be wrong to think of political violence and social justice as a dichotomy, since there are times when social justice calls for the use of political violence, as in the case of just wars, just revolutions, and civil disobedience.

While the justified use of violence during just wars and just revolutions is not a contentious issue, on the condition of course that violence is used appropriately and proportionally within certain limits,[4] the use of violence during acts of civil disobedience is a more controversial issue, which needs to be addressed. The philosophical debate on civil disobedience sees on one side those who argue that by definition civil disobedience cannot allow for the use of any violence, like John Rawls (1971) and Hugo Adam Bedau (1961), and on the other side those who are not opposed to the use of violence, like Michael Walzer (1970) and Howard Zinn (1968). In fact this debate is slightly misleading, as the real question is not whether violence can be used during civil disobedience, but instead what type of violence is legitimate to use. If violence is defined as an act that causes harm or injury to people or property, then most cases of civil disobedience involve violence, since much civil disobedience involves acts of aggression directed towards objects rather than subjects. The suffragette movement in England between 1903 and 1918 was not afraid to use violence as a way of getting its message across, and the Anti-Global movement today feels the same way.[5] Indeed apart from Gandhi, most advocates of civil disobedience are prepared to subscribe to some use of violence, albeit usually never against other people but only against property. This suggests that violence is not excluded from the armoury of those fighting for a more just world. The extent to which something 'wrong' can be availed of for the sake of something 'right' is one of the many question that will be addressed in this book.

This takes us to our second point. Violence has an instrumental value whereas social justice has an intrinsic value. It was Hannah Arendt who in 1969 argued that violence is by nature instrumental. Violence is a means to an end, unlike social justice, which is an end in itself. The vast majority of cases of political violence, and all the paradigm cases, would suggest that in the political arena violence is used as a means to an end.[6] Justice on the other hand is something we value for itself. This is not to deny that a just society will have beneficial consequences, in terms of the well-being of its citizens. But social justice is something we aim at as an ultimate goal. Once again, the question whether violence can be a legitimate means to the ultimate end of promoting justice raises its head.

Thirdly, although political violence can be employed for the sake of justice, it is also true that political violence escalates when social justice breaks down. In other words, the price for failing to promote social justice can be measured in terms of rising levels of political violence. There is empirical evidence for this phenomenon at both the micro and macro level. At the micro level, there appears to be a firm causal correlation between social inequality and higher levels of crime and other social malaise.[7] In 1996, Harvard and Berkeley published separate studies that examined income inequality in all fifty states in the United States.[8] Both studies found that the correlation between income inequality and mortality rates for all ages was significant. The states with higher income inequality have, amongst other things, higher rates of infant mortality, of homicide, of violent crime, of incarceration, of unemployment, of heart disease and of cancer. At the macro level, the experience of Sicily in the nineteenth century and of Russia in the 1990s clearly shows that we can expect the advent of organized crime, including the mafia, whenever state institutions fail to perform their primary function of providing protection for the person and their private property.[9]

At this point it is necessary to take stock of the fact that although violence is the essence of politics, justice is the first virtue of political institutions. Political violence and social justice are inseparable, two sides of the same coin. We cannot evaluate violence without a proper understanding of social justice, but at the same time an improved awareness of the concept of violence contributes to a better understanding of injustice, and therefore to the aims and scope of social justice. The principal aim of this book is to elucidate the relationship between violence, injustice and social justice. The fundamental thesis of the book is to show that at the core of any theory of justice there is a theory of violence.

Questions regarding the justified use of violence have always attracted great interest, from the just war tradition to the ethics of revolution and terrorism, from theories of civil disobedience to theories of punishment. Yet it is virtually impossible for any moral assessment to get off the ground without a clear understanding of the subject-matter that is being investigated. In the last analysis, moral analysis must necessarily follow a two-stage process. The first stage consists in a conceptual analysis of the subject-matter, where the aim is simply to define the key terms in question. The second stage consists in the moral assessment of the concepts defined in the first stage.

This book endorses this two-stage approach. The first five chapters represent the first stage, and their aim is to provide a neutral, amoral definition and analysis of the concept of violence. The subsequent four chapters will perform the second stage, where the concept of violence, as defined in the first five chapters, will come under moral scrutiny, and issues of justification will be addressed. The reason for adopting a two-stage approach is that, contrary to what some people assume, violence is not wrong by definition. To assume that violence is wrong would make violence a normative concept, in the sense that to characterize something as an act of violence would suffice to condemn it. But as Robert Holmes (1989, 37–38) argues, this view does not hold up well under scrutiny. It is crucial to distinguish between a concept being wrong by definition, and it being prima facie wrong:

> if violence is not wrong by definition, it is nonetheless prima facie wrong, or wrong all other things being equal, just by virtue of the fact that it is prima facie wrong to harm people.... while acts of violence are not wrong by definition, they are all of them prima facie wrong and in need of justification.

Chapter One will provide an overview of the many different attempts to define the concept of violence over the last 100 years. There are two dominant ways of thinking about violence: in terms of an act of force, or in terms of a violation. Those who define violence as an intentional act of excessive or destructive force endorse a narrow conception of violence (the Minimalist Conception of Violence), while those who see violence in terms of a violation of rights champion a broader conception of violence (the Comprehensive Conception of Violence). The strengths and weaknesses of both approaches will be duly considered.

Chapter Two will put forward and defend a novel definition of violence as violation of integrity. Being broader than the Minimalist Conception of Violence, but narrower than the Comprehensive Conception of Violence, this definition occupies an intermediate space in the existing literature on violence. This chapter will also argue that violence is, by nature, a social act, which ought to be defined within the logic of the appropriate social dynamics.

Chapter Three will suggest that there are two different ways of doing violence, which may involve either an action or an omission. While an omission is as much an act of violence as an action, the point will be made that from a moral point of view there is a difference between certain omissions and certain acts, even if they have the same consequence.

Chapter Four explores the relationship between violence and intentionality. The received view is that the intentions of the perpetrator of violence are the defining feature of an act of violence, whereby intentionality is the difference between an act of violence and a mere accident. I will call this the intention-oriented approach (I-O approach). All paradigm cases of violence are intentional, nevertheless it is possible for violence to be unintended. This chapter suggests three different ways in which an act of violence can be foreseeable but unintended. In an attempt to move beyond the intentional paradigm, it will be argued that the I-O approach should be supplemented by a new approach, namely the victim-oriented approach (V-O approach), where violence is defined from the perspective of the victim.

Chapter Five, which acts as a transition chapter between the more explicatory account of violence of the previous four chapters, and the normative account of the next four chapters, will present a typology of the concept of violence based around two key issues. First, whether an act of violence requires that the harm done must necessarily have been intended, or is it sufficient for the harm to have been merely foreseen. Secondly, whether the harm in question must necessarily be the result of a direct act, or can violence be done also via an omission. These two set of issues can be arranged as a 2×2 matrix, giving rise to four distinct faces of violence: violence as an intentional action; violence as a foreseeable but unintended action; violence as an intentional omission; violence as a foreseeable but unintended omission. A number of examples will be used to apply this framework to the concept of violence in general, and to political violence in particular.

Having come to terms with the concept of violence, the remaining chapters of the book will explore the similarity between an act of violence and what we consider to be an injustice, and therefore the relationship between violence and the aims of social justice. We will start with a moral assessment of violence. Borrowing from the extensive literature on why death is bad, Chapter Six argues that there are extrinsic and intrinsic reasons why violence is bad. Violence is extrinsically bad because of the experience of injury and suffering, although its importance has perhaps been exaggerated in the literature on violence. Apart from the harm of experiencing violence, violence is also intrinsically bad (the Humiliation Factor) to the extent that it makes the victim feel vulnerable and inferior to the perpetrator of violence. Experiencing violence can undermine a victim's self-respect and self-esteem. The Humiliation Factor states that violence exposes the powerlessness of the victim, making them vulnerable to the perpetrator of violence. The Humiliation Factor explains why violence is both bad and wrong, and in certain cases even worse than death.

Chapter Seven investigates the relationship between the concepts of violence, injustice and social justice. Given that the first task of a theory of justice is to suggest ways of overcoming or even eradicating injustice, this chapter argues that concerns about injustice should be re-instated as the starting point of our theorizing about social justice, and that a theory of violence helps us to understand what an injustice is, and why it is bad. Being a victim of injustice is degrading, in the same way that being a victim of violence is also degrading. Although injustice and violence are distinct concepts, their similarity on this issue can be revealing.

Violence being a more extreme phenomenon than injustice, one can see more clearly what is bad (and wrong) about injustice by exploring the phenomenon of violence. Understanding violence helps us to recognize the true nature of injustice, as well as define the aims of a just society. Like violence, injustice can also be considered the disempowerment of persons. This does not mean that the terms 'violence' and 'injustice' are interchangeable, and yet, since both injustice and violence can be defined from the point of view of the victim, it is through the lenses of violence that theorists of justice can understand the true nature of injustice.

The relationship between violence and injustice, advanced in Chapters Six and Seven, will be put to the test in Chapter Eight. This chapter, which focuses on the concept of exploitation, will argue that it is only with the help of a theory of violence that we can see more clearly what makes the injustice of exploitation both bad and wrong.

The literature on exploitation so far has focussed almost exclusively on the question of the circumstances of exploitation: it is the injustice of institutional circumstances that makes exploitation unjust. This chapter, by contrast, will investigate a different question, namely: what are the motives of exploitation? There are two different motives behind the act of exploitation: to secure an economic gain by using another person to one's advantage, and to humiliate and degrade another person for the sake of identifying with power. The latter is the same motivation we find behind an act of violence. It follows that the injustice of exploitation is wrong for the same reasons that violence is bad and wrong.

Finally, Chapter Nine asks whether social justice can be promoted through the use of violence, or in other words whether violence can be justified on the grounds of promoting justice. Two dominant arguments used to justify violence will come under consideration: the Identity Argument, and the Consequentialist Argument. Although both arguments are in part valid, and ought to be taken seriously, they are also found to be wanting. Yet it would be a mistake to jump to the conclusion that violence can never be justified. There are circumstances when violence can be justified, even extreme violence, but only in exceptional circumstances, and only if five principles are duly respected: Self-defence; Reasonable Success; Proportionality; Last Resort; and Gradual Progression.

In the last and concluding chapter, the question whether violence is the essence of violence will be posed. It will be argued that while it is misleading to see violence as the *essence* of violence, it is nevertheless true that there is a special relationship between violence and politics. The nature of this special relationship will be the focus of this chapter.

Notes

1. For an outstanding account of why social justice matters, see Barry (2005). As I write this introduction, in the British newspapers there is extensive media coverage of Sir Nicholas Stern's report on climate change. This long and complex report has a simple message, namely, that human activity (and intentional omissions) has raised the amount of the key greenhouse gas carbon dioxide in the atmosphere to unsustainable levels. If carbon emissions continue at the present level, we can expect global average temperatures to rise by 2°C above pre-industrial levels. This will have a profound impact on the planet, its weather and its inhabitants. Extreme

weather events and growing water shortages will put millions of lives at risk. Furthermore the impacts of climate change are not evenly distributed, with the poorest nations and its people suffering earliest and most. The Stern report can be found at: http://www.hm-treasury. gov.uk/independent_reviews/stern_review_economics_climate_change/ sternreview_index.cfm.

2. The same message is given extensive treatment by Iris Marion Young (1990).

3. See Barry (1995) and Hampshire (1999).

4. The *locus classicus* on just war theory is still Walzer's (1977) outstanding analysis, indeed his book has had an impact on the literature on the just use of violence during a revolution, as Geras' (1990) analysis clearly shows. For a philosophical account of the justification on revolutions in general, see Nielsen (1976-7).

5. The move for women's vote in England started in 1897 when Millicent Fawcett founded the National Union of Women's Suffrage. But Millicent Fawcett believed in peaceful protest. It was only after 1903, when the Women's Social and Political Union was founded by Emmeline Pankhurst and her daughters, Christabel and Sylvia, that the movement embraced violence. It started by disrupting political meetings, and escalated to include setting fire to churches, vandalising Oxford Street, smashing windows at the residence of the Prime Minister at Downing Street, setting fire to mail boxes, an arson campaign and slashing paintings at art galleries.

6. Not everyone agrees with Arendt on this point. For example Besteman (2002) argues that violence can become an end in and of itself, especially when used by citizens against the state or against each other for control of the state. We are told that the non-instrumental aspect of violence is most evident in the analysis of the cultural dimensions of political violence, which is the focus of Besteman's edited volume. The non-instrumentality of violence is an intriguing thesis, but ultimately it is not convincing. I am not denying that there are a multitude of ends that are pursued by the use of violence, sometimes even simultaneously and in contradictory fashion, but we must not confuse the thesis of the plurality of ends with the claim that violence is both instrumental and non-instrumental. To suggest that violence is an end in and of itself is unhelpful. Violence remains instrumental, even if there is more than one goal being pursued. Violence is a means to an end, even though the end is not always what it seems.

7. See Robert Pear, 'Researchers Link Income Inequality to Higher Mortality Rates', *New York Times*, Friday, April 19, 1996.

8. George A. Kaplan and others, 'Inequality in income and mortality in the United States: analysis of mortality and potential pathways', *British Medical Journal* Vol. 312 (April 20, 1996), pp. 999–1003. Bruce P. Kennedy and others, 'Income distribution and mortality: cross sectional ecological study of the Robin Hood index in the United States', *British Medical Journal* Vol. 312 (April 20, 1996), pp. 1004–1007.

9. See Gambetta (1993) and Varese (2001).

1
The Concept of Violence

Understanding political violence is a principal preoccupation for anyone interested in politics, professional politicians and social scientists alike, which explains why in recent years there has been an influx of books on the topic of political violence, widely defined. The proliferation of interest in political violence in academic circles is to be welcomed. In particular the empirically-driven output from sociologists, psychologists, anthropologists and political scientists has been relentless, impressive in its quantity if not always its quality.

In recent years the bulk of these publications have tended to be edited volumes based on ethnographic case studies rich in the exposé of violence in all its forms, from hate crime to genocide.[1] Generally speaking each case study is informative and revealing, yet the reluctance of the editors to ground the disparate ethnographic case studies on a shared definition of violence takes away from the theoretical value of these books. We may learn a great deal about specific acts of political violence occurring within certain cultures in different parts of the world, without necessarily having a better understanding of the meaning of violence as a universal concept. At best these volumes remind us of the complexity of violence, they do not help us to understand it.

One of the aims of this book is to argue for the need of a clear, universally valid definition of violence, to be formulated with the help of the unfashionable but reliable technique of conceptual analysis. In the last analysis, distinguishing a violent act from an act of violence (Chapter One), attempting a comprehensive definition of violence (Chapter Two), deciding whether omissions that allow harm to occur should count as acts of violence (Chapter Three), specifying the role that intentionality plays in an act of violence (Chapter Four), and highlighting the main features of the concept of violence (Chapter Five) is the sort of invaluable contribution that only philosophical conceptual analysis can make, bringing clarity and precision in an area of research still very much confused and confusing. Furthermore, it is only after the concept of violence has been defined, and its many obscure aspects clarified, that normative questions can be asked about the nature of an act of violence, for example determining why violence is bad and prima facie wrong (Chapter Six), revealing the overlap between political violence and social injustice (Chapter Seven and Eight), or establishing when and how violence can be justified (Chapter Nine).

For the most part this book will ignore the extensive empirical research on political violence, with the exception of specific examples throughout the book which only serve the purpose of elucidating theoretical distinctions or principles, and one longer specific case study on exploitation in Chapter Eight. The decision to restrict the scope of this work to questions of a more theoretical nature should not be interpreted as an indictment on empirical research, since there are some outstanding works in this tradition.[2] But it would be impossible to do justice to the full complexity of the phenomenon of political violence in one short book, therefore our scope will necessarily have to be much more modest, restricted to a philosophical analysis of the concept of violence.

One of the aims of this book is to propose and defend a new definition of the concept of violence. This task will be undertaken in Chapter Two, where an account of violence as a violation of integrity will be put forward. Of course any attempt to present a 'new' definition of a concept necessarily builds upon the previous history of this concept. The concept of violence is not an exception. Thus, the idea of violence as a violation of integrity builds upon two other well-known historical approaches to understanding the nature of violence. The first approach, which takes a minimalist line, defines violence as an act of excessive physical force. The other approach, which takes a broader line, suggests a definition of violence in terms of a violation of rights. These two approaches will be the subject of this first chapter. It is necessary to explore both the strengths and weaknesses of these two approaches not only as a mark of respect for all the important work that philosophers have done over the years, but also in order to show how a new definition of violence, as violation of integrity, goes beyond what we already know about the idea of violence.

The aim of this first chapter is therefore to provide the reader with an overview of the scholarship, over the last 100 years, concerning the concept of violence. Readers who are not interested in the history of this concept may safely skip this chapter and start directly from Chapter Two. But for those who have an interest in seeing how the meaning of a concept, such as violence, has developed over the course of the twentieth century, this chapter will cover the following areas. Parts I and II will start by investigating the syntax and etymology of the word 'violence', followed in Parts III and IV by an account of the two dominant ways of thinking about violence, respectively as an act of excessive force, and as a violation. Part V will suggest that these two approaches correspond to what may be called a Minimalist and a Comprehensive Conception of Violence.

Part I: The syntax of violence

It is important not to confuse 'violent' (the adjective) with 'violence' (the noun), since a violent act is not always an act of violence, and vice-versa an act of violence need not always be violent. As Harris (1980, 14) reminds us, 'the descriptive use of 'violent' concentrates on the quality, the character, of the act itself, while it seems that it is the consequences, or perhaps also the intended consequences of such acts, which lead us to classify them as acts of violence'. The term 'violent' is an adjective, which qualifies a certain act or person. When a certain act is defined as being 'violent', it means that the act has exceeded some generally recognized limit or norm.[3] If I brush my teeth with excessive vigour, causing my gum to bleed, I am performing a violent act, to the extent that some limit regarding how much force to use when brushing one's teeth was exceeded. The fact that I am brushing my teeth violently does not mean that I am indulging in an act of violence.

Similarly while most acts of violence entail violent acts, that is not always the case. Just as there are violent acts that are not acts of violence, there are also acts of violence that do not require violent acts. Slamming the door with all my force is a violent act, which may or may not be an act of violence. If at home alone I slam the door to my room in frustration, I am performing a violent act although not an act of violence. But if I deliberately slam the door on your

Table 1.1 Violent acts and acts of violence

	Act of violence	Act of non-violence
Violent act	Slamming the door on your hand	Slamming the door in frustration
Non-violent act	Gently closing the door of your cell and throwing away the key	Gently closing the door

hand, then I am performing both an act of violence and a violent act. And if I gently close the door to lock you into a cell, and I proceed to carefully dispose of the key leaving you to starve to death, I am performing an act of violence although not a violent act.

Perhaps what distinguishes a violent act from an act of violence is the degree of intentionality intrinsic to the latter. The question of intentionality is extremely complex, and I mention it here only to set it aside until Chapter Four, where the orthodox view whereby an act of violence is automatically equated with an intentional act will be challenged. For the time being, I suggest we work on the assumption that an act of violence is by definition intentional.

Going back to the distinction between violent acts and acts of violence, the permutations of the way violent acts interact with acts of violence are represented in Table 1.1.

Part II: Violence – a linguistic analysis

The term 'violence' is derived from the Latin *violentia*, meaning 'vehemence', a passionate and uncontrolled force. Yet because acts of excessive force frequently result in the violation of norms, rights or rules, the meaning of violence is often conflated with that of 'violation', from the Latin *violare*, meaning 'infringement'. Indeed most attempts to define violence tend to combine the idea of an act of physical force with a violation. Thus for example Honderich (2002, 91; 2003, 15) defines violence as 'a use of physical force that injures, damages, violates or destroys people or things', while Steger (2003, 12) points out that violence 'comprises a range of meanings, including "to force", "to injure", "to dishonor", and "to violate" '.[4]

The prevailing synthesis between 'violence' and 'violation' is not necessarily to be welcomed, as it may lead to growing confusion rather than clarity.[5] In fact while acts of excessive physical force often entail some form of violations, as in the case of rape, there are times when a violation occurs without the need of any excessive physical force, for example when a victim of rape was drugged before the event, or alternatively acts of excessive physical force may take place without anything or anyone being violated, as in the case of consensual sex of a particularly rough nature. For this reason, in what follows the relationship between violence and force, and between violence and violations, will be reviewed independently of each other. Separating issues of physical force from issues of violations has the virtue of identifying two competing perspectives on violence, where the approach taken will determine whether the concept of violence ought to be defined narrowly (violence as force) or more broadly (violence as violation).

Before we move on to examine these two approaches in more detail, it may be useful to clarify how the term violence ought to be distinguished from other terms of a similar nature, such as 'power', 'aggression' and 'coercion'. Arendt (1969), in her still very influential study on violence,[6] suggests two reasons why violence should not be confused with power. First, because power corresponds to the human ability not just to act but to act *in concert*. Secondly, because power is an end in itself, whereas violence is by nature instrumental. Both claims are rather odd to say the least. The claim that power requires concerted action seems totally arbitrary. Whether we follow Weber in defining power as the ability to get outcomes despite resistance, or alternatively we take the more recent rational choice approach whereby power is defined as the ability to change the incentive structures of another actor or actors to bring about certain outcomes,[7] the fact remains that power applies equally to single individuals as it does to groups. It is also puzzling why Arendt feels that power is an end in itself. As Barry (1989, 271) points out, the importance of the desire for power as an end in itself, perhaps because it is intrinsically gratifying, is often overestimated as a motive force in politics:

if we take care to avoid this kind of cheap and fashionable cynicism we shall, I believe, conclude that in the great majority of cases people value power because of the chance it gives them to bring about states of affairs that they desire, and not primarily for any intrinsic gratification that they derive from power itself.

Barry suggests that we adopt an instrumental view of power, as a means to an end, and he is absolutely right on this point.

Notwithstanding my misgivings regarding Arendt's account of power, she is absolutely right in suggesting that we distinguish the concept of power from that of violence. It seems to me that the difference between these two concepts can be expressed more simply in the following terms. Power is, by definition, a dispositional concept, something that people who possess it have the option to use.[8] Violence is different. Violence is not something we possess or not possess, it is not a capability we either have or not have, instead violence is something we do. Violence is the term we use in relation to an act, which refer to the process and/or the consequences of a certain action.

Regarding the distinction between violence and aggression, Bäck (2004, 223), argues that an aggression is made up of three components, namely forcefulness, intentionality and injury: 'We may then define "aggression" as "a forceful action, done intentionally by an agent, of a type of action that tends, or intends, to reduce both the freedom or the genetic fitness of those affected by that action"'. Bäck suggests that violence is in many ways similar to aggression, to the extent that violence also entails forcefulness, intentionality and injury, but with an added twist. Whereas aggression has no moral dimension, violence is morally loaded. That is to say, we may be able to eliminate the notions of moral evil from the concept of aggression, but we cannot do the same with the concept of violence, for as Bäck (2004, 223) points out: 'to call something "violent" is often to give it at least a *prima facie* reason why is it morally wrong'.

For the most part Bäck's account is correct, especially on the moral dimension present in the idea of violence but lacking in the idea of aggression. There are, nevertheless, at least two problematic issues with Bäck's analysis. First, as previously mentioned, it is imperative to distinguish 'violent' from 'violence', something that Bäck fails to do. Violent is to aggressive as violence is to aggression. The difference is that whereas violent and aggressive are adjectives that can be used to describe an agent or an action, violence and aggression refer to the action itself. But as we said before, an act of violence may not be violent, just as an aggression may not require the perpetrator to be aggressive. There is also a problem with the issue of intentionality. Bäck claims that both aggression and violence by definition assume intentionality. That may be the case for aggression, but not for violence, which can be either intentional or unintentional. The question of intentionality (and non-intentionality) is crucial for an accurate understanding of violence, indeed it will be the central issue in Chapter Four.

Finally, the difference between violence and coercion. At the most general level, coercion undermines voluntariness, therefore in order to grasp the concept of coercion, we need to understand the meaning of voluntary and involuntary actions. This is a tall order. As Wertheimer (1987, 4) points out: 'while the principle that coercion undermines voluntariness may be uncontroversial, it is less clear what constitutes the coercion or duress that violates the voluntariness principle'. Much of the debate on coercion deals with the question whether coercion applies specifically and exclusively to interpersonal threats, or whether it also applies to circumstances that limit alternatives.[9] Leaving this issue aside, I suggest we define an act of coercion as any act in which A (a person) directly or indirectly interacts with B (another person) so that B does Y (some action), even though B was in the process of doing, or about to do X (some other action).

Clearly the concepts of violence and coercion are close relatives, but they are not identical twins, therefore they should not be confused. First of all, as Miller (1971) points out, while violence can be used to coerce, in which case violence is a form of coercion, not all acts of violence are necessarily acts of coercion, since it is possible for coercion to occur without violence. For example, when a rapist uses violence to force a woman to have sex with him against her will, violence is used to coerce the woman. But violence and coercion can diverge, as when a deranged, armed individual goes into a public school and starts shooting innocent victims. This person is clearly performing an act of violence, but not an act of coercion, since they are not trying to get the victims to do Y instead of X. In these incidents, which are more common than they ought to be, it would appear that the perpetrator has one tragic aim, namely to kill innocent people, not to change their actions.[10] Similarly, coercion can occur without violence, for example when I use moderate force to restrain a child chasing a football from running across the road. In this case I am using coercion to prevent the child from doing a specific action, against his will, but I am not using or doing violence to the child.

There is also another issue that distinguishes an act of coercion from an act of violence. Coercion is by definition an act that under-mines voluntariness, to the extent that the person being coerced ends up doing something against their will. But this is not always the case with violence. There are times when violence occurs even when the actions of the victim are voluntary, for example when in the past women in China voluntarily endorsed the practice of footbinding,[11] or when someone desperate for a job accepts working conditions that are highly dangerous, as in the case of miners in Africa or South America. In Volume 1 of *Capital* (Chapter XV 9) Marx points out that in a scotching mill at Kildinan, near Cork (Ireland) between 1852 and 1856 there were six fatal accidents and sixty mutilations, which could have been prevented by the simplest appliances, at a very small cost to the mill owners. I would argue that this is a case of violence, even though the workers were not forced by the owners to accept the job, but did so voluntarily.

Having distinguished the idea of violence from the concepts of power, aggression and coercion, we can now return to the task of defining the concept of violence. In what follows, two rival ways of understanding violence will be assessed, namely violence as force and violence as a violation.

Part III: Violence as force

Coady (1986) is probably right when he reminds us that the normal or ordinary understanding of the term 'violence' is in terms of interper-sonal acts of force usually involving the infliction of physical injury, which suggests that the concept of violence cannot be understood independently from the concept of force. Indeed most definitions of violence assume that force plays a determining role. This strong affinity between the terms 'violence' and 'force' would appear to be vindicated by the Oxford English Dictionary, where violence is defined as 'the exercise of physical force so as to inflict injury on, or cause damage to, person or property'.

Notwithstanding its linguistic roots and common perception, the relationship between violence and force is one of the most debated issues in the literature on violence. On one side there are those who have no qualms about defining violence in terms of force.[12] One of the earliest and most authoritative representatives of this group is the American pragmatist John Dewey. In a series of articles originally published in 1916, Dewey (1980, 246) argues that violence is force gone wrong, or in other terms force that is destructive and harmful: 'energy becomes violence when it defeats or frustrates purposes instead of executing or realizing it. When the dynamite charge blows up human beings instead of rocks, when its outcome is waste instead of production, destruction instead of construction, we call it not energy or power but violence'.

It is important to emphasize that Dewey is not saying that force and violence are synonymous. Clearly not all force is violence (rescuing someone from drowning or preventing someone from harming themselves), just as not all acts of violence require the use of force (murder by poisoning). Instead according to Dewey it is only when force becomes destructive and harmful that it turns into an act of violence.[13] Apart from being destructive, it is generally assumed that an act of excessive force must also be deliberate (by the perpetrator) and unwanted (by the victim). Thus Gert (1969, 616) says that 'some might define an 'act of violence' as an unwanted intentional violation', and Keane (1996, 66–67) defines violence as 'the unwanted physical interference by groups and/or individuals with the bodies of others, which are consequentially made to suffer a series of effects ranging from shock, bruises, scratches, swelling or headaches to broken bones, heart attack, loss of limbs or even death'.

The reason for specifying the unwanted nature of an act of violence is in order to distinguish an act of violence, like torture, from other acts of intentional, excessive force that are clearly not acts of violence, such as surgery. The qualification of what is wanted or unwanted is revealed by what one consents to as opposed to what one does not consent to, where the implication is that what is being consented to, be it a wanted intentional violation or a wanted physical interference, cannot be an act of violence. The simple equation from what is being consented (not consented) to what is wanted (unwanted), is perhaps too simplistic, and should be resisted. Just like in the case of actions that do not always reveal our preferences, consent is a poor indicator of what is wanted or unwanted.[14] It follows that simply assuming that an act of violence is always 'unwanted' increases the risks that clear examples of violence, of a structural or institutional nature, are not recognized for what they really are.

Just because people consent to certain practices, and may even appear as if these practices are not unwanted, it does not mean that violence is not taking place. Rape laws in most parts of the world, including many states in the US, continue to require proof of physical force, where the 'force' must physically compel the woman to submit. But as Schulhofer (1998, ix–x) argues, there is a great deal of unwanted sex, which results from threats, coercive 'offers', and abuses of power, trust, and professional authority, that is considered consensual simply because it does not leave signs of severe physical abuse:

> unwanted sex pervades the landscape of workplace interactions, relationships with doctors and lawyers, and contacts with strangers, acquaintances, and even our dating partners. Physically violent rape is its most obvious instance, but not its most common form. Sex can be compelled by overt brutality, by physical intimidation, by the coercive effects of status, power, or authority, and by the manipulative abuse of trust. . . . Sex can be coerced in a multitude of ways that the law tolerates and sometimes tacitly encourages.

Fully consensual acts of sexual perversions may also lead to some confusion about what is wanted and what is an act of violence. There is a tendency to suggest that acts of BDSM (bondage, discipline, dominance, submission) do not constitute acts of violence. This is in fact incorrect. Those who support BDSM and other erotic power exchange practices argue that such activities are morally acceptable because they are fully consented by the participating agents, and indeed they are right.[15] Yet the fact that there is voluntary, informed consent between adults of a clear mind engaging in acts of BDSM does not mean that there is no violence being done. It only means that the violence being done or received can be justified on ethical grounds, but these remain acts of violence nevertheless. The definition of violence should not be confused with the justification of violence, and wanted violent physical violations remain acts of violence.

Apart from wrongly assuming that acts of violence are always unwanted, there also appears to be an underlying problem with any attempt to define violence in terms of excessive force.[16] Wolff (1969, 604) defines force as 'the ability to work some change in the world by the expenditure of physical effort', and Hannah Arendt (1969, 44–45) points out that

> *Force*, which we often use in speech as a synonym for violence, especially if violence serves as a means of coercion, should be reserved, in terminological language, for the 'forces of nature' or the 'force of circumstances' (*la force des choses*), that is, to indicate the energy released by physical or social movements.

These two definitions underscore a fundamental qualitative difference between 'force' and 'violence'. First, force (like power) is a dispositional concept, to the extent that it refers to an ability or potentiality. Violence on the other hand refers to the action itself, or as Audi (1971, 50) points out, 'violence in this sense is always *done*, and it is always done *to* something, typically a person, animal or piece of property'. Secondly, violence is an evaluative concept, perhaps even a normative concept, while force (like aggression) is not.[17] It is perhaps the moral neutrality of the concept of force that leads Hannah Arendt (1969) to dismiss its usefulness when searching for the meaning of violence.

So far we have explored the possibility of defining violence in terms of excessive force. While this approach has the merit of explaining many cases of violence, it also fails to explain many other cases that ought to be classified under the heading of violence. This suggests that perhaps we need to rethink the idea of violence along different lines, whereby it is not the forcefulness of the act that determines whether it qualifies as an act of violence, instead it is the violation endured by the victim that becomes the central issue.

Part IV: Violence as violation

We have seen that violence can be defined in terms of the notion of force. Alternatively, violence can be conceptualized in terms of the verb 'to violate', meaning to infringe, or transgress, or to exceed some limit or norm. Newton Garver (1973) goes as far as to suggest that the idea of violence is much more closely connected with the idea of violation than it is with the idea of force.[18] Following Garver, many contemporary theorists of violence have converged on the idea of defining violence in terms of a violation, although there seems to be some disagreement about what exactly is being violated when an act of violence takes place.[19]

The most popular answer to the question 'violation of what?' is 'violation of rights'. Unfortunately the immediate appeal of this answer is misleading. If violence is the violation of rights, then naturally one ought to say something about the nature of rights being violated. This next step is imbued with difficulty. There are at least three distinct ways of conceptualizing the set of rights that are being violated by an act of violence. First, we could be talking about the violation of personal rights, or those rights essential to personality. Garver (1968; 1973) is the best known exponent of this position. He argues that rights are of two kinds, referring to either the body or the dignity of the person.[20] Secondly, we could be talking about the violation of the right to ourselves, widely defined. This answer finds favour with those political philosophers who endorse the thesis of self-ownership, thus for example Nozick (1974, ix) famously tells us that 'individuals have rights, and there are things no person or group may do to them (without violating their rights).... any more extensive state [beyond a minimal state] will violate persons' rights not to be forced to do certain things, and is unjustified'. Finally, we could be talking about the violation of human rights, widely defined to include any obstacle or impediment to the fulfilment of a basic need. Galtung (1969) is perhaps the best-known advocates of this position, which is still very popular especially amongst radical opponents of globalization. For example Jamil Salmi (1993, 17) defines violence as 'any avoidable action that constitutes a violation of a human right, in its widest meaning, or which prevents the fulfilment of a basic human need'. He goes on to say that each time human beings starve or are undernourished because of social or political reasons, it is legitimate to consider these people as the victims of social violence.

The appeal of defining violence in terms of the violation of rights is evident, but once again further analysis exposes at least two intrinsic problems with this line of reasoning. Albeit rare, there are cases of violence occurring without rights being violated. This point has been made by Audi (1971, 59): '[while] in the most usual cases violence involves the violation of some moral right.... there are also cases, like wrestling and boxing, in which even paradigmatic violence can occur without the violation of any moral right'. Another objection regards the all-inclusive concept of rights being violated. Apart from the violation of our basic rights, such as the right to life, to personal security and to liberty, violence is understood to include also the violation of our socioeconomic rights. Yet the broader our definition of human rights, the more pervasive and inescapable violence becomes. Almost any act can be said to violate someone's rights, making violence ubiquitous and therefore meaningless. As Joseph Betz (1977, 341) points out: 'If violence is violating a person or a person's rights, then every social wrong is a violent one, every crime against another a violent crime, every sin against one's neighbour an act of violence'.

Part V: Minimalist vs comprehensive violence

So far two different ways of approaching the idea of violence have been investigated: violence as excessive force and violence as a violation. The first approach leads to a narrow conception of violence, while the second approach leads to a broader conception. Defining violence in terms of excessive or destructive force has the important advantage of delineating clear boundaries around what constitutes an act of violence, avoiding therefore the tendency to use the term violence as synonymous for everything that is evil or morally wrong.[21] This in part explains why Norman Geras (1990, 22) suggests that violence be defined simply as 'the exercise of physical force so as to kill or injure, inflict direct harm or pain on, human beings', while Bill Starr (2006, 55) restricts his analysis of violence to physical violence: 'the notion of the use of physical force to the extent that it damages the recipient of the physical force will suffice as a working stipulation of what constitutes violence'. Definitions of violence that emphasize the notion of physical force deliberately used to cause suffering or injury will be referred to as the Minimalist Conception of Violence (MCV).[22]

There is much to be said for precise, tight definitions of key concepts, therefore from a purely analytical point of view the MCV is to be welcomed. The problem with the MCV is that by restricting acts of violence to intentional, direct, physical acts against other persons the MCV misses out on too many other important dimensions of the phenomenon of violence. For example, in his influential and still powerful definition of violence, Audi (1971, 59) reminds us that an act of violence can be physical or psychological, aimed at persons, animals, or property, as suggested by his definition of violence:

> Violence is the physical attack upon, or the vigorous physical abuse of, or vigorous physical struggle against, a person or animal; or the highly vigorous psychological abuse of, or the sharp, caustic psychological attack upon, a person or animal; or the highly vigorous, or incendiary, or malicious and vigorous, destruction or damaging of property or potential property.

One of the major virtues of Audi's definition is the acknowledgement that violence has a psychological dimension. This has particular resonance within the growing literature on family violence, where the psychological impairment that comes from living under constant threat and fear of violence is recognized as being part of what constitutes domestic violence.[23] Similarly the growing literature of testimonies from genocide or torture survivors also suggests that psychological violence may be the worst aspect of an act of violence, even worse than physical violence.[24]

Another problem with the MCV is that it seems to be oblivious to the most pervasive and destructive form of violence: structural or institutional violence. In his ground-breaking article on violence, peace and peace research, Galtung (1969) distinguishes between 'direct violence', where the instigator of an act of violence can be traced to a person or persons, and 'structural violence', where there may not be any person who directly harms another person. In structural violence the violence is built into the structure, and shows up as unequal power and consequently as unequal life chances. Galtung is undoubtedly right when he reminds us that structural violence is more deadly and destructive than direct violence.[25]

The attempt to broaden our understanding of violence, either along Audi's or Galtung's lines, may be referred to as the Comprehensive Conception of Violence (CCV).[26] As we have already seen, advocates of the CCV maintain that there are some notable advantages with going beyond the MCV, yet there are also serious problems with the CCV that must be confronted. For example, by introducing a psychological component Audi would appear to offer only a more obscure and less precise definition of violence. It is true that according to Audi not all psychological abuses are acts of violence, but only 'vigorous' psychological abuses, yet as Audi himself recognizes, the term 'vigorous' is inherently vague, and perhaps even subjective.[27] A problem of an analogous nature troubles Galtung's notion of structural violence. When Galtung (1969, 168) explains that 'violence is present when human beings are being influenced so that their actual somatic and mental realizations are below their potential realizations', he fails to appreciate that this definition is much too inclusive, its scope much too broad. Not surprisingly Galtung has attracted much criticism, for example from Keane (1996, 66) who takes a very dismissive stand: 'attempts (such as John Galtung's) to stretch its meaning to include "anything avoidable that impedes human realization" effectively makes a nonsense of the concept [of violence], linking it to a questionable ontological account of "the satisfaction of human needs" and making it indistinguishable from "misery", "alienation" and "repression" '.[28]

For definitional purposes, it is crucial to delineate the boundaries of what constitutes an act of violence. At present there appears to be no agreement regarding this issue, with some arguing for a narrower scope (MCV), while others defend a broader scope (CCV). This debate cannot be settled here, although it is important to emphasize that behind the controversy between the MCV and the CCV, there is a fundamental disagreement of a different nature, namely whether violence should be defined from the point of view of the perpetrators (violence as intentional, destructive force) or alternatively from the point of view of the victims (violence as a violation). There is of course a third alternative, yet not fully explored in the literature, which is to define violence from the point of view of an impartial spectator or third-party. This approach will be the subject of the next chapter, together with a working definition of the concept of violence that falls between the MCV and the CCV; namely, violence as loss of integrity.

Part VI: Conclusion

The problems of violence may be cardinal to a proper understanding of political life, yet the concept of violence remains elusive and often misunderstood. It was 1906 when Georges Sorel (1961, 60), the French social theorist of anarcho-syndicalism, remarked: 'the

problems of violence still remain very obscure'.[29] Writing sixty years
later, Arendt (1969, 35) commented that 'what Sorel remarked sixty
years ago ... is as true today as it was then'. We can confidently say
that what Arendt remarked forty years ago is also as true today as it
was then.

Compared to Sorel's time, or even Arendt's time, today we have
access to a much greater pool of empirical case studies on violence.
The many different forms of political violence, including terrorism,
civil disobedience, genocide, war and revolutions, all enjoy their
own growing and specialized bodies of literature, while philosophical
investigations of the concept of violence seem to be lagging behind.[30]
In undertaking the almost impossible task of trying to make sense
of the many definitions of violence, this chapter has focused on two
predominant ways of thinking about this concept. The minimalist
approach (MCV) sees violence as an act of intentional, excessive force,
while the comprehensive approach (CCV) sees violence as a violation
of rights. The ideological and methodological gulf between these two
approaches is so fierce and deep-seated that one is left wondering
whether there are not one but two concepts of violence. In the next
chapter, an alternative to these two approaches will be put forward,
which may succeed in capturing the virtues of these two rival concep-
tions while avoiding the pitfalls: the theory of violence as violation
of integrity.

Notes

1. Recently published edited volumes on violence include Apter (1997);
   Turpin and Kurtz (1997); Besteman (2002); Worcester *et al.* (2002); Stanko
   (2003); Scheper-Hughes and Bourgois (2004a).
2. See for example Gurr (1989; 1993), and Fearon and Laitin (1996; 2000).
3. Wolin (1963, 23–24) argues that 'violence' derives from either the Latin
   violentia, which meant 'vehemence', or from the verb *violare*, which
   means 'to treat with violence'. The latter carries the additional notion of
   exceeding some limit or norm. These meanings are reflected in the verb
   'to violate'.
4. See also Riga (1969); Wade (1971).
5. See Van den Haag (1972).
6. See for example Bar On (2002).
7. Weber's analysis of power can be found in Weber (1978). For the rational
   choice approach to the concept of power, see Dowding (1991; 1996).

8. The best philosophical account of power is still, arguably, to be found in Morriss (1987).
9. Nozick (1969) famously argues that coercion does not apply to circumstances, but only to interpersonal threats.
10. While most people are familiar with the tragic events in Dunblane, Scotland (March 13, 1996), where sixteen children and one teacher lost their lives, and Columbine High School in Littleton, Colorado (April 20, 1999), where fourteen students (including two killers) and one teacher were killed, it may come as a surprise that since 1996 there have been fourteen different incidents of school shootings worldwide.
11. Footbinding will be discussed in more detail in Chapter 2.
12. Apart from Coady (1986) see also Graham and Gurr (1969); Nieburg (1969); Audi (1971); Gotesky (1974); Geras (1990); Keane (1996); Steger (2003).
13. Ladd (1991, 27) goes as far as to say that 'destructiveness is the essence of violence'.
14. On the problem of revealed preferences, see Sen (1982).
15. On consent and the ethics of BDSM, see Archard (1998).
16. See Miller (1971).
17. Wolff (1969) argues that force, unlike violence, is morally neutral; Holmes (1973) suggests that the concept of violence is evaluative, although this does not make violence wrong by definition; Garver (1973) maintains that the concept of violence is a moral concept.
18. In 1973 Garver revised and expanded his original article 'What Violence Is' first published in 1968. See Garver (1968; 1973).
19. Waldenfels (2006, 80) argues that from the victim's point of view there are three possible answers to the question 'who or what can be violated?': something, a general rule, or somebody. He goes on to dismiss the first two, on the grounds that violence against things can be interpreted as an indirect violence against persons, and that not every case of breach of a rule is an act of violence. That leaves the third option, where violence ascribes the violation to somebody to whom it is done: 'Thus, violence has an addressee, someone from whom life is taken, to whom death is given or to whom something is done'.
20. Garver argues that one has the right to one's body and the right to autonomy; Holmes (1971, 112) defends a position similar to Garver, although he emphasizes the non-bodily side of violence: 'to do violence to someone... is to diminish him as a person, where what is central to this notion is the inflicting of mental harm'. See also Scheper-Hughes and Bourgois (2004b).
21. The problems encountered by a definition of violence that is too broad will be discussed more fully in Chapter 6.
22. The Minimalist Conception of violence echoes what Coady (1986) calls the 'restricted' definition of violence, what Grundy and Weinstein (1974) refer to as the 'observational' definition, and what Platt (1992) identifies as the 'descriptive' concept of violence.

23. For an overview of the voluminous literature on domestic and family violence, see Breines and Gordon (1983); French *et al.* (1996); Daniels (1997); Bar On (1998).
24. Taking the Guatemalan genocide as a representative case study, see Zur (1998); Green (1999); North and Simmons (1999).
25. See also Garver (1973); Galtung (1996); Lee (1996); Curtin and Litke (1999). For an overview of Galtung's contribution to the study of violence and peace, see Lawler (1995).
26. The Comprehensive Conception of Violence echoes what Coady (1986) calls the 'wide' definition of violence, what Grundy and Weinstein (1974) refer to as the 'expansive' definition, and what Platt (1992) identifies as the 'polemic' concept of violence.
27. At the same time it is debatable whether the term 'vigorous' in 'vigorous psychological abuse' is more vague than the term 'excessive' in 'excessive physical force'.
28. See also Coady (1986).
29. On Sorel see King (2003); Jennings (1985); Roth (1980).
30. It is worth mentioning that there is an excellent anthology in French that looks at the meaning of violence in the history of philosophy. *La Violence*, edited by Frappat (2000), reproduces the relevant extracts from the usual suspects in the history of European thought, including Plato, Machiavelli, Spinoza, Hobbes, Rousseau, Kant, Hegel, Engels, Nietzsche, Sorel, Schmitt, Freud, Benjamin, Weber, Foucault, Arendt and Derrida.

2
Violence and Integrity

In the previous chapter it was suggested that the current state of play in the literature on violence reflects a disquieting schism between two rival positions, with one faction defining violence narrowly around the notion of excessive force, while the other defines violence more broadly around the notion of a violation of rights. These two rival positions were labelled respectively the Minimalist Conception of Violence (MCV) and the Comprehensive Conception of Violence (CCV), and it was even suggested that perhaps there are not one but two concepts of violence.

The lack of concurrence at this most basic level in defining the concept of violence is not only awkward, but it can also have serious detrimental effects on future efforts to study this key phenomenon within the social sciences. In particular, there is a growing risk that the idea of violence becomes associated with the growing list of concepts carrying the warning sign of being 'essentially contested', which in turn is the first step on the well-trotted road that leads to a subjectivist outlook, and eventually to ethical relativism.

In an effort to redeem the concept of violence from the threat of subjectivism, the aim of this chapter is to provide a definition of violence that aspires to be universally valid. Part I will alert the reader to the growing wave of research that refuses to acknowledge that violence has a universal meaning. Part II will explore the social dynamics of those acts that we think of as acts of violence; it will be argued that violence is essentially a social act, captured by a trilateral relationship featuring the perpetrator, the victim and a hypothetical impartial spectator, and not simply a bilateral relationship between perpetrator and victim. The point of view of the impartial spectator is what makes it possible to define the concept of violence on non-subjective grounds. Parts III and IV will put forward and defend an original definition of violence, based around the idea of violence as a violation of integrity. Part V will attempt to settle, once and for all, the dispute between the narrow MCV and the broad CCV regarding the scope of violence. It will be suggested that one of the advantages of thinking of violence in terms of a violation of integrity is that it allows for the possibility to conceptualize an intermediate space between these two rival positions.

Part I: The subjectivist threat

It is becoming increasingly fashionable to argue that the concept of violence does not lend itself to any single, universal, all-purpose theory. This position, which tends to be popular with some anthropologists, has of late found increasing resonance amongst sociologists and even political scientists. While it is not possible, nor desirable, to give an exhaustive review of this growing body of literature, it may be useful to analyse a representative sample of this popular trend.

In their book *Violence: Theory and Ethnography*, Stewart and Strathern (2002) endorse the somewhat predictable thesis that violence is defined differently within each culture, defending an analysis of violence based on subjectivity and contested claims of legitimacy. According to Stewart and Strathern (2002, 3) violence can be seen as either destroying order or creating it, yet the issue turns on the question of whose perception of order is at stake: 'Violence pinpoints the differences between people's perceptions of what is proper and appropriate in different contexts of conflict. This explains why it is praised by some and condemned by others. The perception of what is violence may also be subjective'. Stewart and Strathern conclude that one cannot speak of violence as a universal concept, instead the social meaning of violence is determined within the context in which the act is being performed, and by the social agents who occupy this cultural space. The closest Stewart and Strathern come to a definition of violence is the rather unhelpful and excessively vague claim referring to physical action that harms another person, and that the legitimacy of this act may be contested.

While the emphasis on subjectivity and contested legitimacy is not shared by every anthropologist, it is safe to assume that their position still reflects the dominant view within the discipline. Fortunately things seem to be changing. Based on her work in Sudan, Fluehr-Lobban (1995) feels that the issue of violence against women throws the perils of cultural relativism into stark relief, and such violence cannot be excused or justified on cultural grounds. She also argues that anthropologists have a duty to challenge violations and promote education about human rights. This 'committed' approach to public anthropology is fully endorsed, amongst others, by Sanford (2003, 24), whose research as a forensic anthropologist on human rights, truth and memory in the aftermath of the Guatemalan army geno-cide campaigns against the Maya in the 1980s has focused on the exhumations of clandestine cemeteries in isolated Maya villages:

> Anthropology can make connections among the local, national, and international expressions of human rights practices as well as local appropriations of global rights discourses. Because anthro-pologists can have close relationships with those who are the victims of human rights violations and those who organize their communities for recognition of their rights, anthropologists can greatly enhance legally bound understandings of human rights.

Sanford goes on to quote approvingly Magnarella (1993, 7): 'owing to our knowledge and experience, our theoretical and practical research skills, we are in a unique position to further the causes of human rights and justice'.

It would not only be unwise to abandon the concept of violence to the sirens of subjectivism, but from a moral point of view it might even be unforgivable.[1] There is no doubt that the subjectivist posi-tion may have the advantage of short-circuiting all the difficulties we encountered in Chapter One, but expediency and convenience are poor counsel for proper explanations in the social sciences, since what is being gained in terms of simplicity is lost on the front of explan-ation, and perhaps even justification. From a normative point of view, if violence can only be legitimately defined within a predefined cultural practice, it will also become illegitimate to pass judgement on practices of violence that on moral grounds ought to be rebuked, if not altogether censured. This strikes one as profoundly misguided.

Paradoxically, the subjectivist approach to violence popular amongst most anthropologists and hermeneutically inclined social theorists echoes the philosophical contempt of ethics as a serious topic for philosophical discussion by the adherents of logical positivism in the early part of the twentieth century. In his *Language, Truth and Logic*, Ayer (1936) took the view that ethical judgements were not cognitive but emotive, thus nothing more than expressions of and incitements to feeling. This dismissive attitude to ethics was later developed by Stevenson (1944) in *Ethics and Language*, and it contributed to Laslett's (1956, vii) famous proclamation in 1956 that 'for the moment, anyway, political philosophy is dead'. Laslett was clearly exaggerating, indeed as Barry (1990, xxxii) points out, it would have been more accurate to say that political philosophy was not dead but moribund, or that political philosophy in the late 1950s was certainly in the margins of the discipline but not completely out in the cold.[2]

The point here is that just as logical positivism was able to strike a nearly fatal blow to ethical theory, the present fashionable inclination to confer excessive subjectivism on our understanding of violence could seriously undermine any hope of reaching a universal moral condemnation, grounded on reason, on this pervasive phenomenon. Torture *is* wrong, and what makes it wrong has nothing to do with the fact that torture happens not to be the subjective preference of the torture victim. Similarly rape is wrong, even within wedlock. Likewise the death penalty is wrong, because it is a form of torture.[3] Torture, rape and the death penalty are acts of violence, and as such they are to be identified, and condemned, on objective grounds, notwithstanding the fact that torture, rape or the death penalty may be acceptable within certain cultures. The first step towards a universal condemnation of such practices is to recognize these as universally recognized acts of violence.

Sadly, the tendency to argue that violence defies a universal, objective definition has spread outside of the discipline of anthropology. In the introduction to her edited volume on *The Meanings of Violence*, sociologist Stanko (2003, 3) wants to promote an approach to the study of violence that does not assume a standard definition, suggesting that violence as a phenomenon can no longer be conceptualized as fixed: 'In order to advance our thinking, I suggest that what violence *means* is and will always be fluid, not fixed; it is mutable. This is why it is crucial that a programme on violence *not* be framed through definitions of violence as found in the criminal statuses'. The position defended in this book is the exact antithesis of what Stanko recommends. It will be argued that we need a definition of violence that is universally valid, and that the meaning of violence should be fixed rather than fluid. In an effort to argue for an analysis of violence that goes beyond subjectivity and contested claims of legitimacy, in what follows the phenomenon of violence will be approached from the point of view of its social dynamics. This will make it possible to formulate a more objective definition of the concept of violence.

Part II: The social dynamics of violence

Violence does not just happen; instead violence is something that people do. More specifically, violence is not something that people do in general, but it is always done to something or someone in particular.[4] And usually we know that violence has been done when something or someone has been violated.[5] Our next task is to explore the social dynamics within which the act of violence is performed.

Defining violence on objective grounds does not preclude the fact that an act of violence, or doing violence, always occurs within a social context.[6] In fact, one can make sense of violence only within a social context. Swinging a baseball bat is not per se an act of violence, but it becomes an act of violence when another person is injured by this act (X crushed Y's head with a baseball bat). The social aspect of violence suggests that an act of violence is, first and foremost, a relational proposition. At the most basic level, violence is captured by a bilateral relationship involving a perpetrator and a victim, as shown in Figure 2.1.

The terms 'Perpetrator' and 'Victim' are notoriously difficult to define, and therefore subject to controversy. The following minimal definitions will apply to this chapter and throughout the book. The term 'Perpetrator' refers to the social agent whose performance causes or contributes to the violation of integrity of another social agent.

Perpetrator ⟶ Victim

Figure 2.1 The bilateral relationship of violence

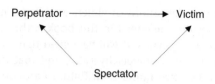

Figure 2.2   The trilateral relationship of violence

The term 'Victim' will refer to the social agent whose integrity has been violated by the performance of a Perpetrator.

Most acts of violence can be explained in terms of the abusive relationship between the Perpetrator and the Victim, yet the bilateral relationship does not capture the full complexity of an act of violence. The social dynamics of an act of violence is more accurately captured by a trilateral social relationship involving a perpetrator, a victim, and a spectator,[7] as shown in Figure 2.2. The arrow ⟶ stands for 'doing violence to', the broken arrow ┈┈▶ stands for 'being aware of'.

The advantage of thinking of violence as a trilateral relationship rather than a bilateral relationship is that the Spectator in the trilateral relationship performs the crucial role of providing the perspective from which the claims of the other two agents can be critically examined. The potential problem with the other views-points, namely those of the Perpetrator and Victim, is their subjectivity. This is not to suggest that per se subjectivity is a problem. On the contrary, there is no doubt that the most powerful and important voice in the dynamics of violence is that of the victim. That is why the first-person narrative is crucial for a proper understanding of violence. One only needs to think of the inestimable insights we have gained from reading the testimonial evidence by genocide survivors like Levi (1988) to realize that the voice of the victim should not be silenced. Yet as Brison (2002, 34) reminds us, while first-person accounts of experiences of victimization are of the essence, these narratives cannot be taken simply at face value: 'If a claim of victimization is made on behalf of a group, for example, or because of one's membership in a group, the past and present victimization of the group in question needs to be critically examined'. Brison is specifically concerned that 'victim talk' tends to provoke counter-'victim talk', hence the importance to evaluate all claims, in order to separate legitimate from less-legitimate claims of victimization.

A similar point is made by Schirmer (2003) regarding the type of testimonies that are gathered worldwide by Commissions of Truth and Reconciliation. She argues that in the aftermath of the Guatemalan genocide (1981–1983), the only voices represented in the debate are those of the victims or the anthropologists whose narratives claim to represent them: 'without denying the crucial importance of those voices' Schirmer (2003, 61) points out, 'what we have lost sight of is what the armed actors in this story might tell us about why and how the violence occurred'. Schirmer (2003, 62) goes on to explain why listening to the voices of the victims may not be sufficient: 'Many of us, for political and moral reasons, choose to believe the veracity of the testimony of the powerless victim . . . . But one is caught in a paradox. If one accepts the truth of any particular perspective because it is true from the perspective of the teller, then to claim it as a broader, more historical truth is to be merely dogmatic'.

All the same, the ability to distinguish between legitimate and less-legitimate claims of victimization (Brison), or assessing the veracity of any perspective by applying standards of truth that are external to the perspective itself (Schirmer), are not the only advantages of having narratives of victimization critically examined from the point of view of the spectator. The other advantage is that the spectator may alert us to problems of violence even when we do not hear the voice of the victims. That is because violence can occur when the Perpetrator and/or the Victim are either not aware of the violence, or when the awareness is suppressed, or even when the violence is not unwanted. This is often the state of affairs with cases of structural violence, as suggested by the well-known cultural custom of footbinding among Chinese women.

Footbinding in China

Footbinding was introduced in some regions in China in the eleventh century, and continued to be practiced until the late 19th century. It was widespread and not just practiced among the nobility. Girls as young as three or four would have their feet bound tightly with bandages, folding all the toes except the big one under the sole to make the foot slender and pointed. After a couple of years, the big toe and heel were brought together, bending the arch, causing constant pain and hindering free movement. The ideal length was three inches. Footbinding was believed to have an erotic effect on Chinese men, who generally believed that the smaller the woman's foot, the more wondrous become the folds of the vagina. Not surprisingly footbinding became crucial for securing a husband. A girl's beauty and desirability were counted more by the size of her feet than by the beauty of her face. Match-makers were not asked, 'Is she beautiful?' but 'How small are her feet?'.[8]

For these reasons, and not unlike women today who assist in clit-oridectomies or infibulations, Chinese women are believed to have been complicit cultural gatekeepers. The fact that footbinding was a cultural practice, which mothers forced upon their daughters, does not make it any more acceptable, or any less an act of violence. Much violence is done in the name of culture.[9] According to Dworkin (1974) the connection between beauty rituals and pain is not acci-dental, the tolerance of pain and the socialization of that tolerance begins in preadolescence, and serves to prepare women for lives of self-abnegation and husband-pleasing.

In order for footbinding to be seen for what it is, namely an act of violence, it is crucial to endorse a trilateral relationship, whereby the act of violence is also defined from the point of view of the spectator, since this is one of those cases when the voice of the victims cannot always be clearly heard. As Simpson (1970) rightly reminds us, in a hostile environment one may become inured to almost anything, including injury, therefore someone raised in the midst of turbulence or social decay may fail to recognize that they are being subjected to violence. The same can be said for cultural environments that condone inegalitarian practices of subjugation and oppression, where the victims may not be aware that they are being violated, or where the perpetrators may not realize that they are doing violence.

The fact that a certain act occurs with the consent of the victim does not mean that the act in question is not an act of violence. The principle of consensuality can, in most cases, justify or legitimize an act that without consent would be wrong. But the normative issue of consent should not be confused with the analytical effort of defining a certain act. Consent has nothing to do with the definition of an act of violence, hence the question 'is act X justified if consented to?' is not to be confused with the question 'is act X an act of violence?'.

Boxers consent to the violence which occurs in a boxing ring, and occasionally some boxers even lose their lives after receiving repeated blows to the head, yet consent does not take away from the fact that boxing is quite simply legitimate violence. Consent may determine the legitimacy of the act, not its nature. On a more serious note, there are many millions of people around the world who suffer injuries after consenting to work in hazardous working conditions, having become bonded labourers by taking a loan for as little as the cost of medicine for a sick child, which they may never be able to pay off.[10] Their consent, often reinforced by cultural imperatives, does not invalidate the claim that they are still victims of violence. For all these reasons, it is crucial to define an act of violence from different points of view, including the point of view of the Spectator.

Given the role of the Spectator in critically examining, and therefore defining, an act of violence, it is crucial to specify exactly who or what the Spectator is. I want to suggest that the Spectator, who performs the crucial role of evaluating (and perhaps even judging) the activities of the Perpetrator and Victim, represents a hypothetical perspective operating from an ideal position. The Spectator's view is the view-from-nowhere. It may help to think of the spectator along the lines suggested by Adam Smith in *The Theory of Moral Sentiment* (Part III, Section 1.6):

> When I endeavour to examine my own conduct, when I endeavour to pass sentence upon it, either to approve or condemn it, it is evident that, in all such cases, I divide myself, as it were into two persons; and that I, the examiner and judge, represent a different character from that other I, the person whose conduct is examined into and judged of. The first is the spectator, whose sentiments with regard to my own conduct I endeavour to enter into, by placing myself in his situation, and by considering how it would appear to me, when seen from that particular point of view. The second is the agent, the person who I properly call myself, and of whose conduct, under the character of a spectator, I was endeavouring to form some opinion. The first is the judge; the second the person judged of. But that the judge should, in every respect, be the same with the person judged of, is as impossible that the cause should, in every respect, be the same with the effect.

In the trilateral relationship of violence, as in Adam Smith's ideal spectator, the Spectator can be anyone who is able to form a judgement as to the propriety or impropriety of the conduct observed, whether they are directly involved (or even present) in the act in question or not. The Spectator provides a more objective assessment, unlike the more subjective standpoints of the perpetrator and the victim, which is why it is necessary to think of an act of violence as a trilateral social relationship rather than a bilateral social relationship involving only perpetrators and victims.

Part III: Towards an objective definition of violence

The role of the Spectator in the trilateral analysis of violence provides an impartial standpoint from which to assess violence beyond subjectivity. On the closely related question of pain, Nagel (1986, 160) defends this objective standpoint, suggesting that suffering is a bad thing, and not just for the sufferer:

> But the pain, though it comes attached to a person and his individual perspective, is just as clearly hateful to the objective self as to the subjective individual. I know what it's like even when I contemplate myself from outside, as one person among countless others. And the same applies when I think about anyone else in this way. The pain can be detached in thought from the fact that it is mine without losing any of its dreadfulness. It has, so to speak, a life of its own. That is why it is natural to ascribe to it a value of its own.

This perspective will make it possible for certain practices to be classified as acts of violence, even when they were not considered as such from the subjective point of view of the Perpetrator or the Victim. As we have seen, from the point of view of the Spectator the cultural ritual of footbinding can be seen for what it really is, namely a practice of violence. The next step is to ascertain what the Spectator should be looking for when identifying a certain act as an act of violence.

The general consensus is that the essence of violence is the harm, injury or suffering it causes. Even the two rival approaches to violence, the narrower perspective based on acts of excessive force (the Minimalist Conception of Violence, or MCV) and the broader perspective based on the idea of violation of rights (the Comprehensive Conception of Rights, or CCV), for all their fundamental differences, share the view that violence is fundamentally about harm or injury. They may disagree on the question of how the harm and injury comes about, whether it is as a result of an act of excessive force or as a result of rights being violated, but the fact that violence is primarily about harm and injury is a shared starting point for both MCV and CCV.

The same assumption can be found in the work of Audi (1971, 97–98), whose famous definition of violence could be seen as capturing an intermediate position between the MCV and the CCV:

> The physical attack upon, or the vigorous physical abuse of, or vigorous physical struggle against, a person or animal; or the highly vigorous psychological abuse of, or the sharp, caustic psychological attack upon, a person or animal; or the highly vigorous, or incendiary, or malicious and vigorous, destruction or damaging of property or potential property.

According to Audi, violence constitutes an extreme physical or psychological attack on a person, animal or property. Audi's definition has the virtue of including under one category a variety of disparate phenomena, being broader than the MCV by virtue of including a psychological dimension, but narrower than the CCV for not going as far as any violation of rights. Yet the problem with Audi's account is that it appears to be a description of violence rather than a definition. Even Audi seems to be aware of this problem. Faced with the objection that his definition does not capture the essence of violence, but merely introduces three subsidiary concepts of violence (physical violence; psychological violence; and violence to inanimate objects), Audi (1971, 63) retorts that in the case of the concept of violence it is apparent that the notion of vigorous abuse comes very close to forming a kind of core: 'for virtually all instances of violence involve vigorous abuse, and those that do not can be seen to exhibit important resemblances to it or a clear potential for it'.

Audi's intuition that an act of violence essentially involves 'vigorous abuse' finds favour with most standard definitions of violence, which emphasize the element of harm, injury or suffering. Indeed from that point of view there seems to be unanimous agreement between the narrow MVC, the broad CCV, as well as Audi's intermediate account. But are the notions of injury, harm or vigorous abuse, the essence of violence? Is the job of the Spectator to decide where and when injury, harm or vigorous abuse is occurring?

In what follows, an alternative starting point from which to define violence will be put forward, one that is not centred on the notions of injury, harm or vigorous abuse. The problem with adopting the notions of injury, harm or vigorous abuse as the groundwork from which to define the concept of violence, is that, apart from the notorious difficulties one encounters when trying to define these terms,[11] there is also the problem that injury, harm or vigorous abuse may themselves be secondary symptoms of an even more foundational issue. In other words, injury and harm and vigorous abuse are terms we use to describe the consequences of violence, but they are not necessarily what constitute the act of violence in itself. There is a different, and perhaps superior, way of understanding the nature of violence, namely, as a violation of integrity. According to this way of thinking about violence, injury, harm and vigorous abuse are only the epiphenomena of an even more fundamental cause, the violation of integrity.

Part IV: Violence as a violation of integrity

The claim that the concept of violence can be defined in terms of a violation of integrity needs to be substantiated, as this idea does not have a history in the literature on violence.[12] In particular, the notion of 'integrity' needs closer analysis. In defining violence as the violation of integrity, the term integrity is used here in a strictly non-philosophical sense, meaning wholeness or intactness. The term 'integrity' here simply refers to something that has not been broken, or that has not lost its original form.

The notion of 'integrity' in the idea of violence as violation of integrity is fundamentally different from the way this term is commonly used in moral philosophy. Integrity can be understood in two different ways, as a moral concept or as an amoral concept. The moral connotation of integrity is perhaps captured by the notion of 'honesty'. This makes 'integrity' a term of art in moral philosophy, holding a place of honour in virtue ethics. In moral philosophy integrity refers to the quality of a person's moral character, denoting the attribute of incorruptibility and perhaps even purity. For many years philosophers have been debating what it means to be a person *of* integrity, from Frankfurt's (1987) idea of a fully integrated self, or someone who is able to bring harmony to their hierarchically arranged volitions and desires to Williams' (1981) idea of integrity as maintenance of identity-conferring commitments.

But integrity can be stripped of its moral coating, whereby the amoral definition of integrity simply points to the notion of 'unity', or to the quality or state of being complete or undivided. It is the latter idea of integrity as wholeness that I want to suggest is crucial for an accurate definition of violence. Thus, an act of violence is fundamentally a violation of integrity, to the extent that it damages or destroys a pre-existing unity. It may be easier to see this violation of unity in terms of violence against an inanimate object, although the same violation also applies to people and other animals. When a bomb falls on a house reducing it to a heap of rubble, a process of transformation as degradation takes place which alters the pre-existing entity of the structure as a house. Similarly when a person becomes the victim of an act of violence, it is one's integrity as a person that is being infringed, since in the process of being violated one is reduced to a lesser being, in physical and/or psychological terms.

The concept of violence as violation of integrity should not be confused with Newton Garver's idea of violence as violation of personhood, although there are important similarities between the two positions. According to Garver (1973, 257), 'what is fundamental about violence in human affairs is that a person is violated'. He goes on to explain what it means to talk about 'violating a person' as follows: 'if it makes sense to talk about violating a person, that just is because a person has certain rights which are undeniably, indissolubly, connected with his being a person'. There are two main differences between the idea of violence as violation of integrity, and Garver's notion of violating a person. First of all, violation of integrity takes into account the fact that apart from a person, violence can also be done to objects or animals. Secondly, in embracing the idea of natural rights in order to understand the moral dimension of violence, Garver is falling back to the broad and vague idea of violence as a violation of rights. It may be worth recalling that the impetus to define violence as a violation of integrity stems in part from an effort to avoid the indeterminacy of rights-violation.[13]

The idea of violence as violation of integrity echoes MacCallum's (1993) views on the subject. In a piece originally written between 1969 and 1970, but only published posthumously in 1993, MacCallum argues that violence is wrong because it damages, destroys, or violates the integrity of the things so changed. The way MacCallum (1993, 243–244) uses the term integrity here is very similar to the way I am suggesting it should be employed, meaning wholeness or completeness:

> The human body is normally viewed as not merely an assemblage of parts but a system of more or less harmoniously integrated parts. When speaking of its integrity we can thus be speaking of its completeness or wholeness as such a system. When so viewed, the integrity of the body will have both inward-looking and outward-looking aspects.

This distinction between inward and outward-looking aspects is crucial. The inward-looking aspect will emphasize the integration of the body's parts within a system, whereas the outward-looking aspect will emphasize the autonomy of the system itself. As MacCallum (1993, 244) explains: 'the upshot is that the integrity of the body is seen to be a function both of the relations of its parts to each other and of its relations to other things'. Underpinning MacCallum's views on integrity is a certain metaphysical view about persons and their autonomy, where persons are viewed as bounded and at least somewhat autonomous entities, and the aspect of autonomy generally most at issue in discussions of the integrity of persons is that concerned with self-determination.

The idea of violence as violation of integrity assumes a metaphysical conception of the self as something violable, which is related to but at the same time distinct from a person's body, or as Waldenfels (2006, 81) puts it, we should think in terms of an integrated sphere of life, namely 'bodily existence as a sphere of vulnerability'.[14] In her remarkable book *Aftermath: Violence and the Remaking of a Self*, Brison (2002) analyses the impact on her conception of her 'self' of surviving a nearly fatal attempted sexual murder. The language Brison uses clearly suggests that the violence she suffered cannot simply be reduced to the physical harm or injury she suffered. Instead, it is the violation of her integrity, in all its different forms, that perhaps comes closest to doing justice to what she is describing.

For example, Brison tries to make sense of her experience by referring to the self being 'undone':

> In this book. . . . I develop and defend a view of the self as fundamentally relational – capable of being undone by violence (xi)

> The undoing of a self in trauma involves a radical disruption of memory, a severing of past from present, and, typically, an inability to envision a future (68)

Brison also describes how the violence she suffered 'demolished' or 'shattered' her world:

> I had my world demolished for me. The fact that I could be walking down a quiet, sunlit country road at one moment and be battling a murderous attacker the next undermined my most fundamental assumptions about the world (25–26)

> When the trauma is of human origin and is intentionally inflicted. . . . it not only shatters one's fundamental assumptions about the world and one's safety in it, but it also severs the sustaining connection between the self and the rest of humanity (40)

In the end, Brison (2002, 110) tells us that violence destroys the self: 'A perfectly good, intact, life was destroyed'. What is most interesting about this last quote is that, as Brison reminds us, in order for something to be destroyed, it must first exist as intact. It is precisely this notion of something being intact that the notion of violence as a violation of integrity is trying to capture.[15]

The experience of injury, suffering or harm is a consequence or symptom of having one's integrity violated. It is the violation of integrity that is the essence of an act of violence, not the injury, suffering or harm. To define violence in terms of the harm rather than violation is to mistake the symptom for the disease. Thus for the rest of the book the following definition of violence will be adopted: *An act of violence occurs when the integrity or unity of a subject (person or animal) or object (property) is being intentionally or unintentionally violated, as a result of an action or an omission. The violation may occur at the physical or psychological level, through physical or psychological means. A violation of integrity will usually result in the subject being harmed or injured, or the object being destroyed or damaged.*

Part V: The scope of violence

Armed with this definition of violence as violation of integrity, we can finally return to the debate discussed in the previous chapter between two rival definitions of violence, namely the MCV which defines violence as an act of intentional, excessive force, and the Comprehensive Conception of Violence (CCV) which sees violence as a violation of rights. The dispute between these two approaches regards the scope or magnitude of violence, the MCV being less inclusive, perhaps inadequately so, while the CCV tends to be more inclusive, perhaps excessively so.

In this chapter it was suggested that there is an alternative to the MCV and the CCV, namely, to define violence in terms of a violation of integrity. One advantage of defining violence as a violation of integrity is that it provides a solution to the puzzle regarding how narrowly or how broadly the concept of violence is to be defined. In fact the idea of violence as violation of integrity could be said to capture the intermediate space between the narrower idea of excessive force and the broader idea of violation of rights.

Like the MCV, the idea of violence as violation of integrity resists the temptation of defining violence so broadly as to incorporate any violation of rights, as suggested by the CCV. At the same time, the notion of violation of integrity includes more cases of violence than the MCV, where violence is defined merely as an act of intentional, excessive physical force. The difference between the idea of violence as violation of integrity and the CCV comes down to what is being violated, with the CCV suggesting that violence refers to a violation of rights, whereas the alternative approach recommends that we think of violence more stringently as a violation of integrity. Of course, there are times when a violation of integrity overlaps with a violation of rights, but not every violation of rights entails a violation of integrity.

A violation of integrity can take the form of an act of excessive physical force, for example when a blow to the head damages the physical integrity of a person, but as in the case of much sexual violence, a violation of integrity can occur even when it is not a case of violent physical rape. As MacKinnon (2001, 778) says:

> What is the injury of rape? What is harmful about sexual abuse? Some dimensions of the harm include the intimate intrusion on the body, including delicate tissues; the attack on the self, which can be shattered; the degradation of human dignity; the violation of trust and destruction of spirit. Can you name others? Rape can destroy one's sense of safety, belief in integrity and worth, belief in and enjoyment of intimate relationships, and faith in one's place of respect in family or community.

Similarly a violation of integrity can coincide with a violation of rights, again as in the case of sexual violence. Yet the concept of integrity, as used here, does not lend itself to the accusations of being excessively broad and all-encompassing, as often the case with attempts to defend the controversial thesis that violence occurs whenever rights are being violated. Thus when Galtung (1969) claims that violence is present whenever our somatic and mental realizations are being impeded, or when Salmi (1993) defines violence as any avoidable action which prevents the fulfilment of a basic human need, they are assuming a conception of rights that covers every aspect of rights, legal and moral, political, social and economic. This may be necessary for an account of social justice (or injustice), but not for a definition of violence. The latter can be captured more successfully, and succinctly, by the idea of a violation of integrity.

Part VI: Conclusion

While both the MCV and the CCV make valid contributions to our understanding of violence, each approach shedding its light on a different facet of this extremely complex phenomenon, this chapter suggests a different way of thinking about violence, which combines elements from the two other approaches in an original definition of the concept of violence. This alternative way of thinking about violence, which tries to capture the intermediate position somewhere between the narrow MCV and the broad CCV, is in terms of violence as the violation of integrity.

The notion of integrity at the core of the idea of violence as violation of integrity should not be confused with the moral ideal of integrity as purity and honesty (being true to oneself) so dear to virtue ethicists. Instead the idea of integrity in this definition of violence refers to the amoral notion of integrity as unity or wholeness. An act of violence is fundamentally a violation of the integrity of the subject or object that suffers the violence, to the extent that the act of violence takes something away from the victim, therefore shattering the pre-existing psychological and/or physical unity that was in place before the violence took place.

In focusing on the violation of integrity, this way of thinking about violence has the important advantage of identifying more clearly why an act of violence is prima facie bad and wrong. This will be crucial in the second half of the book when we undertake a moral assessment of violence, especially the arguments for justifying violence. But before we can engage with matters of a moral nature, there are a number of issues regarding the act of violence that have to be clarified, including the distinction between acts and omissions, and the small matter of intentionality by part of the perpetrator. It is to these questions that we turn to next.

Notes

1. I am using the term 'subjectivism' here in the way it is used by Nagel (1997).
2. The general view now is that two books in particular were instrumental in 'reviving' political philosophy in the 1960s, Hart's (1961) *The Concept of Law* and Barry's (1965) *Political Argument*. The process of resuscitation was of course completed in 1971 with the publication of John Rawls's *A Theory of Justice*.
3. See Bufacchi and Fairrie (2001).
4. See Audi (1971, 50).
5. See Holmes (1971, 110).
6. To say that all violence occurs within a social relationship would seem to neglect the reality of self-violence, including self-inflicted harm or self-injurious behaviours. In fact, following the groundbreaking work of Ronald Laing in 1960, any act of self-violence can be seen as part of the process by which an individual retreats from the world of consensual experience and enters the fantastic world of psychosis. Here we find that self-violence involves a social relationship between the 'false' and the 'real' selves, hence even in cases of self-violence a type of social relationship is present. See Laing (1990).

7. The trilateral relationship of violence, which echoes Foucault's (1977) triadic structure of victim – audience – sovereign, is not to be confused with David Riches's idea of the triangle of violence, in which the viewpoints of performer, victim, and witness are distinguished. My analysis of violence differs from Riches's triangle of violence on at least two points. First, Riches fails to distinguish between violent acts and acts of violence. Secondly, Riches defends a relativist position, whereby the performance of violence is inherently liable to be contested on the question of legitimacy, depending on the perspective of the performer, victim of witness. According to my trilateral analysis of violence the 'spectator' provides an impartial perspective which allows for an objective assessment of violence. For a sympathetic account of Riches's model, see Stewart and Strathern (2002).

8. See Mackie (1996); Spence and Ching (1996).

9. See Barry (2001).

10. On bonded labour and other forms of modern slavery, see *www.antislavery.org*.

11. Joel Feinberg's four volumes treatise on *The Moral Limits of the Criminal Law* is the best effort to come to terms with the concept of harm, as well as a reminder of just how thorny the concept of harm really is. See Feinberg (1984; 1985; 1986; 1988). Feinberg's pathbreaking four-volume study was the subject of a special issue of the *Buffalo Criminal Law Review*, Vol.5, No.2, 2002. See also Coleman and Buchanan (1994).

12. To his credit, Salmi (1993, 17) also defines direct violence as an attack on integrity, but he fails to specify what he means by integrity: 'Direct violence refers to acts of deliberate violence resulting in a direct attack on a person's physical or psychological integrity'.

13. As Betz (1977, 341) says: 'The problem with Garver's analysis of the concept of violence arises from the extension implied by his definition. The definition is just too broad'.

14. Waldenfels asks: 'in what form has somebody been violated or injured? Here we run into dubious distinctions such as bodily violence and mental cruelty.... But such distinctions always tend to play off one form of violence against the other, as if for example an attack on the Other's dignity were less offensive than a punch'.

15. Brison also quotes Judith Herman, who argues that 'the traumatic event thus destroys the belief that one can *be oneself* in relation to others' (Herman, *Trauma and Recovery*, 1992, p. 53, in Brison, p. 40), and Primo Levi, who remarks that 'our language lacks words to express this offense, the demolition of a man' (Levi, *If Not Now, When?*, 1985, p. 9, in Brison, p. 50).

3
Violence by Omission

When thinking or reading about violence, most people conjure up the picture of a distinctive act being performed by the perpetrator of violence, with destructive or harmful consequences for the victim; a mugging, a rape, or flying an airplane into a tall building. For example, when reading the following passage from Glover's (2001, 120) account of one of the many genocidal massacres in Rwanda in 1994, the act of violence that comes to mind is the dismembering of a fellow human being by machete blows: 'A massacre at Kibeho was seen by a schoolgirl, Yvette. She saw many brutal killings, including a baby killed with a machete and thrown down the toilet. Yvette received two blows which nearly killed her. Later she was interrogated, beaten, raped and made pregnant'.

It is beyond doubt that murdering someone by machete blows constitutes an act of violence. And yet, while this is a paradigm case of violence, it would be wrong to assume that all acts of violence follow a similar configuration. Above all, apart from direct acts of destructive or harmful conduct, an act of violence can also be done through an inaction or omission. Violence by omission is an aspect of the act of violence that often gets overlooked. It is precisely this hidden type of violence that will be explored in this chapter. In what follows, it will be argued that in terms of doing violence, there is no difference between a direct action and an omission, even though violence by direct action and violence by omission may not always carry the same moral weight.

Part I: How violence is done

'Doing something' usually entails the performance of a direct action with certain consequences: 'doing the dishes' involves the physical action of scrubbing a plate with a sponge; 'doing homework' implies the physical action of writing in a notebook; etc. We can also do something by not performing an action, for example when we burn the toast by not switching off the grill before the slice of bread is incinerated. In the latter case, which will be referred to by the generic term of 'omissions', we do something by doing nothing.[1]

'Doing violence' is not different from doing anything else. In all paradigm cases of violence, when an act of violence occurs, the perpetrator performs a direct action (punching, kicking, dispensing machete blows, etc.) that has the effect of violating the victim's integrity, by inflicting injury or suffering on the victim. Not surprisingly, most definitions of violence suggest that an act of violence necessarily entails a direct physical act that causes harm or destruction. Thus Honderich (2002, 91; 2003, 15) defines violence as 'a use of physical force that injures, damages, violates or destroys people or things'; Keane (1996, 66–67) describes an act of violence in terms of 'the unwanted physical interference by groups and/or individuals with the bodies of others, which are consequentially made to suffer a series of effects ranging from shock, bruises, scratches, swelling or headaches to broken bones, heart attack, loss of limbs or even death'; and Geras (1990, 22) suggests that violence can be defined simply as 'the exercise of physical force so as to kill or injure, inflict direct harm or pain on, human beings'.

The above definitions capture our basic intuitions about violence, and they certainly cover the majority of cases of violence. Yet there are other instances of violence that cannot be accounted for by these definitions. For example, the most extreme cases of neglect are also a form of violence, even if neglect entails doing nothing. Neglect can take different forms, from abandonment to merely overlooking or ignoring certain situations. Yvette, the child who witnessed the massacre at Kibeho in Rwanda, who received two blows of machete, and who was beaten and raped, was arguably the victim of two separate acts of violence: the direct action of her aggressors and rapists, and the indirect omission of the international community who failed to intervene to avoid this genocide.

The above example suggests that violence is done by either doing something (a direct action) or by not doing something (an omission). The fact that violence can be done via an omission adds a different dimension to the meaning of violence, although not necessarily a new dimension. In *On Liberty* Mill (1991, 15) was already addressing the question of the evil effects of certain inactions, with characteristic clarity: 'A person may cause evil to others not only by his actions but by his inaction, and in either case he is justly accountable to them for the injury'. Mill (1991, 16) goes on to explain that inactions that cause evil require a much more cautions exercise of compulsion compared to actions that have the same effect, nevertheless this does not take away from the basic principle: 'To make any one answerable for doing evil to others, is the rule; to make him answerable for not preventing evil, is, comparatively speaking, the exception. Yet there are many cases clear enough and grave enough to justify that exception'.

Part II: Omissions

Defining an omission in terms of 'not doing something' has the drawback of there being more than one-way of not doing something. It is useful therefore to make three sets of distinctions regarding the nature of omissions: the first between an omitted action and an omitting action; the second between negative causation and negative action; the third between bilateral and trilateral omissions.[2]

Ted Honderich deserves credit for introducing the first distinction. An omitted action describes a mere nothing, or what Honderich calls 'an unrealized possibility', whereas an omitting action is an action done instead of another action. Honderich (1989, 68) explains this point by way of the example of omitting to turn off the radio at 12 noon:

> How did I not turn off the radio at noon? As it happened, I did not turn off the radio at noon by *staying my hand*, be performing that little action after having made a first move towards turning off the radio. My staying my hand *was* or *was identical with* my not turning off the radio at noon.

In this example, not turning off the radio was an act performed by the omitting action of staying my hand.

There are two types of omitting actions, negative causation and negative action. This distinction was first introduced by Harris (1980, 45):

Negative causation – A's failure to do X caused Y where A could have done X and X would have prevented Y.

Negative action – A's failure to do X with the result Y will make the doing of Y a negative action of A's only where A's doing X would have prevented Y and A knew, or ought reasonably to have known this, and where A could have done X and knew, or ought reasonably to have known, this.

The difference between negative causation and negative action is particularly important in terms of allocating moral responsibility for one's omitting actions. According to negative causation, one is responsible for everything and anything one failed to do. If I meet a friend on Saturday at 3 pm for a game of tennis, I am responsible for causing the death of a stranger in my local hospital who could have been saved had I been donating blood at 3 pm on Saturday rather than playing tennis. On the other hand according to negative action I am responsible for the death of the stranger in the hospital if and only if I knew that he could have been saved by my donation of blood, or that his death was foreseeable if I failed to donate blood, but nevertheless I proceeded to play tennis on Saturday at 3 pm.

There is also a third type of distinction that needs to be introduced, between bilateral and trilateral omissions. In a bilateral relationship, Perpetrator (P) does violence to Victim V through an omitting action. For example, if an elderly father has a heart attack, in the presence of his son, who withholds the medications necessary to keep his father alive (perhaps because he will inherit a massive fortune when his father dies), the son is committing an act of violence through omission. In a trilateral relationship, a third party is involved, Witness W, who by not intervening allows P to do violence to V. If apart from the father dying of a heart attack and his son withholding the medications to save his life, there is also a daughter present at the scene, who fails to intervene either by trying to get the medications from his brother or by calling for help, she is also doing violence by omission. In this case both P and W are doing violence to V, in the case of P for his omitting action of not giving his father the medications, and in the case of W for allowing P's negative action to take effect.

The concept of 'allowing' something to happen is crucial here. As Foot (1978, 26) points out, *allowing* here means forbearing to prevent: 'For this we need a sequence thought of as somehow already in train, and something that an agent could do to intervene. (The agent must be able to intervene, but does not do so.)'. Being a witness to an act of violence, W is doing violence to V when W is aware of P's act of violence, is in a position to intervene, but does nothing to stop P or to rescue V. The condition of being 'aware' of what P is doing to V is crucial here, especially in terms of the distinction we encountered before between Negative Causation and Negative Action. In the case of Negative Action, unlike merely Negative Causation, W's action X would have prevented P from doing violence to V, and W knows, or ought reasonably to have known, that doing X will prevent P from doing violence to V.

The three sets of distinctions regarding violence by omission are represented graphically in Figure 3.1.

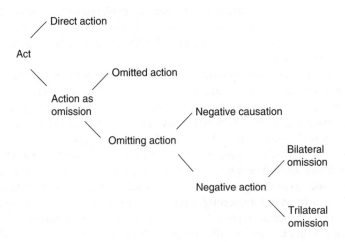

Figure 3.1   Acts and omissions

Part III: The Equivalence Thesis

So far it has been suggested that there is more to an act of violence than a direct action with harmful consequences; violence can also be done through an omission. The remaining part of this chapter will consider the moral status of an act of violence by omission. It will be argued that while in most cases, there is no difference from a moral point of view between violence by direct action and violence by omission (the Equivalence Thesis), this is not necessarily always the case. This is where the distinction between bilateral and trilateral omissions becomes crucial; there are times when violence by omission in a trilateral relationship carries less moral weight than violence by omission in a bilateral relationship or indeed less than violence by direct action.

In recent years the debate whether there is a moral difference between an act and an omission has evolved in response to Philippa Foot's claim that there is a moral distinction to be made between acts and omissions, for example the act of sending poisoned food to underdeveloped countries, and the omission of allowing people in the underdeveloped world to die of starvation. Foot (1978, 26–27) is not saying that allowing people to die of starvation is not morally problematic, especially since at some level all of us living in the West contribute to their misery, nevertheless from a moral point of view she argues that there is a distinction between what one does or causes and what one merely allows:

> Most of us allow people to die of starvation in India and Africa, and there is surely something wrong with us that we do; it would be nonsense, however, to pretend that it is only in law that we make the distinction between allowing people in the underdeveloped countries to die of starvation and sending them poisoned food.

According to Foot, even though our omissions carry some moral weight, an omission is morally speaking less serious than the act.[3] Unfortunately Foot's argument is based on certain moral intuitions which are never fully explained or justified. For example Foot makes an attempt at providing a theoretical basis for treating some omissions as morally different from certain acts when she introduces the distinction between positive and negative duties. Negative duties describe our obligations not to intentionally harm others, while positive duties refer to our obligation to positively benefit someone. Foot holds that we are generally more stringently bound by a negative duty than by a positive duty, and that violating a negative duty is worse than violating a positive duty, even if not violating a negative duty has the consequence of harming a greater number of people.[4] In what follows an attempt will be made to justify Foot's moral intuitions by providing an argument based on the distinction between bilateral and trilateral omissions.

Foot's position is captured by Glover (1977, 92) as follows: 'in certain circumstances, failure to perform an act, with certain foreseen bad consequences of that failure, is morally less bad than to perform a different act which has the identical foreseen bad consequences'. Glover rejects Foot's position, which he refers to as 'the act and omission doctrine', on the grounds that the reasons usually presented in its defence are found lacking. Of course Glover is prepared to accept that many acts are worse than their (apparently) corresponding omissions, to the extent that the bad consequences of the act may be worse or more inevitable than the bad consequences of the omission; there may be various side-effects that stem uniquely from certain actions but not from omissions, and more inevitable because the consequences of an actions are more direct than the consequences of an omission. This suggests that in most cases the consequences of a direct act tend to be worse than the consequences of an omission, although the mere fact that a particular consequence results from an omission rather than an act is of no moral significance

Glover considers the case where a government official fails to provide an adequate allowance for old age pensioners in his yearly budget when doing so is known to provide a greater number of deaths among the elderly. Glover admits that there are at least two reasons why it would be morally worse if this official went into a retirement home and shot the same number of people as would have died as a result of his policy on pensions. First, there may be various negative side effects that stem uniquely from shooting the pensioners. For example the other residents might be terrified and experience psychological harm or at least have their sense of security undermined, not to mention the effect on the loved ones of the deceased. Secondly, the direct action of shooting the pensioners ensures their deaths to a far greater degree, while the omission (in terms of the policy) still leaves open the possibility that the people who would be affected might be assisted and saved by others. Yet this case suggests that the moral difference between an act and an omission exists only because the consequences of the act tend to be more severe than the consequences of the omission. The fact remains that there is no moral significance whether similar consequences result from an omission rather than an act.

Glover is not alone in his negative assessment of Foot's act and omission doctrine, with Harris and Honderich being two other authoritative, like-minded exponents of the same view. Harris (1980, 9) argues that 'there can be no moral difference between positive and negative actions with the same consequences', while Honderich (1989, 100) endorses the belief that 'by our ordinary omissions we do as wrong as we might by certain awful acts'. I suggest we refer to the position defended by Glover, Harris and Honderich as the Equivalence Thesis. The issue here is not simply whether omissions qualify as acts of violence, since clearly they do. It is not even whether omissions carry moral weight, again clearly they do. Instead, the issue is whether acts and omissions are equally wrong, or wrong to the same degree. The Equivalence Thesis takes an uncompromising position on this issue, recommending that we measure the moral weight of our omissions on the same scale as the moral weight of certain acts.

It is this position that is defended by Glover, Harris and Honderich. When Glover denies that our omissions are 'morally less bad' than certain acts, he is saying that omissions are at least as morally bad as certain acts. When Harris says that there is 'no moral difference' between omissions and acts, he is saying that from a moral point of view certain omissions cannot be distinguished from certain acts. When Honderich says that 'by our ordinary omissions we do as wrong as we might by certain awful acts', he is saying that on moral grounds omissions are on a par with certain acts.

It seems to me that in order for the Equivalence Thesis to hold, two conditions must be met: foreseeability and alternativity. The condition of foreseeability is straightforward; the agent in question must be in a position to be able to predict the harmful consequence of their omitting action. The condition of alternativity, or the possibility of alternative action, is more complex, being constituted by two different components: first, it must be *possible* to act in a different way (the choice-set must hold more than one option); second, it must be *viable* to act in a different way (the different options within the choice-set must be more or less comparable in terms of facility of access).[5]

There are cases when both conditions are met, and the Equivalence Thesis holds. Consider the following example:

The Inheritance Case

A man will inherit a fortune when his father dies. With this in mind, when the father has a heart attack, the man omits to give his father medicine necessary for keeping him alive.

In the Inheritance Case, introduced by Glover (1977, 95), the foreseeability condition is met, to the extent that the man knows, or ought reasonably to have known, that his actions would result in the death of his father. The alternativity condition is also met to the extent that the alternative to the omitting action, namely to give the father the necessary medicine, was not only a possible option, but it was also viable. Because all the conditions are met, in the Inheritance Case we can agree with Glover, Harris and Honderich that there is no moral difference between the omitting action of withholding the medicine and the act of killing the father.

While the Equivalence Thesis holds in the Inheritance Case, this is not always the case. In fact, in the vast majority of cases of omitting actions the Equivalence Thesis does not hold, to the extent that the conditions of foreseeability and alternativity are either not met, or they apply only to a lesser degree. Consider the following example:

The Oxfam Case

Take my action today of paying $1,200 for the air fares to Venice, giving my credit card number on the phone to the travel agent. That was an ordinary action with an ordinary effect, getting the seats. In doing the thing, I omitted to contribute $1,200 to Oxfam. If I had done that instead, some lives would have been saved.

In the Oxfam Case, discussed in great detail by Honderich (2002, 74), the foreseeability condition is met, to the extent that no one could plead ignorance to the gross inequalities in the world today, or to the existence of charities such as Oxfam that are the only reason preventing the statistics on global starvation from making even more depressing reading. Of course one has only a vague idea of who will be suffering for one's omitting action, or who exactly will benefit from one's charity, unlike in the Inheritance Case, but that is irrelevant. From a moral point of view everyone has the same moral standing, whether at home or abroad, no matter the race, gender or nationality, therefore it could be argued that we have a duty to take equal account of the interests of everyone, whoever they are and wherever they happen to be.[6]

As for the alternativity condition, it is a different story. It cannot be denied that technically speaking it is *possible* to forego a trip to Venice in order to make a donation to Oxfam, but there is more to alternativity than merely the possibility of performing an alternative action. Apart from being possible, the alternative must also be *viable*. In the Oxfam Case, strange as it may sound, it may not always be viable to expect a person to forego a trip to Venice. In order to see why an alternative action is not always viable, it may help to rewrite the Oxfam Case without any reference to Venice or $1,200, as follows:

The Oxfam Case (2)
Take X's action today of paying Y for the air fares to Z. That was an ordinary action with an ordinary effect, getting the seats. In doing the thing, X omitted to contribute Y to Oxfam. If X had done that instead, some lives would have been saved.

Z, the desired holiday destination, does not have to be Venice, and Y, the cost of the holiday, does not have to be $1200. Does the Equivalence Thesis still hold if Y is $200 rather than $1200 and Z is, say, Blackpool rather than Venice? Let's assume that instead of spending $1,200 on Venice, X spends $200 on a holiday in Blackpool,[7] would X be off the moral hook? According to my understanding of the Equivalence Thesis the answer would have to be 'no', since X could have sent Oxfam the $200 if only X had the decency to spend his holiday at home, doing gardening and reading a novel, rather than going to Blackpool. Clearly it is *possible* to donate money to Oxfam anytime one thinks of going on holiday, but I would argue it is not *viable* to expect that to be always the case.

There are times when donating money to Oxfam rather than going on holiday is not viable. Refusing to take my wife on holiday, because I feel under a moral obligation to donate all the money I would have spent on the holiday to Oxfam, is problematic not so much because I would be depriving my wife of experiencing the beauty of Venice, but because in doing so I am not performing the action of a loving husband, which is a crucial aspect of the person I want to be.[8] In this example, and contrary to what may seem at first, what is viable is not determined by the subjective preferences one happens to have. Instead, what is viable is defined impartially in terms of what all suitably qualified impartial rational persons would agree on. Gert (1998, 222) defends this impartial approach in his account of justifying violations to the moral rule:

> Justifying violations of the moral rules is similar to justifying the moral rules themselves. It consists in showing that all suitably qualified impartial rational persons can or would publicly allow this kind of violation of the moral rules.... [A]ll rational persons agree on the procedure by which a violation can be justified. This procedure must be such that it can be part of a public system that applies to all rational persons, which means that it must be understandable to all rational persons and not irrational for them to use it in making decisions about how to act and judgments on the actions of others.

Leaving aside the well-known controversy over rationality and irrationality, Gert's account of morality as impartiality causes problems for the Equivalence Thesis, since all suitably qualified impartial rational persons would agree that it is not always viable to expect people to forego their holiday in exchange for a donation to Oxfam. In other words, while the Equivalence Thesis holds that there is no moral difference between the act of sending poisoned food to Africa and the omission of not donating money to Oxfam, I am suggesting that there is a difference, and the difference is captured by the alternativity condition. If my grandmother dies of hypothermia in a cold flat in London while I'm on holiday in Venice with my wife, then the Equivalence Thesis would hold, as all suitably qualified impartial rational persons would agree that there is no moral difference between the positive action of killing my grandmother and the omitting action of going on holiday with the same consequences. But by the same token it is not always viable to expect people never to go on holiday on the grounds that the money could have been spend differently, with more beneficial consequences for someone on the other side of the world. The alternativity condition (in terms of what is viable) is much weaker in the Oxfam Case compared to the Inheritance Case.

The conclusion to be drawn from the above analysis is that, contrary to the arguments put forward by Glover, Harris and Honderich, sometimes omissions and actions carry different moral weight. There are degrees of moral wrongness, and while to some extent we all share the burden for the starvation occurring today in certain parts of the world, and we all could (and should) do a lot more to prevent it, it does not follow that an omission always carries the same moral weight as an action which has the same consequences.[9] Honderich (2002, 75 emphasis added) says that the omitting action of not giving $1200 to Oxfam 'has the effect of some lives being lost, *the same effect as* the possible action of ordering your armed forces to stop the food convoys getting through for a while'. Even if an omission and an action have the effect of some lives being lost, it does not follow that there is no difference between certain omissions and certain acts. The difference is determined by the fact that the foreseeability and/or alternativity conditions may not be fully met.

Part IV: Moral absolutism and moral dilemmas

Underpinning the Equivalence Thesis there appears to be a commitment to what can be labelled 'moral absolutism'; namely the view that the value of an action, unless it is morally neutral, is either morally good or evil. The alternative to moral absolutism is the kind of 'moral gradualism' embraced by Foot, whereby certain actions and omissions carry different moral weight, hence in certain cases an action can be morally worse than an omission.

Of the authors we have discussed so far who champion the Equivalence Thesis, Honderich is the one who most clearly embraces moral absolutism. In a recent chapter, Honderich (2003, 180) makes the following point:

There are degrees of moral responsibility, and shares of moral responsibility for things, and degrees of humanity or decency in a whole life. But there are not degrees of being right or degrees of being wrong. The question of which action is right is a question to which the only relevant response is a verdict. You do not have three possible answers.

It is precisely this assumption of moral absolutism that is most problematic about the Equivalence Thesis.

The limits of moral absolutism, or extreme universal moral realism,[10] can be exposed by what in the literature is called a 'moral dilemma'. Following Sinnott-Armstrong (1987, 266), we can define a moral dilemmas as 'situations where there is a moral requirement for an agent to adopt each of incompatible alternatives, but where neither moral requirements is overridden in any way that is both morally relevant and realistic'. The term 'realistic' has a specific meaning here, referring to a moral requirement that is so strong that anyone who violates it does what is morally wrong. Paradoxically the example Honderich uses to defend the Equivalence Thesis, the Oxfam Case, is a perfect example of a moral dilemma.

The problem with moral absolutism or extreme universal moral realism can be exposed by working through certain moral dilemmas, like the Oxfam case, where different agents can still personally favour different alternatives, and their personal rankings or choices will determine what they ought to do. As Sinnott-Armstrong (1987, 267) points out, 'since [extreme universal] moral realists deny that any moral judgments depend on such mental factors as moral beliefs or choices, extreme universal moral realism is false'. Elaborating on the Oxfam case, suppose that I have to choose between paying $1200 for the airfare to Venice, a surprise gift for my wife's 40th birthday, and not taking my wife to Venice but instead donating the same amount to Oxfam. The conflicting moral requirements might be described as equal, since on one side there is the omission to help Oxfam, and on the other side there is the omission not to take my wife to Venice on her 40th birthday. Both omissions carry moral weight. The choice between omissions reflects what Sinnott-Armstrong (1987, 270–271) calls 'a way of life':

this notion is vague, but what is important here is that a way of life includes a tendency to rank one kind of value above another and to choose accordingly. Such rankings are moral beliefs, and such ways of life can be chosen . . . . . such ways of life *do* affect what agents ought to do in some moral dilemmas.

The point about 'a way of life' is that this is what makes our life meaningful. The choice I make not only reflects the person that I am but also the person I want to be. This, in part, is the moral significance of choice. Scanlon (1988, 179) refers to this as the 'demonstrative value' of choice:

On our anniversary, I want not only to have a present for my wife but also to have chosen that present myself. This is not because I think this process is the one best calculated to produce a present she will like (for that, it would be better to let her choose the present herself). The reason rather, is that the gift will have a special meaning if I choose it – if it reflects my feelings about her and my thoughts about the occasion.

If Sinnott-Armstrong and Scanlon are right, then there is a fundamental problem with the type of moral absolutism, or extreme universal moral realism, which is assumed as valid by the Equivalence Thesis.

The shortcomings of the Equivalence Thesis become even more evident if we examine the failure to rescue Jews during the Nazi occupation of Europe. This example has the advantage of being a less abstract nature compared to the Inheritance Case or the Oxfam Case.

Part V: The case of the rescuers

The rescue of Jews in Nazi Europe, and in particular the moral standing of bystanders, is one of the most complex and controversial moral issues coming out of the Holocaust. The issue of bystanders is particularly interesting for our account of violence and omissions because, by virtue of allowing the violence to continue, or by not rescuing the Jews, the bystanders are themselves doing violence to the victims.

While all bystanders carry some blame for the death of many Jews, it will be argued that there is a moral difference between the omitting actions of at least some bystanders and the direct actions of the perpetrators of the Holocaust. The difference will be highlighted not by comparing bystanders to perpetrators, but by comparing two different sets of bystanders. If it can be shown that there is a moral difference between the omitting actions of two different sets of bystanders, then it must follow that there is also a moral difference between bystanders and perpetrators.

It is not my intention to review the extensive literature on the bystanders during the Holocaust;[11] instead I will focus on one specific empirical fact about the rescue operation that has only recently come to surface. In their important contribution to the literature on rescuers and the Holocaust, Varese and Yaish (2000) analyse the most extensive available data set on rescuers,[12] and conclude that *being asked* is a significant predictor of helping behaviour. Two-thirds of the rescuers were asked to help, and only one third initiated their action. Moreover nearly all (96%) of those who were asked to help Jews did so. The statistical analysis provided by Varese and Yaish is much more sophisticated than I can give it credit for here, taking into account a number of variables such as religion, gender, economic conditions, geography, identity of asker, etc. But for our purposes we can focus on one simple basic fact: the vast majority of rescuers needed an extra reason to stimulate their helping behaviour, and 'being asked' seemed to work as a trigger mechanism.[13]

Let us now consider the following two hypothetical scenarios: Anton and Beatrice are both living in France under the Vichy government in the 1940s, and although they are both opposed to the Nazi regime, and they are both equally appalled by the mistreatment of the Jews, yet neither Anton nor Beatrice become rescuers. Notwithstanding the fact that they are both non-rescuers, there is an important difference between Anton and Beatrice; namely, Anton does not become a rescuer even after being asked to do so (he belongs to the minority 4% according to the statistical analysis provided by Varese and Yaish), whereas Beatrice was never asked to rescue anyone, not by a friend, or stranger, or by a Jewish family looking for shelter. Is there a moral difference between their omissions? In both cases the omission has the same effect; some Jewish people lost their lives when they could have been saved. Yet, I would argue that being asked rather than not being asked to become a rescuer makes a difference in terms of the moral weigh of their omissions. The difference is that the alternativity condition is much weaker in Beatrice's case than in Anton's case.

As previously argued, there are two parts to the alternativity condition: first, the alternative action (to become a rescuer) must be a possible alternative. That condition clearly holds for both Anton and Beatrice, since becoming a rescuer was an option (admittedly not an easy one) for all non-Jews living in Europe at the time. Secondly, the alternative action must be viable. This condition holds for Anton more so than for Beatrice. In the context of life under German occupation in the Vichy government, even if we do not anticipate someone to spontaneously look for Jews in need of rescuing, we would expect them to assist the vulnerable when directly asked for help. To become a rescuer was a more viable alternative in the case of Anton than in the case of Beatrice. The fact that Anton was asked to become a rescuer suggests that the opportunity to become a rescuer presented itself as a viable option,[14] unlike in the case of Beatrice, who was never asked, hence in her case becoming a rescuer was a more difficult option compared to Anton.

The reason for distinguishing between Anton and Beatrice is not to suggest that Anton was morally responsible for his omissions whereas Beatrice was not. Anton and Beatrice, like all bystanders, must shoulder some of the responsibility for what happened. Having said that, to paint all non-rescuers with the same moral brush is inaccurate, and perhaps even unfair on some bystanders in comparison to other bystanders. There are moral differences between non-rescuers that must be acknowledged, and even thought all bystanders carry some blame for the plight of the Jews, from a moral point of view they are not all the same. The fact that there is a moral difference between bystanders suggests that there must also be a moral difference between bystanders and perpetrators, and if that is the case, the Equivalence Thesis does not always hold.

Part VI: Conclusion

The aim of this chapter was to highlight a hidden feature of what constitutes an act of violence, namely the fact that violence can be done through an omission. Assuming the validity of this claim, the chapter went on to tackle the question whether there is a moral difference between an omission and a direct action, when both have the same consequence. It was argued that while in many cases there is no difference between a direct action and an omission, and therefore an omission can be as bad or as wrong as a direct action, there are times when an action and an omission carry different moral weight. This is not to deny that an omission can be as much an act of violence as a direct action, or that violence by omission often carries the same moral weight as violence by direct action. At the same time, depending on the circumstances dictated by the conditions of foreseeability and alternativity, certain omissions carry less moral weight than certain direct actions, even if they have the same consequences.

Notes

1. Occasionally it is even possible for the same act, such as doing a musical performance, to be done either by performing a certain action – hitting the keys on the piano keyboard – or by not performing a certain action – sitting perfectly still in front of the keyboard without generating any sounds from the piano, as suggested by John Cage's famous piece for piano, 4"33'.
2. In this chapter we are not going to distinguish between intentional and unintentional omissions. The question of intentionality is very complex, and will be tackled in some detail in the next chapter.
3. Foot's thesis is about moral weight rather than moral responsibility. The question of moral responsibility raises a number of other issues, fundamentally about determinism and free-will, which will not be addressed in this chapter. For those interested in issues of moral responsibility, an argument roughly along the same lines as Foot's has been defended by Fischer and Ravizza (1993).
4. Quinn (1989, 289), in an effort to find a formulation of the distinction between doing and allowing (he refers to Foot's thesis as the Doctrine of Doing and Allowing) that best fits our moral intuitions, switches the attention from our duties to our rights: 'The basic thing is not that killing is intrinsically worse than letting die, or more generally that harming is worse than failing to save from harm, but that these different choices run up against different kinds of rights – one of which is stronger than the other in the sense that it is less easily defeated. But its greater strength in this sense does not entail that its *violation* need be noticeably worse'. Clearly Quinn is assuming that an act of violence is a violation of rights.
5. I am grateful to Brian Burgess for a very helpful discussion about these two conditions.

6. There is still some debate on the type of duty we have. Echoing Philippa Foot, Pogge (2002) also appeals to the distinction between positive duties (to help people in need even though we have not done anything unjust) and negative duties (not to do unjust things).

7. Blackpool, in the north-west of England, is a small seaside resort famous for its shoddy hotels, cheap food and tacky entertainment. In the 1950s and 1960s it used to be the destination of many working class families who could not afford to go abroad.

8. The significance of this choice will be explained in Part V below.

9. It may be the case that advocates of the Equivalence Thesis mistakenly regard praise and blame as opposites, thus while it is praiseworthy to donate money to Oxfam, there may not be any blame in not donating the money. As Gert (1998, 323) argues: 'The usual way of talking about praise and blame have obscured the distinction between moral standards and responsibility standards. Praise is not the opposite of blame, but of condemnation, and is related to moral standards. Blame and its opposite, credit, are related to responsibility standards'.

10. Extreme universal moral realism is the view that moral judgments are true if and only if certain conditions hold which are independent of the actual and ideal moral beliefs and choices of the judger and the judged. The condition of 'actual and ideal' is what distinguishes this extreme version of moral realism from a weaker or moderate moral realism, which claims independence from actual, but not ideal, mental states. An ideal mental state is captured by a fully informed, rational, impartial spectator.

11. For an excellent analysis by a political philosopher of the many issues regarding bystanders, see Geras (1998). See also Glover (2001, Ch. 40, pp. 379–393).

12. The data collected by the Altruistic Personality and Prosocial Behaviour Institute (APPBI), which contains a sample of 346 identified Jewish rescuers and 164 non-rescuers. This data was used by Oliner and Oliner (1988).

13. In a more recent chapter Varese and Yaish (2005) explore the interaction between pre-existing dispositions (a pro-social personality) and situational factors (direct request for help). They reach three important conclusions: First, rescuers were more likely to help the more pro-social their personality was. Second, being directly asked for help increased the likelihood that a person with a pro-social personality would help. Third, the stronger a given pro-social disposition is, the more likely it is that a situational factor activates that existing inclination.

14. As Gross (1997) points out, in some cases the asking party was someone from the resistance movement, who may even have offered economic incentives to the rescuers.

4
Violence and Intentionality

It is a generally held view that an act of violence is, first and foremost, an intentional act. Most definitions of violence suggest that an act of violence occurs when the perpetrator deliberately and voluntarily aims at causing injury or suffering to the victim, or in other words injuring the victim is his or her purpose in acting. I will refer to this view as the intention-oriented (I-O) approach. The aim of this chapter is to challenge the received view that violence must always be defined in terms of the intentions of the perpetrator. This is not to suggest that intentionality never plays any role in an accurate account of violence. On the contrary, the intention to cause harm is often the determining issue whether a certain act qualifies as an act of violence. Nevertheless there are times when it is possible, and necessary, to relax the prerequisite of intentionality, and replace it with other necessary conditions such as knowledge or foreseeability of inevitable consequences to one's actions.

Intentionality is crucial for understanding violence on at least two different levels. First, intentionality enables us to distinguish between benevolent and malevolent actions that involve inflicting suffering on others. A surgeon does not perform an act of violence when she performs surgery on a patient, since her intention or goal is not to cause injury, even if the patient suffers pain during the surgery. On the other hand Dr. Josef Mengele, who in the 1940s in Auschwitz experimented on helpless victims with terrifying consequences, is guilty of performing acts of violence. Secondly, intentionality is often the difference between an act of violence and a mere accident. The difference between the events of September 11 2001, and the crash of the American Airlines jetliner in Queens NY on 12 November 2001, is that the former was an act of violence whereas the latter was a mere accident.

Notwithstanding its indisputable merits, I want to argue that the I-O approach is inadequately limited, reflecting an insufficiently narrow conception of violence. Apart from the intentionality of the perpetrator of the action, it will be argued that violence occurs when an action carries harmful consequences which were foreseeable but unintended. The idea of foreseeable but unintended violence becomes intelligible when we take into account the perspective of the victim. This perspective will be referred to as the victim-oriented (V-O) approach. Defining violence from this perspective downplays the issue whether or not their injury or suffering was intended by anyone. As I said before, the aim of this chapter is not to reject the I-O approach, but merely to suggest that the I-O approach ought to be complemented by the V-O approach.

Perhaps the only way to combine both the I-O approach and the V-O approach into one unified account of violence is once again to think of violence as a violation of integrity, to be analysed within the framework of a trilateral relationship involving perpetrators, victims and spectators, as suggested in the previous chapters. The role of the spectator is crucial since the spectator is in the unique position to evaluate an act not only in terms of the intentionality of the agent performing the action but also in terms of the consequences of the act in question on its victims. The spectator will be asking not only whether the perpetrator was acting with the intent to cause harm but also whether the perpetrator should have known or foreseen that such actions were likely to violate the integrity of the victim, notwithstanding the original intention of the perpetrator.

Part I: The Intention-Oriented (I-O) approach

When it comes to defining violence, the central role of intentionality enjoys almost universal approval. This can be explained in part by the fact that intentionality is seen by many as the moral line which differentiates a benevolent from a malevolent action, even if both actions result in suffering. The fact that intentionality plays a dominant role in the work of early Christian theologians as well as in Kant's moral philosophy greatly contributes to this factor.

The moral distinction captured by the intent requirement informs the Doctrine of Double Effect (DDE), which articulates a dominant position in Just War Doctrine. The DDE asserts that it is worse (from a moral point of view) to intentionally cause harm than to cause harm with foresight but without intention. The earliest version of DDE can be found in Thomas Aquinas' *Summa Theologica* (II-II, Qu. 64, Art.6), and it has been a key concept in Catholic ethics ever since. As defined by Mangan (1949), this doctrine stipulates that an agent may licitly perform an action that will produce both a good effect and a bad effect provided that four conditions are met: (1) that the action is good in itself or at least indifferent; (2) that the good effect and not the evil effect be intended; (3) that the good effect be not produced by means of the evil effect and (4) that there be a proportionately grave reason for permitting the evil effect.

The DDE has proved to be immensely influential in the literature on lawful killing and the ethics of war. For example Anscombe (1961) famously endorses the DDE in order to illustrate the case of killing in self-defence, while Walzer (1977) recognizes the DDE as a principal component in his account of Just War Doctrine, but adds another condition to the ones already discussed, which stipulates that the foreseeable evil be reduced as far as possible, even if this involves accepting costs to the agent.[1]

Apart from forming the crucial backbone to the DDE, the notion of intentionality is also pivotal to the 1948 Convention on the Prevention and Punishment of the Crime of Genocide, where intent is singled out as integral to the legal definition of genocide, as unambiguously stated in Article 2 of the Convention:

[G]enocide means any of the following acts committed with intent to destroy, in whole or in part, a national, ethical, racial, or religious group, as such:

(a) Killing members of the group;
(b) Causing serious bodily or mental harm to members of the group;
(c) Deliberately inflicting on the group conditions of life calculated to bring about its physical destruction in whole or in part....[2]

We have seen that the concept of intentionality makes it possible to distinguish between a benevolent from a malevolent will. Yet there is more, since intentionality is also important for another reason, namely for distinguishing between an act of violence and a mere accident. If I drive within the speed limit and a dog runs in front of my car and I'm unable to break or swerve in time before making impact, killing the dog in the process, the resulting death of the animal is seen as an accident. But if I see the dog on the side of the road and I deliberately increase my speed and change the direction of my route with the intent to run him over, my actions are now an act of violence against the dog. Similarly the tragedy of September 11 2001 was an act of violence because the suicide hijackers acted with the intent of causing harm and misery, unlike the tragedy of 12 November 2001 which was not the result of the pilot's intentions.

For all these reasons, many commentators include the require-ment of intent in their definition of violence. Thus Pogge (1991, 67 emphasis added) claims that 'a person uses physical violence if he *deliberately* acts is a way that blocks another's exercise of her legitimate claim-rights by physical means'; Steger (2003, 13 emphasis added) argues that 'violence is the *intentional* infliction of physical or psycho-logical injury on a person or persons'; Graham and Gurr (1969) define violence as behaviour 'designed' to inflict physical injury to people or damage to property.[3]

Notwithstanding its undeniable importance for defining viol-ence and determining related issues of responsibility, intentionality remains an awkward concept that has puzzled philosophers of actions over many generations. In a famous essay originally published in 1971, the late Davidson (1980, 43) ponders on the relationship between agency, events and action: 'What events in the life of a person reveal agency; what are his deeds and his doings in contrast to mere happenings in his history; what is the mark that distinguishes his actions?'. Davidson argues that there is an important distinction to be made between actions and mere happenings. If I slam the door of my room, I am performing an action, but if it is the wind that shuts the door it is a mere happening. This distinction between actions and happenings is essential if we are to see ourselves as endowed with (some) free will, therefore in (some) control of what goes on in our lives, and not mere passive spectators of the unfolding of history. Clearly what is behind the idea of actions is the notion of agency.

Intentionality implies reason. To say that person P acted intention-ally is to say that P performed action φ because P had a reason to φ.[4] It follows that 'intentionality' stands for 'intention with which', which is roughly equivalent to the purpose, aim or end one wants to fulfil through one's action.

Miller (1971) is one of the many commentators who highlight the determining role of intentionality in defining an act of violence. It is worth quoting Miller (1971, 16–17) at some length to see the full strength of this argument:

> Consider the case where A intends to shake B's hand in a gesture of friendship but, not realizing how weak B is or how strong he himself is, breaks three bones in B's hand. Has A committed an act of violence? Obviously the act of shaking B's hand was done intentionally, but the act of breaking three bones in B's hand – or perhaps it is better to say 'the breaking of the bones in B's hand' – was *not* intentional. The breaking of the three bones in B's hand was an *accident*. I think we would all agree that A's was not an act of violence . . .

It is to those actions in which the harm, injury or destruction does *not* seem to have been *accidental* that we are wont to affix the label 'violence'. In cases where A appears to have been mentally deranged or deficient at the time of the act of violence, we pause to consider whether A was responsible for his actions, and consequently to what degree he should be treated or punished. But as long as the incident was not an accident, we do not withdraw our description of the act as an act of violence.

Miller appears to be making two distinctions here. The first is between a mere accident and an act of violence. The second distinc-tion, which mirrors the first, is between two levels of intentionality. There is the 'minimal' intentional action of shaking B's hand, and the 'full' intentional action of shaking B's hand in order to break three bones in his hand. According to Miller, for an act to qualify as violence it must entail the full intention to cause injury or suffering to another person.

Admittedly the I-O approach to violence has many merits. It correctly highlights the conceptual and moral difference between acts of violence and mere accidents. Furthermore not all acts that cause injury and suffering are acts of violence, and intentionality, or the intent to cause harm, is often what makes the difference. This is of course the most significant difference between a dentist and a torturer. Yet, while it cannot be denied that many acts of violence are intentional, and that intentionality is what determines whether a certain act is an act of violence or not, that is only part of the story. There is more to an act of violence than the intent by its perpetrator to cause harm. It is only when we start questioning the hegemony of the I-O approach that incidents of foreseeable but unintended harm enter the picture as legitimate concerns for a theory of violence.

Part II: Foreseeable violence in theory

The belief that intentionality is intrinsic to an act of violence is the orthodox view in the literature on violence, yet not everyone is fully convinced. One of the most authoritative dissenting voices is that of Audi (1971, 58):

> Must violence be done intentionally? It is not implausible to main-tain that it must be. We might note, for instance, that most of the examples of violence on the above list [raping, beating up, and storming a city] are actions and activities that are inconceiv-able except as intentional... But even if the vast majority of cases of violence, and all the paradigm cases, are intentional, it never-theless seems possible for violence to be unintentional... Thus, although there are ways of doing violence which can be conceived only as intentional, not all violence need be intentional.

Audi uses the example of someone who suffers from serious psychosis. When provoked into a rage, this person inadvertently and unintentionally tramples three children and knocks over two old ladies. According to Audi, this person would still be guilty of viol-ence, even though such violence was unintentional. Audi's attempt to explore the notion of 'unintentional violence' deserves praise, although his example of someone who suffers from serious psychosis is problematic, partly because this person's ability to reason comes into question, but also because this example fails to capture the complexity of the issue.

In order to appreciate the full strength of the idea of uninten-tional violence, it will be necessary to go back to the literature on philosophy of action and dig deeper into the notion of intentionality. Following Bratman (1987) we can say that there are two ways of understanding what it means to act intentionally, the Simple View and the Alternative View. The Simple View states that action A is intentional whenever the agent performing the action intends to do A. There is no difference between an action being intentional and an agent intending to do the action. In other words, an action is intentional because it arises out of an intention on the part of the agent to perform an action of that type. This is straightforward. For example, I intentionally book a table for two for my wife and I at our favourite restaurant because I intend to surprise her with this treat on her birthday.

But on closer inspection there is more to intentionality than the Simple View suggests. As Bratman says, it is necessary to distinguish between what I intend and the motivational potential of my intention.[5] The problem with the Simple View is that there are times when what we do intentionally does not fully match with what we intended to do. When an intended action has foreseen but undesired side effects, the agent will have brought about the effect intentionally, but not to have intended to bring it about. For example the intended action of taking my wife to our favourite restaurant on her birthday could have the foreseeable but undesired side effect that she will feel bad for having to contravene her strict diet on her birthday. Thus the Alternative View states that an agent does action A intentionally without intending to do B, as long as the agent knows the implications of B, that B was foreseeable given A, and the agent is willing to accept B as a consequence of A.[6]

At the core of this discrepancy between the Simple View and the Alternative View we find the important distinction between the intentionality of an action, and the foreseen but unintended consequences of the same. We have already seen that most commentators include intentionality (understood according to the Simple View) in their definition of violence. The question is whether an act of violence should be defined not so much in terms of the intentions of the perpetrator, but on the issue whether the consequences of certain actions were foreseeable. In other words, should a definition of violence take into account the Alternative View of intentionality?

This seems to be the way Harris (1980, 19) is encouraging us to think. In his definition of violence, there is no mention of intentionality but only of foreseeability: 'an act of violence occurs when injury or suffering is inflicted upon a person or persons by an agent who knows (or ought reasonably to have known), that his actions would result in the harm in question'. Knowing about the likely consequences of one's actions is different from intending such consequences, for sometimes the consequences of certain actions can be foreseen although not intended. By putting the emphasis on what is foreseeable rather than what is intended, Harris is broadening the scope of an act of violence. His definition of violence makes it possible for us to analyse hard cases that fall between the stools of what is clearly intended and what is a mere accident.

For example, there are cases where certain actions bring about unintended suffering and injury to others, where these actions are avoidable, but nothing is done to prevent these actions from taking place. In the previous chapter we came across the notion of *allowing* something to happen, meaning forbearing to prevent. In the literature on violence, the same idea is expressed in terms of the concept of not preventing an avoidable evil. Defining violence in terms of not preventing an avoidable evil is a popular approach for those who advocate the idea of structural violence.[7] For example Galtung (1969, 168) defines violence as the cause of the difference between the potential and the actual, between what could have been and what is, and when the difference between the potential and the actual is avoidable, then violence is present:

> if a person dies from tuberculosis in the eighteenth century it would be hard to conceive of this as violence since it might have been quite unavoidable, but if he dies from it today, despite all the medical resources in the world, then violence is present according to our definition'.

I will return to Galtung's idea of structural violence in Part V.

Once again, the important lesson we must take from attempts to define violence as a foreseeable, avoidable action which causes harm, even if the harm is not intended, is that it forces us to accept a broader conception of violence. In Chapter One the distinction between the

Minimalist Conception of Violence and the Comprehensive Conception of Violence was introduced. One way of depicting this distinction is between merely intentional violence and foreseeable but unintended violence. In what follows, the idea of foreseeable but unintended violence will come into closer scrutiny, by exploring some empirical examples of acts of violence where the consequence was foreseen or avoidable, even if not intended.

Part III: Foreseeable violence in practice

Harman (1986, 97), whose views on intentionality are not dissimilar to those of Bratman mentioned before, argues that in a typical intentional action, apart from end E which one intends to achieve by means M, we must also consider possibly foreseeable side effects S of M, and consequences C of E:

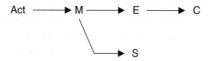

We suppose that M and E are intended, but what about S and C? Could S and C be foreseen, and perhaps avoidable, but not intended? Harman and Bratman both reject the holistic thesis that holds that all foreseen aspects of one's actions are intended, suggesting instead that S and C are not intended. In what follows the positions defended by Harman and Bratman against holism will be taken as valid, in order to explore the notion of a foreseeable but unintended act of violence. Three different cases of foreseeable violence will be considered, each referring to an instance of political violence.

1) P performs action A intending to achieve end E, for the benefit of B, by means M, foreseeing side-effect S which unintentionally injures V.

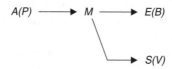

P (the perpetrator of violence) did not act with the full intention of inflicting injury or suffering on V (the victim), indeed to the extent that the injury was an unintended consequence, one could argue that the injury was accidental. Yet from the point of view of V, to the extent that S was foreseen (and perhaps avoidable) P performed an act of violence.

The fact that an act can have unintended consequences does not preclude the possibility that it can also be an act of violence. A famous example in the literature is from Hart (1968), who describes the famous nineteenth century case of *R.* v. *Desmond, Barrett and Others*, Irish Nationalists (IN) whose political actions had tragic unintended consequences:

The Irish Nationalists[8]

In 1868 there lay in jail two Irish Fenians, whom the accused attempted to liberate. For the purpose, one of them dynamited the prison wall outside the area where it was believed the inmates would be at exercise. Though the ploy failed, the explosion killed some persons living nearby. The point to be observed here is that, for the law, a foreseen outcome is enough, even if it was unwanted by the agent, even if he thought of it as an undesirable by-product of his activities. It was no part of the Irish National-ists' purpose or aim to kill or injure anyone; the victims' deaths were not a means to their end; to bring them about was not their reason or part of their reason for igniting the fuse, but they were convicted on the ground that they foresaw their death or serious injury.[9]

The deaths caused by the actions of the INs were not a means to his end but only an undesirable by-product of their actions. In Hart's opinion, whether they intended to kill anyone or not is irrelevant, and they should be rightfully convicted of murder. Leaving aside the legal issue of the right punishment for this offence, or the appropriate words for describing this case, the question for us is whether or not the civilian bystanders were killed by an act of violence. I would argue that this is a case of violence, not because the INs intended to kill anyone (they clearly did not), but because the fatalities were foreseeable, therefore the deaths were avoidable.

Another example which fits the model is the tragic case of the many thousands of Chinese immigrant workers who died in the United States in the 1860s during the construction of a transcontinental railroad.[10]

Chinese Immigrants and the Transcontinental Railroad

In 1862 the US Congress authorized the most ambitious project that the country had ever undertaken, to link the country's two coasts by way of a continuous stretch of railroad tracks from the Atlantic to the Pacific. Two companies divided the task of actual construction: the Central Pacific Railroad Corporation and Union Pacific. Central Pacific went for a major recruitment drive for 5,000 white workers, but the appeal secured only 800 men. Central Pacific then turned to Chinese immigrants, who were cheap, plentiful and easily exploitable. At the peak of construction, Central Pacific would employ more than 10,000 Chinese men. These men often performed the most dangerous tasks, with tragic outcomes. On average, for each two miles of track laid, three Chinese labourers were killed by accidents. Many more died from smallpox and other diseases.[11]

The intention behind this project was to set up a train service that would benefit all Americans, both politically and economically, and not to kill Chinese immigrants. While it is true that Chinese immigrants were paid less than white workers,[12] their suffering and death was never intended. The hundreds who died in accidents and the thousands who died of smallpox were an unintended consequence of building the transcontinental railroad. Yet, even if unintended, these deaths were foreseeable, and avoidable, therefore one might still want to consider these deaths as the result of violence.

(2) P performs action A intending to achieve end E, to the detriment or harm of H, by means of M, foreseeing side-effect S which unintentionally also harms V.

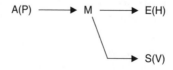

The difference between cases (1) and (2) is that in the first case the purpose behind the action is to benefit someone, whereas in the second case the purpose is to harm someone.[13] Apart from that, in both cases the means (M) has an unintended victim (V).

In the literature on DDE there is a widely discussed example which compares the actions of two agents, a strategic bomber (SB) and a terror bomber (TB). SBs destroy military targets with the intention of bringing the war to an end as quickly as possible. In so doing, SBs often kill civilians, whose deaths are unintended but foreseen. TBs on the other hand intentionally aim at population centres, with the intention of killing civilians, acting on the belief that this will help to bring an end to the war they are fighting. According to the DDE, although foreseeable, the unintentional deaths caused by SB are permitted, whereas the intentional deaths caused by TB are not. Once again, leaving aside the moral assessment of the situation, from the point of view of defining an act of violence there seems to be no difference between SB and TB. In both cases, people died as a result of an act of violence.

In fact, one could go as far as to suggest that there is no difference between the SB and the IN from Hart's example. As Gross (2005–2006, 560) argues:

> it is difficult to see, then, why SB should not be convicted of killing civilians and how he could turn to the DDE to not only mitigate his punishment but to erase the badness of the act itself. The only difference between SB and IN is, if anything, the good end that SB invokes; their intentions are equally pure. Because neither intends to kill civilians, we are left judging the act not by intention but by the goodness of goal.

On a similar note, Harman uses the hypothetical example of an army commander who intends to kill the enemy hidden in a village by bombing the village, realizing this will as a side effect also kill non-combatants in the village. Clearly the non-combatants were killed by an act of violence, and it becomes increasingly difficult to tell the difference between the army commander and a terrorist.

This example is not as hypothetical as may appear. Two disturbing real-life examples of foreseeable but unintended violence, which have been in the news in the last few years, also relate to instances of war: the (not-so-smart) smart-bombs, and death by friendly fire during combat.

Smart Bombs

Smart bombs were first used on Iraq during Operation Desert Storm in 1991, then on Kosovo eight years later, and in 2002 on Afghanistan in the War Against Terrorism. Whereas only about 10 percent of the weapons used in Operation Desert Storm were 'smart bombs,' a US Department of Defense (DOD) report estimated that in Afghanistan about 60 percent of the bombs dropped were precision-guided weapons, many using sophisticated satellite guidance for higher accuracy. According to the DOD report, the U.S. air campaign in Afghanistan achieved a 75 to 85 percent success rate. By comparison, in the 1991 Gulf War and the 1999 Kosovo conflict less than half such weapons hit their targets.[14]

The disconcerting aspect of these statistics is of course what to make of the 15 to 25 % of smart-bombs that went astray in Afghanistan and never reached the intended target. For example, the smart-bomb that missed its target by a mile, hitting a residential area in Kabul and killing up to four civilians,[15] or the 60 % of smart-bombs that hit the wrong targets in Kosovo and Iraq. It would appear that at least 2,500 Iraqi civilians died as a result of 'smart bombing' in Iraq in 1991.[16] Many more Iraqi civilians have died as a result of the Iraq War started by George W. Bush in 19 March 2003.[17] The case of friendly fire is similar to the smart bombs.

Friendly-Fire

In April 2002 during the War in Afghanistan, a US fighter pilot dropped a laser-guided 500-pound bomb killing four Canadian soldiers and wounding another eight. This is after a U.S. warplane mistakenly dropped 1,000-pound bombs on three Red Cross warehouses in Kabul. Friendly fire has always been an unintended consequence of war. It has been calculated that 21 per cent of U.S. casualties in the Second World War were from friendly fire. In Korea it was 18 per cent, in Vietnam 39 and in the Gulf War a whopping 49 per cent.[18]

The victims of friendly fire are unintentionally harmed by acts of war that are intentionally harmful: Action A (US bombing of enemy lines) may be intentionally directed towards B (Taliban soldiers), but may end up unintentionally harming C (Canadian soldiers or Red Cross offices). Clearly the act of dropping bombs is an act of violence, which has intended victims and unintended victims. If the intended victims are the result of intentional violence, the foreseeable but unintended victims must be the result of foreseeable but unintended violence.

(3) P performs action A intending to achieve end E, harming H only to a certain degree (H1) by means of M, although M has the unintended consequence UC of harming H to a much greater degree than intended (H2).

$$A(P) \longrightarrow M \longrightarrow E(H1) \longrightarrow UC(H2)$$

The third type of unintentional violence is restricted to a bilateral relationship between the perpetrator of violence (P) and the victim who is harmed (H). The interesting point here is that H is the victim of both intended and unintended violence, as in the case of the Chinese immigrant workers who worked and died during the construction of the transcontinental railroads. The Chinese immigrants were intentionally being exploited, but unintentionally many of them (perhaps thousands) died because of the living and working conditions, although such deaths were both foreseeable and avoidable. It seems absurd to suggest that while the act of exploitation was intentional, the resulting deaths were purely accidental. Like in the previous two cases, this example suggests that violence should be defined from the perspective of those who find themselves at the receiving end of such acts; in particular whether the harm caused was foreseeable and avoidable, not in terms of the intentions of the perpetrators of violence.

Part IV: Rethinking violence

The orthodox view, based on the I-O approach, draws a sharp line between acts of violence and mere accidents. A closer analysis of intentional action suggests that it is possible for an act of violence to occur even when the resulting suffering and injury was not intended. The problem with the I-O approach is that instances of 'foreseeable but unintended violence', which fall between the stools of intentional violence and mere accidents, remain invisible unless a different, less orthodox approach to issues of violence is implemented. In what follows it will be suggested that instead of defining violence only from the point of view of the perpetrator (the I-O approach), violence should also be defined from the point of view of its victims (the V-O approach).

Cases of double-effect such as the casualties of errant smart bombs or friendly fire, or extreme cases of exploitation such as the suffering of Chinese immigrants working on America's transcontinental railroads, are not mere accidents, even though these undesirable consequences may have been unintentional. From both a moral and a political point of view it is important that such incidents, which abound in history, are categorized as acts of violence, not as mere accidents. As Table 4.1 shows, instead of the binary distinction between violence and accidents, it is more accurate to think in terms of three categories: intentional violence, foreseeable but unintended violence, and mere accidents. The V-O approach covers those cases of foreseeable but unintended violence that are beyond the grasp of the I-O approach.

Table 4.1   Two types of violence

Intentional violence	Foreseeable but unintended violence	Mere accidents
Killing of innocent people in New York, Washington and Virginia on September 11 2001	Death of Chinese immigrants working on the transcontinental railroad Death as result of smart bombs gone astray Death by friendly fire Strategic and terror bombers	Accidental deaths caused by the crash of American Airline flight 587 on 12 November 2002

The reason for introducing the V-O approach is not to dismiss the I-O approach *tout-court*, by denying that intentions are part of the equation, or refusing to distinguish between acts of violence and mere accidents. That would clearly be wrong, as intentions play an important role in our understanding of violence, and victims of accidents are not to be confused with victims of violence. The problem with the I-O approach is simply that it is too limited in its scope, therefore the definition of violence it supports is much too narrow. By defining acts of violence in terms of the intention of the perpetrator to inflict injury or suffering on the victim, the I-O approach excludes many cases of abuse from being categorized as instances of violence. The issue here is not merely linguistic, pertaining to the way certain abusive acts are classified. It is a more fundamental issue, which challenges the way we think about violence. By referring to certain instances of foreseeable but unintended injury or suffering as acts of violence, the scope of the concept of violence is stretched beyond the narrow confines of intentionality.

In the previous section it was suggested that extreme cases of exploitation, or the use of smart bombs, or even friendly fire, should be recognized as acts of violence. There are good reasons, of a moral and political nature, for redefining the concept of violence to include such instances of foreseeable but unintended violence, and therefore for broadening our conception of violence. Above all, the concept of 'violence' is morally and politically transformative. An act of violence alters the normative relationship between perpetrators and victims, therefore classifying certain events as acts of violence sheds a new light on the moral accountability of social actors.

Reiman (2004, 55, emphasis in original) feels very strongly about not using the term 'accident' when referring to deaths that could have been prevented. In particular, he feels that that deaths caused as a result of unhealthy and unsafe conditions in the work place are not mere 'accidents' and should not be referred to as such, but acts of 'violence', 'crime', even 'murder':

> If it takes you an hour to read this chapter, by the time you reach the last page, two of your fellow citizens will have been murdered. *During that same time, more than six Americans will die as a result of unhealthy or unsafe conditions in the workplace!* Although these work-related deaths could have been prevented, they are not called

murders. Why not? Doesn't a crime by any other name still cause misery and suffering? What's in a name?

To refer to a certain event as the result of an act of violence rather than an accident transforms the way we perceive the individuals involved in that episode, to the extent that we demand a justification from perpetrators of violence for their actions. After all, violence is *prima facie* bad and wrong, as Chapter Six will suggest, which is why morality requires that an act of violence must always be justified. Albeit reluctantly, we accept accidents as mere happenings, but when violence occurs we demand a justification. The concept of foreseen but unintended violence reclaims under the rubric of justification instances that would otherwise be dismissed as mere accidents, and therefore would not require a justification. To rethink certain events as acts of violence, on the grounds that the resulting suffering and injury to the victims was foreseen and/or avoidable even if not intended, means that questions will be asked of the perpetrators and issues of accountability will arise. Mere accidents are bad, as the families of the 260 casualties of American Airlines flight 587 on 12 November 2002 will testify. But the violence suffered by the Chinese immigrants working on the transcontinental railroads in the 1860s, of the families of civilians killed during war, or the families of soldiers killed by friendly fire, is not only bad, but it may also be wrong. That is why an act of violence ought to be defined from the point of view of the victims, not the perpetrators.

Part V: The Victim-Oriented (V-O) approach

In what follows, the V-O approach will come under closer scrutiny. This approach has the merit of uncovering cases of violence that would otherwise go undetected. The idea is not to supersede the I-O approach with the V-O approach but to broaden the scope of the concept of violence by using the V-O approach in conjunction with the I-O approach.

The major difference between these two approaches is that while the I-O approach is motivational, the V-O approach is consequentialist. That is to say, an act of violence is not defined solely from the point of view of the perpetrator but also from the point of view of the victim (or potential victim) of violence. A victim of violence is any living creature that is injured by, or suffers as a result of, the direct or indirect act of another person. In other words, the term 'victim' will be used as a short cut for all those instances where a person or animal finds itself at the receiving end of vigorous abuse.[19]

Arguably the most famous endorsement of the V-O approach is by Galtung (1969, 171–172) who defends a definition of violence 'entirely located on the consequence side'. The advantage of Galtung's approach is that apart from cases of direct, personal violence, it also captures cases of indirect, structural violence. The difference between direct, personal violence and indirect, structural violence is that in the first case the consequences of an act of violence can be traced back to specific persons as actors, while in the second case there may not be any person directly responsible for harming another person. In structural violence the violence is built into the system and shows up as unequal power and consequently as unequal life chances. If people are starving under conditions that are foreseeable, and avoidable, then violence is occurring, regardless of whether there is a clear subject–action–object relation.

There are some well-known problems with Galtung's notion of structural violence. When Galtung (1969, 168) explains that 'violence is present when human beings are being influenced so that their actual somatic and mental realizations are below their potential realizations', he fails to appreciate that this definition risks being much too inclusive, its scope being much too broad. Defining the victims of violence as anyone who is effectively prevented from realizing their potentialities makes violence ubiquitous and arguably inevitable. Not surprisingly Galtung has attracted much criticism for this, for example by Keane (1996, 66) who takes a very dismissive stand: 'attempts (such as John Galtung's) to stretch its meaning to include "anything avoidable that impedes human realization" effectively makes a nonsense of the concept, linking it to a questionable ontological account of "the satisfaction of human needs" and making it indistinguishable from "misery", "alienation" and "repression" '.

While Galtung's general conception of violence needs rethinking, there is some value to the notion of structural violence, in particular in the fact that it forces us to think of violence from the perspective of those who are at the receiving end of such acts. Even though Galtung does not use the vocabulary of 'victims', he would appear to be endorsing what I am calling the V-O approach. In Galtung's (1969, 172) own words, the biggest disadvantage of the conventional notion of violence is that it 'may hence be catching the small fry and letting the big fish loose'. The same could be said for the I-O approach.

Two other authors who could be read as championing the V-O approach are Ted Honderich and Jamil Salmi. Honderich (1989) argues that facts of violence and facts of inequality are irrefutably (even if not directly) linked. Although Galtung is not mentioned, Honderich's (1989, 64–65) analysis echoes Galtung's notion of indirect, structural violence:

> By our ordinary lives we contribute to certain terrible circumstances. We make essential contributions to the shortening of the lifetimes of whole peoples and classes, and to many kinds of suffering and distress and degradation, and to denials of autonomy and of freedoms. In fact, we ensure by our ordinary lives that multitudes of individuals die before time, that families exist in single wretched rooms, and that this or that people are powerless in their homeland, or subservient in it, or driven from it.

The 'contribution' to the facts of inequality Honderich speaks of is often not intentional. It is instead a foreseeable but unintended consequence of pursuing our ordinary lives. But that does not take away from its violence. The fact that violence may not be intended adds weight to the claim that violence ought to be defined from the perspective of those whose lifetimes are shortened, who live a life of suffering, distress and degradation, without autonomy or freedom.[20]

Salmi's analysis of violence owes much to the influence of Galtung, which perhaps accounts for what is most laudable but also most problematic about his analysis. Salmi's (1993, 17) definition of violence as 'any avoidable action that constitutes a violation of a human right, in its widest meaning, or which prevents the fulfilment of a basic human need' has a distinctive Galtungian resonance, and his notion of indirect violence is very similar, if not identical, to Galtung's notion of structural violence. Yet just like Galtung, Salmi can also be faulted for defending a conception of violence which is perhaps too broad.

Notwithstanding this problem, what is particularly interesting about Salmi's analysis is that he explicitly refers to the category of 'victims' in his account of violence. Salmi (1993, 16) unequivocally states that 'the viewpoint of the victims should be the guiding principle in considering any objective classification of human rights violations'. Thus in the many examples of violence he uses throughout his book, such as starvation or under-nourishment, Salmi (1993, 18) always reminds us that we should define violence from the perspective of its victims: 'each time human beings starve or are undernourished, not because of an absolute lack of food after a natural disaster but simply because food is not available for social or political reasons.... it is legitimate to consider these people as the victims of a form of social violence'.

The works of Galtung, Honderich and Salmi suggest that there is more to the study of violence than can be captured by the I-O approach. The V-O approach adopts a consequentialist reasoning by favouring the perspective of the victims of violence. This is radically different from the motivational reasoning we find in the I-O approach, which starts by looking at the intentions of those who perform acts of violence.

Part VI: Conclusion

This chapter argued that there are valid reasons for endorsing a two-pronged approach to the study of violence, made up of the I-O approach and the V-O approach. Contrary to what is generally believed, violence should not be defined exclusively from the point of view of the perpetrators of violence and their intentions, instead we should also look at violence from the point of view of the victims. The major advantage of endorsing a V-O approach is that it makes the category of unintentional violence intelligible, therefore extending the way we define violence beyond the narrow confines of the intentional stand. According to unintentional violence, an act of violence occurs when injury or suffering is inflicted upon a person or persons by an agent, and the injury or suffering is either foreseeable and/or avoidable.

Violence is morally and politically transformative, in the sense that it alters the relationship between perpetrators and victims. Perpetrators of violence ought to be held accountable for their actions. By endorsing the V-O approach, this demand for justification is extended to cases of foreseeable but unintended violence. One major advantage of taking the V-O approach seriously is that avoidable will no longer go undetected.

Notes

1. The literature on the Doctrine of Double Effect is very extensive, and the brief account in this chapter does not pretend to do justice to this complex body of literature. Marquis (1991) suggests that there is no longer one Doctrine of Double Effect, but at least four different versions of it. For an overview of the literature see Glover (1977, Chapter 6); McIntyre (2004).
2. On the role of intent in the Genocide Convention, and in particular whether intent is a too stringent requirement, see Gordon (2002).
3. Intentionality also plays a central role in the definitions of violence by Coady (1986) and Bäck (2004).
4. On the relationship between intentionality and reason, not only in philosophy of action but also in moral philosophy, see Davidson (1980), Gibbard (1990) and Scanlon (1998).
5. Bratman is challenging the validity of the desire–belief model, which sees intentional action as action that stands in appropriate relations to the agent's desires and beliefs. Instead, Bratman argues that we are planning creatures. We settle in advance on plans for the future. Intentions are typically elements in such coordinating plans. It follows that intentions are distinctive states of mind, not to be reduced to clusters of desires and beliefs.
6. Bratman gives the example of someone who intends to run the marathon, and in doing so will wear down their sneakers. It does not follow that this person intended to wear down their sneakers, even though their intention is to run the marathon, and they know or believe that running the marathon will thereby wear down the sneakers.
7. The theory of structural violence will be discussed in full in Chapter Seven.
8. Needless to say, the fact that in Hart's famous example these actions were undertaken by Irish Nationalists has nothing to do with the assessment of the situation. The same analysis and conclusions would apply if the actions were taken by Loyalists.
9. HLA Hart (1968, 119–120). Hart goes on to say that outside the law a merely foreseen, though unwanted, outcome is not usually considered as intended.
10. See Ambrose (2002).
11. Chang (2003).

12. Chinese immigrant workers received $26–35 a month and had to provide their own food and tents, while white workers were paid $35 a month and were furnished with food and shelter.

13. Knobe (2003) suggests that people's judgement whether an agent intentionally brought about 'some side effect *x*', depends in a crucial way on what *x* happens to be. In particular whether they think that *x* is something good or something bad.

14. Source: *Center for Defense Information*, 7 August 2002.

15. Source: 'Even Smart Bombs Miss Their Mark Sometimes', by David Tarrant, *The Dallas Morning News*, October 18, 2001.

16. Source: 'Already, One Smart Bomb Has Proved Dumb', by Derrick Z Jackson, *Boston Globe*, October 10, 2001.

17. It is hard to put a precise number to the civilian casualties of the Iraq War. As of February 2007 the website *www.iraqbodycount.net* estimates that the casualties are somewhere between a minimum of 55,441 and a maximum of 61,133. According to the *Washington Post* the number may be as high as 100,000: '100,000 Estimated Civilian Deaths since Invasion', *The Washington Post*, October 29, 2004. In January 2007, the United Nations estimated that 34,452 Iraqi civilians were killed in violence and more than 36,000 were wounded during 2006: 'UN Clashes with Iraq on Civilian Death Toll', *The Guardian*, January 17, 2007.

18. Source: 'Friendly-Fire A Common Widowmaker', by Jim Hume, *Times Colonist* (Victoria BC, Canada), July 28, 2002.

19. Here I am following Audi (1971, 63) when he claims, 'all instances of violence involve vigorous abuse'.

20. Honderich (1989, 183) reminds us that 'the average life-expectancy in the economically less developed societies is about forty-five years, as against seventy-four in the developed societies'. See also Honderich (2002, 1–29).

5
Four Faces of Violence

Violence is an exceptionally complex and still very obscure concept. The difficulty one faces when trying to come to terms with the meaning of violence is that this single term is used in a number of different ways, and it covers a vast array of different phenomena. Reading the literature on violence one usually is confronted with the following scenarios: we speak of someone 'being violent' (Anthony forced his way through the crowd), or someone 'doing violence to' something or someone (Bill's interpretation of the play does violence to the text). Sometimes violence refers to an outcome (Daniel raped Elizabeth), although other times it is the intention rather than the outcome that defines violence (Daniel tried to rape Elizabeth). Sometimes violence takes the form of an act (Fred killed Gina by lethal injection), although other times violence takes the form of an omission (Fred killed Gina by not giving her the medications she needed). Violence can be directed to other people (Harry punched Ivan), to inanimate objects (Jack smashed the door), to animals (Kendy hanged the cat by the tail) or to oneself (Louise slashed her wrist). Violence can be physical (Monica punched Nancy, breaking her nose in the process) or psychological (Orlando verbally assaulted Patrick in public, inflicting psychological harm on Patrick). Violence can be direct (Quinn punched Robert), indirect (Steve was aversely affected after seeing Ted punch Ursula) or structural (Victoria died from lead poisoning as a result of working in a mine). Finally, violence can be immediate (Will stabbed Xavier) or it may involve a time lag (Yolanda left Zach to starve).

Taking into account all of the above, there are, I believe, three basic things that can be said about violence, in all its forms and permutations. First of all, *all violence is a violation of integrity*. If the concept of violence has an essence, this is it. As explained in Chapter One, the fact that harm, suffering and injury are inflicted upon the victim is only the epiphenomena of an even more fundamental cause, namely the violation of the integrity of the victim. The term 'integrity' should be interpreted in a strictly non-philosophical sense here, meaning wholeness or intactness. Integrity refers simply to the quality or state of being complete or undivided. An act of violence is fundamentally a violation of integrity, to the extent that it damages or destroys a pre-existing unity, where the unity can be physiological or psychological. The experience of injury, suffering or harm is a consequence or symptom of having one's integrity violated, but it is the violation of integrity that is the essence of violence. To define violence in terms of the harm or suffering rather than violation of integrity is to mistake the effect for the cause. Although the idea of violation of integrity forms the basis of our definition of violence, this is only a starting point. In order to have a more accurate picture of what violence entails, it is necessary to introduce two further distinctions.

This takes us to our second point. That the violation of integrity caused by the act of violence is the result of an action is trivially true. The violence reported in our newspapers on a daily basis is a chronicle of such actions. Yet, integrity can be violated by an omission as much as by a direct action. Consider the example introduced by Singer (1972) of someone who does not help or does not rescue a child who is drowning in a pond. Singer uses this example to make the point that, from a moral point of view, there is no distinctions between cases in which I am the only person who could possibly help and cases in which I am just one among millions in the same position to help. Leaving the question of moral responsibility aside (this was discussed in some detail in Chapter Three), the omission of not helping a person in need is causally equivalent to the action of harming that same person, and therefore must also be considered an act of violence.

Thirdly, apart from taking the form of an action or an omission, the violation of integrity can be either intended, or it can be foreseen even if unintended. Intentionality is a complex and contested concept in the philosophy of action, as the discussion in Chapter

Four indicates. Intentionality refers to a general 'purpose' or 'aim', an 'intention with which', and it can entail both a minimal intentional action (picking a flower while walking along a path) and a full intentional action (my intention to visit a friend next week). Intentional acts of violence are so abundant that there is no need to elaborate on them. Street crimes, sexual violence and the bombing of a city are all valid examples of this disturbing reality. Yet the harm caused by the violation of integrity can take place without the harm being intended, a fact that needs to be explained. There are three general types of unintentional harmful acts. First, action A was not intended to harm anyone, but it unintentionally (although foreseeably) harmed B. Secondly, action A may have been intended to harm B, but unintentionally (although foreseeably) it also harmed C. Finally action A may have been intended to harm B only to a certain degree, but unintentionally (although foreseeably) it ended up harming B to a much greater degree. The point here is that instead of thinking of violence strictly in terms of what the perpetrator intended to do, we should also think in terms of the foreseen consequences of the same act, or even in terms of avoidable evil. To focus exclusively on the intentions of the perpetrator is to assume that an act of violence is by definition intentional, whereas to include foreseen and avoidable consequences is to allow an act of violence to be intentional as well as unintentional. In terms of Singer's example of someone who does not help or does not rescue a child who is drowning in a pond, this qualifies as an act of violence to the extent that the consequences on the child of this non-action were both foreseen and avoidable.

The essence of violence (violation of integrity) analysed through these two variable (action versus omission; intentionality versus foreseeability) forms the basis of our definition of violence:

(1) An act of violence occurs when the integrity or unity of a subject (person or animal) or object (property) is being violated.

> *a. The violation of integrity may occur at the physical or psychological level, through physical or psychological means.*
> *b. A typical consequence of the violation of integrity is that a person or animal will be harmed or injured, or an object will be destroyed or damaged.*

(2) *An act of violence occurs when integrity is violated intentionally, or when the violation of integrity is foreseen and avoidable but unintended.*

(3) *An act of violence occurs when a violation of integrity is the result of an action, or of an omission.*

Part I: The four faces of violence

So far I have argued that all violence involves a violation of integrity; that violence can be an act or an omission; and that violence can be intentional or unintentional. These pointers combine to form an analytical framework, giving rise to four distinct faces of violence: when integrity is violated intentionally by means of a direct action; when integrity is violated intentionally by means of an omission; when the violation of integrity is foreseeable (even if not intended) as a result of certain actions and when the violation of integrity is foreseeable (even if not intended) as a result of certain omissions. In what follows example of each of the four faces of violence will be put forward, followed in Part II by the same analysis but this time regarding political violence.

It may be necessary to point out that these four faces are not meant to represent mutually exclusive ideal types, nor am I suggesting that each act of violence falls under one and only one of these categories. Violence is a difficult concept to analyse precisely because most instances of violence would include elements of more than one face of violence. For example, during bombing raids two different types of violence will occur simultaneously: the intentional violence caused by the deliberate act of dropping bombs on certain enemy targets, as well as the foreseeable violence caused by a percentage of bombs that will unintentionally hit civilian targets. Notwithstanding this undeniable truth about violence, the exercise of distinguishing between four different faces of violence is a useful analytical exercise that tries to bring clarity to the complexity of this phenomenon by breaking it down into its different component parts.

Violence as intentional action

Intentional violence abounds, and sexual violence provides a myriad of examples of this hideous offensive abuse. The case of the Central

Park Jogger, as told by the victim Meili (2004) in her recent book, is a good example of sexual violence as intentional violence.

The Central Park Jogger
Trisha Meili was a young New York stockbroker. On April 19th, 1989, she went for a run in Central Park (in New York) after work at 9.35 p.m. She was attacked, raped, savagely beaten and left for dead. She is found hours later by two men wandering the park. When she arrives in the emergency room she is in a coma.

This well-known story is one of many instances of sexual violence against women.[1] In the case of Trisha Meili the rapist was a complete stranger, but often the violence comes from people of trust, be it a friend, boyfriend, parent, husband or family relative. Women are also the targets of sexual violence during wartime, as the recurring, systematic rape of women during warfare testifies.[2] In each of those cases, the act of violence is an intentional act, to the extent that the perpetrator fully intended to violate the integrity of the victim. In the case of sexual violence, the violation occurs via a direct action, although there are also cases where the violation of integrity suffered by the victim occurs as a result of an omission rather than an action.

Violence as intentional omission
The tragic case of Anna Climbie is an example of how an act of violence, apart from involving direct actions, can also occur via an omission. In the case of Anna Climbie the omission in question took the form of intentional, gross neglect.

Anna Climbie
In 1997 Anna Climbie came to Britain from the Ivory Coast. Just over a year after leaving Ivory Coast, Anna Climbie was dead at the age of eight. The victim of horrendous physical and emotional abuse, she was failed by all who were bound up in her care. Her death was the worst case of child abuse the Home Office pathologist who examined her body had ever seen. She was bound hand and foot, naked, in a bathtub in a tiny flat in Tottenham [London] in the middle of winter. Instead of being fed she was starved: what little food she was given were scraps, fed to her in the bath on a

piece of plastic bag. Instead of being clothed, she was stuck in a black binbag which caught her excrement and trapped acids that burned her body. Anna Climbie died from hypothermia due to exposure to cold and wet conditions. The underlying cause of her death was severe neglect and malnutrition.[3]

Anna Climbie was the victim of many aspects of violence. The 128 marks on her body found by the pathologist are a clear indication of direct acts of physical violence. We now know that Anna was beaten with a variety of weapons including belt buckles, bicycle chains, coat hangers and shoes. We also know that razor blades were taken to her fingers and a hammer to her toes. But apart from these direct acts of violence, Anna also suffered from certain intentional non-acts or omissions. Anna was not fed properly. She was not given adequate clothing. She was not cared for. She was not loved. As the coroner said, in the last analysis the underlying cause of her death was severe neglect and malnutrition, in other words it was omissions of an intentional nature that killed Anna Climbie. These intentional omissions are as much a form of violence as the more obvious direct acts of abuse. Had Anna Climbie only been subjected to the deliberate omissions and not to the direct physical abuses, she would still be the victim of violence.

Foreseeable violence by actions

In Chapter Four the idea of foreseeable but unintended violence was discussed in some detail. Without going over the same material, suffice to say that foreseeable violence occurs when the violation of integrity, albeit unintended, was foreseen and/or avoidable. Foreseeable violence stands to intentional violence as manslaughter stands to murder. The legal definition of manslaughter is the unlawful killing of a human being without malice or premeditation, whereas murder requires malicious intent. Manslaughter can be either voluntary, when it happens in the heat of passion caused by adequate provocation, or involuntary, when the person's act was by its nature dangerous to human life or was done with reckless disregard for human life, and the person knew (or could foresee) that such conduct was a threat to the lives of others. The distinction between manslaughter and murder is important from a legal point of view, just as the distinction between intentional and foreseeable violence is important from an analytical and perhaps even moral point of view. The point here is simply that foreseeable violence is as much an act of violence as intentional violence, the same way that manslaughter and murder are both acts of violence.

The following example highlights the fact that a certain act, albeit unintended, is still an act of violence, since the resulting violation of integrity was both foreseen and avoidable.

Deaths Caused by Drink-Driving in the UK

Since the early 1980s, there has been a substantial decline in drinking and driving and in the number of alcohol-related deaths and injuries on the road, which reached their lowest level in 1998 and 1999. However, since 2000 the number of casualties has been rising again. The provisional figures for 2002 are the highest since 1990, with a total of 20,000 casualties and 560 deaths. Around half of the casualties were people other than the drinking drivers themselves. There were probably an additional 250 people killed in accidents involving drivers and riders with raised blood alcohol levels but still below the current legal limit. Altogether, therefore, around one in five road deaths are alcohol related.[4]

In The Case of the Deaths Caused by Drink-Driving, the casualties may not have been intended by drivers, but at the same there is an important difference to be made between these deaths and other road deaths. To the extent that driving under the influence of alcohol has the possible foreseen consequence of causing road deaths, and it is widely known that alcohol is an impairment on our driving, the deaths caused by drink-driving are the result of an act of foreseeable violence, even if unintended.

Foreseeable violence by omission

So far I have argued that violence can take the form of intentional or unintentional action, or intentional omissions. But there is a fourth face of violence we need to consider: foreseeable violence by omission, where the violence was never intended. This is perhaps the least visible type of violence, which explains why it often goes undetected. The famous case of Kitty Genovese reminds us that violence often lurks where we least expect it.

Kitty Genovese

At approximately 3:20 on the morning of March 13, 1964, twenty-eight-year-old Kitty Genovese was returning to her home in a nice middle-class area of Queens, NY. She parked her car and started the walk to her apartment some 35 yards away. She got as far as a streetlight when a man grabbed her. She screamed. Lights went on in the 10-floor apartment building nearby. She yelled, 'Oh, my God, he stabbed me! Please help me!' Windows opened in the apartment building and a man's voice shouted, 'Let that girl alone.' The attacker looked up, shrugged and walked-off down the street. Ms Genovese struggled to get to her feet. Lights went back off in the apartments. The attacker came back and stabbed her again. She again cried out, 'I'm dying! I'm dying!' And again the lights came on and windows opened in many of the nearby apartments. The assailant again left and got into his car and drove away. Ms Genovese staggered to her feet as a city bus drove by. It was now 3:35 a.m. The attacker returned once again. He found her in a doorway at the foot of the stairs and he stabbed her a third time – this time with a fatal consequence. It was 3:50 when the police received the first call. They responded quickly and within two minutes were at the scene. Ms Genovese was already dead. The only person to call, a neighbor of Ms Genovese, revealed that he had phoned only after much thought and an earlier phone call to a friend. He said, 'I didn't want to get involved'.[5]

Kitty Genovese's murder is one of the most studied murder cases in the sociology of group behaviour. This disturbing event raises many questions about selfishness and the lack of altruism. In terms of our analysis of violence, we must try to account for the fact that her murder was witnessed by 38 onlookers who did nothing to help her. One possible explanation is that each one of the 38 onlookers assumed that one of the other 37 onlookers was going to assist Kitty Genovese or even only call the police. If we give the onlookers the benefit of the doubt, it follows that their non-actions were not intended to harm Kitty Genovese, unlike in the case of Anna Climbie whose neglect was very much intended. Nevertheless, the death of Kitty Genovese was both foreseeable and avoidable, and therefore the omissions of the bystanders should be seen for what it is: foreseeable violence by omission.

Table 5.1   The four faces of violence

	Intentional	Foreseeable
Action	• Sexual violence	• Drink driving
Omission	• Extreme neglect	• Bystanders

As I said before, these four faces of violence are not meant to be mutually exclusive, since most cases of violence would fall under more than one category. In fact it would be more accurate to portray the four faces as overlapping spheres in a Venn diagram. For example, the killing of Anna Climbie is an example of both an intentional act of violence (the beatings with belt buckles, bicycle chains, hammer and razor blades), and of an intentional omission (the malnutrition and severe neglect). The four faces of violence we talked about so far refer to violence in general. In what follows, the more specific case of political violence will be put to the test.

Part II: Political violence defined

Political violence is a subset of the more generic category of violence, therefore we should expect the analysis of violence above also to apply to specific cases of political violence.

At the most basic level politics is essentially about power relations, where the aim of political violence is either to change or to uphold existing power structures or relations. To identify politics with power relations is a fairly standard move. Dahl (1999, 15) suggests the following definition: 'A political system is any persistent pattern of human relationships that involves, to a significant extent, power, rule or authority'. One important virtue of this definition is that many associations that most people do not ordinarily regard as 'political' possess the attributes of what Dahl calls 'political systems', including private clubs, business firms, religious organizations, civic groups and of course families. Politics exists outside of the public sphere, or in other words there is more to politics than what we find in the institutions of the State. This (and much more) we owe to the feminist challenges to mainstream political science over the last forty years.[6] Another virtue of Dahl's definition is that power always involves social relationships, hence power without anything or anyone to exercise it against is meaningless. The same is true for violence. Although there are notable differences between the concepts of power and violence, and these terms should not be used interchangeably, as already argued in Chapter One, there are also some important similarities: violence like power involves a social relationship, which explains why an astute commentator of politics like Max Weber considered violence to be central to the definition of politics.[7]

The other point about politics worth mentioning is the fact that the aim of political violence is not restricted exclusively to forcing change in the existing power structure, even though images of revolutions and terrorism are the first things that come to mind when we utter the words 'political violence'. Instead, a great deal of political violence occurs when those in power try to maintain the existing power structure. A white policeman punching a peaceful demonstrator in 1955 in Montgomery, Alabama, is as much an act of political violence as the massacre of Sharpeville by the Apartheid regime in South Africa on 21 March 1960. The Sharpeville massacre took place during a peaceful protest organized by the Pan Africanist Congress (PAC) against the pass laws, which restricted the movements of black South Africans. Sixty-seven people were killed, and over 180 injured, when the police opened fire against the protesters. Most of those killed and injured were women and children. By using violence against the peaceful demonstrators, the white policemen in Alabama and South Africa were intending to maintain or prolong a certain political order, grounded on certain relations of power, in this case a racist state of affairs.

This way of thinking about political violence has certain advantages compared to the definitions of political violence by Georges Sorel and Ted Honderich. In their view, for violence to be political it must occur within the public sphere, and it must be aimed at promoting change. Thus Sorel (1961, 195) tells us that political violence applies exclusively to acts of rebellion against the State: 'the term violence should be employed only for acts of revolt; we should say, therefore, that the object of force is to impose a certain social order in which the minority governs, while violence tends to the destruction of that order'. Somewhat similarly Honderich (1989, 8) defines political violence as 'a considerable or destroying use of force against persons or things, a use of force prohibited by law, directed to a change in the policies, personnel or system of government, and hence also directed to changes in the existence of individuals in the society and perhaps other societies'.[8]

The problem, or limitation, with Sorel and Honderich's accounts of political violence is that they fail to appreciate two important aspects of political violence. First, that political relations can occur outside the realm of the public sphere. Secondly, that political violence can be exercised in order to maintain the status quo rather than to force changes. Sexual or domestic violence highlight these points. This type of violence falls beyond the scope of what Sorel and Honderich consider to be 'political', and its goal is often to preserve (rather than change) a certain unequal power relationship already existing between the perpetrator and the victim.[9]

Part III: The four faces of political violence

Political violence has the same four faces as the more generic idea violence: we are looking at intentional or foreseeable action or omissions that cause a violation of integrity. Furthermore, just as for violence more generally, most cases of political violence would also be multi-faceted. Table 5.2 below tries to captures the full complexity of political violence.

Political violence as intentional actions

This is the most obvious of the four permutations. It comprises all deliberate acts of violence performed for the sake of either altering

Table 5.2   The four faces of political violence

	Intentional	Foreseeable
Action	• Terrorism • Torture • Revolutions • Domestic violence	• Smart-bombs • Friendly fire • Arms trade
Omission	• Economic sanctions	• Bystanders • Cover-ups • Insufficient global health fund

or upholding the existing power relations. One obvious example is terrorism:

Terrorism
The deliberate killing of innocent people, at random, in order to spread fear through a whole population and force the hand of its political leaders (Walzer 2002, 5).

Walzer's definition of terrorism is as well known as it is controversial. Whether terrorism always targets innocent people, and whether it always aims to kill people at random, is the subject of much debate.[10] Yet what no one would question is the claim that acts of terrorist are always intentional. It is important for Walzer that we recognize the actions of terrorists as deliberate, since this makes the practice even less morally defensible: 'Terrorists are like killers on a rampage, except that their rampage is not just expressive of rage or madness; the rage is purposeful and programmatic. It aims at a general vulnerability: Kill these people in order to terrify those'. (Walzer 1988, 238).

Similarly the idea of revolution or civil disobedience would not make much sense unless those participating in these acts were doing so deliberately. If one morning I decide to walk to work totally unaware that on that same day the civil rights movement had called for a boycott of the local bus company, I could not take credit for supporting the civil rights movement for having taken part in an act of civil disobedience, even though my actions are in all other respects identical to those taking part in the protest.

Terrorism, revolution and some forms of civil disobedience[11] are three examples of political violence where the objective is to bring about a change, more or less radical, in the existing power relations. Yet intentionality is also present in political violence that seeks to uphold or defend the existing power relations, in the public or private sphere, as in the case of state terrorism, police violence or domestic violence. One poignant example here is the large and increasing support for the use of torture interrogation of terrorists by US state officials after 9/11.

Torture
Any act by which severe pain or suffering, whether physical or mental, is intentionally inflicted on a person for such purposes as

obtaining from him or a third person information or a confession, punishing him for an act he or a third person has committed or is suspected of having committed, or intimidating or coercing him or a third person.

The above definition of torture, taken from Article 1 of the 1984 Convention Against Torture and Other Cruel, Inhuman or Degrading Treatment or Punishment, clearly states that torture is an act where pain and suffering is intentionally inflicted on a person. This includes torture interrogation of terrorists. Thus the hypothetical 'ticking bomb' scenario, where a terrorist is tortured in order to extract information of a bomb planted somewhere in the city and ticking away, is the standard justification given for condoning the act of torturing a presumed terrorist.[12]

Political violence as intentional omissions

As in the case of violence in general, the same is true for political violence: omissions can be as harmful as actions. An intentional omission, or non-action, can be the most devastating way to violate the integrity of someone or something. A recent example of intentional omission is the case of economic sanctions. As Mueller and Mueller (1999) argue, if the U.N. estimates of the human damage in Iraq are even roughly correct, economic sanctions may have killed more people in Iraq in the 1990s than have been slain by all so-called weapons of mass destruction throughout history.

Economic Sanctions against Iraq

No one knows with any precision how many Iraqi civilians have died as a result [of economic sanctions], but various agencies of the United Nations, which oversees the sanctions, have estimated that they have contributed to hundreds of thousands of deaths. By 1998 Iraqi infant mortality had reportedly risen from the pre-Gulf War rate of 3.7 per cent to 12 per cent. Inadequate food and medical supplies, as well as breakdowns in sewage and sanitation systems and in the electrical power systems needed to run them, reportedly cause an increase of 40,000 deaths annually of children under the age of 5 and of 50,000 deaths annually of older Iraqis (Mueller and Mueller, 1999, p.49).

The UN Security Council approved Resolution 661 on 6 August 1990. The effects on the Iraqi people have been devastating. Hunger is endemic. In resigning from his post as first UN Assistant Secretary General and Humanitarian Coordinator in Iraq, Denis Halliday said: 'We are in the process of destroying an entire society. It is as simple and terrifying as that. It is illegal and immoral'.[13] Denis Halliday even went as far as to claim that the systematic, highly planned imposition of a policy with such devastating effects can rightly be termed genocide.

Perhaps to equate economic sanctions with genocide is somewhat disingenuous,[14] even though the sanctions were meant to put pressure on the Iraqi power structure, by way of making millions of innocent Iraqi people suffer.[15] A more fruitful line of attack is to compare economic sanctions with war terrorism. Walzer (2002, 5) defines war terrorism as the effort to kill civilians in such large numbers that their government is forced to surrender, furthermore 'they [ordinary people] aren't killed incidentally in the course of actions aimed elsewhere; they are killed intentionally'. Walzer mentions Hiroshima as the classic case, yet economic sanctions against Iraq has the same characteristics: the people who are targeted, and therefore who suffer the most, are non-combatants, and the 5,300 Iraqi children who died every month from disease, malnutrition and related conditions, were not killed incidentally, but intentionally. The fact that Denis Halliday resigned from his post of UN Assistant Secretary General and Humanitarian Coordinator in Iraq adds credence to the view that economic sanctions are a form of intentional violence by omission.[16]

Political violence by foreseeable actions

Political violence, like violence in general, is not always intentional. In Chapter Four the cases of smart bombs and friendly fire were mentioned as examples of foreseeable but unintentional violence. In what follows, I want to suggest another example that fits the bill of foreseeable but unintended political violence by actions: global arms trade.

Global Arms Trade

The arms trade is big business. In 2003 global military expenditure and arms trade is the largest spending in the world at over 950 billion dollars per year, as reported by the Stockholm International

Peace Research Institute (SPIRI). USA, Russia, France and Britain do the largest businesses of arms trade in the world. Sometimes, these arms sales are made secretly and sometimes knowingly to human rights violators, military dictatorships and corrupt governments. In 2002, developing nations accounted for 60.6% of all arms transfer agreements made worldwide. Arms trade contributes to political oppression and human rights abuse in those nations. In 1997 alone, half of USA's aid was related to military aid/trade. Turkey is the biggest importer of US arms and the largest recipient of USA military aid, even though Turkey does not meet basic US criteria for arms exports. Civilians are the main landmine casualties, yet in 1997 the USA refused to sign an international treaty to ban the use of landmines.[17]

As in the case of smart bombs and friendly fire, with global arms trade we are looking at action that were not intended to cause suffering to innocent people, but given the fact that such suffering is both foreseeable (given the track record of human rights abuses of the countries purchasing the arms from the West) and avoidable, global arms trade has all the features of foreseeable but unintended violence.

Let us consider the specific case of the genocide against the Iraqi Kurds by Saddam Hussein. During the Iran–Iraq war in the early 1980s, the USA was supporting the Iraqi war effort by selling them their arms, but in 1988 began a military operation against Iraqi Kurds in northern Iraq, which included the use of chemical and biological weapons on Kurdish towns and villages. During this operation, some 1,200 villages were destroyed, and more than 180,000 persons were killed. While to the best of our knowledge the USA did not supply Saddam Hussein the chemical and biological weapons used against the Kurds, they are in part responsible for creating a strong Iraqi army. This begs the question whether the USA are in part also responsible for the Kurdish genocide.[18]

Another example, even more evident than the previous one, is the genocide of the indigenous Mayas in Guatemala between 1981 and 1983.

The Guatemalan Genocide

President Rios Montt, who came to power after a military coup in March 1982, presided over the bloodiest era in recent Guatemalan history. He implemented a 'scorched earth policy' targeting rural indigenous communities, which killed up to 150,000 civilians, and internally displaced 1.5 million people. In 1999 the Truth Commission (Commission for Historical Clarification) concluded that between 1981 and 1983 the indigenous Mayas were the victims of genocide.

The USA has been directly involved in Guatemalan affairs since it helped to overthrow the democratically elected government of Arbenz in 1954 and replace him with the first of many military dictators. In the 1960s the USA became directly involved in counter-insurgency operations in order to keep Guatemala from becoming a 'second Cuba', playing a crucial role in professionalizing and training the Guatemalan army. As Jonas (2000, 120) points out: 'This was the origin of the killing machine known as the Guatemalan counterinsurgency army'. The election of Jimmy Carter to the White House temporarily changed the nature of US–Guatemala relations, as the Carter administration imposed conditions on US aid and suspended direct military assistance. Yet this did not prevent the incoming new president Ronald Reagan from finding indirect ways of supporting the counterinsurgency war in Guatemala, including covert CIA assistance, until open military aid was restored. During his visit to Guatemala, Reagan referred to the then Guatemalan president Efrain Rios Montt as 'a friend of democracy'. Today there is an ongoing effort to bring Rios Montt to justice, by charging him with crimes against humanity. Given the close relationship between the USA and the Guatemalan army, it is not unreasonable to suggest that the USA must take some responsibility for the political violence which took place, especially between 1981 and 1983. By giving military aid to Rios Montt, and to many other dictators before and after him, the USA committed acts of unintended but foreseeable political violence against hundred of thousands of civilians in Guatemala.

Political violence as foreseeable omissions

As in the case of violence in general, this is the most obscure type of political violence, therefore it will need a more detailed inspection. We already encountered an example of violence as foreseeable omission in Chapter Three, where the case of bystanders during the Nazi occupation of Europe was discussed. We can safely assume that the vast majority of bystanders did not agree with the anti-Semitic laws of the Nazi regime, and did not intend to harm any Jewish person by their inability to become rescuers. Nevertheless, their non-action contributed to the suffering of the Jews, hence the foreseeable consequences of their omissions makes this a case of violence. In what follows I want to consider two more examples, the cover-up of the sexual abuses within the Church and the insufficient aid by rich countries to poor countries.

The persistent and systematic cover-up by the Catholic Church of the rape and sexual harassment of small children by members of the clergy over the last 50 years presents us with a very disturbing case study. The problem has worldwide implications for the Church. In January 2003, the Catholic Church in Ireland agreed to a landmark $110 million payment to children abused by clergy over decades, where more than 20 priests, brothers and nuns have been convicted of molesting children. Sexual abuse cases involving cover-ups have also been reported in England, France, Australia and the United States. For years, the Vatican viewed such reports as attempts to discredit the Church or as part of an orchestrated campaign against celibacy.

Sex and the Church

Allegations against paedophile priests have convulsed the Catholic Church in Ireland this month, forcing the resignation of the long-serving Bishop of Ferns, Dr. Brendan Comiskey, and further undermining trust in the hierarchy. The latest scandal, highlighted in a television documentary, added to the growing demands for the church to end its instinctive protection of clergymen accused of sex crimes and purge its ranks of those suspected of exploiting their privileged position in society. Dr. Comiskey's departure followed criticism of the way in which he handled child sex abuse allegations against Father Sean Fortune, a priest who committed suicide in 1999 shortly before he was due to stand trial on 29 charges of sexually assaulting young boys. Some of the allegations against the priest dated back to the 1970s when he worked at a south Belfast orphanage. More than 2,500 people have asked to give evidence to an official commission of inquiry in Dublin which is investigating child abuse in Irish state and religious institutions. The statements dated back to the 1950s and 1960s. One of Ireland's most notorious cases involved Fr. Brendan Smyth who was sentenced to 12 years for a total of 74 sexual assaults. His church superiors were said to have known about his behaviour in 1969.[19]

In the case of sexual abuses within the Catholic Church, the violence came in the form of actions (by the clergy who violated the children) as well as omissions (by higher Church authorities in its effort to cover-up the abuses). While the decision to cover-up the scandal was deliberate, the unintended consequence of this cover-up operation was that the violence persisted, since the molesting perverts operating within the Church were allowed to continue to commit more abuses. No one is suggesting that the Church authorities intended for the children to be sexually molested, even though what the children suffered could have been prevented had the Church acted responsibly, at the same time this enduring violence was both foreseeable and avoidable, hence the omissions of the Church must be seen as acts of violence. Furthermore, since this cover-up was motivated by political reasons, we are looking at political violence. By covering-up these sexual abuses the Church was trying to uphold (or at least not undermine) its status of power within society. The rapes that could have been prevented must have been deemed a foreseeable but nevertheless acceptable cost needed to protect the power of the Church.

The second example of violence by foreseeable omission I want to discuss is the well-known case of the unwillingness by OECD countries to contribute 0.7% of their gross national product towards world aid.

Insufficient Aid to Poor Countries

The gap between the rich and poor has widened steadily. Estimates based on World Bank data suggest that over 40% of the 614 million people in less developed countries live in absolute poverty and that average life expectancy is now 25 years less than it is in developed countries. Ten years ago the countries of the Organization for Economic Cooperation and Development (OECD) promised to scale up their development assistance. Since then the flow of aid has actually decreased to its lowest level (in relation to members' combined gross national product) for 20 years. Oxfam describes the rich country record on aid as 'derisory' and their trade policies akin to 'highway robbery'.[20]

Table 5.3 Overseas development aid in 1999

Country	% of GDP	$bn
United States	0.10	9.15
Italy	0.15	1.81
Greece	0.15	0.19
Spain	0.23	1.36
United Kingdom	0.23	3.40
Australia	0.26	0.98
Portugal	0.26	0.28
Austria	0.26	0.53
Germany	0.26	5.52
New Zealand	0.26	0.13
Canada	0.28	1.70
Belgium	0.30	0.76
Ireland	0.31	0.25
Finland	0.33	0.42
Japan	0.35	15.32
Switzerland	0.35	0.97
France	0.39	5.64
Luxemburg	0.66	0.12
Sweden	0.70	1.63
Netherlands	0.79	3.13
Norway	0.91	1.37
Denmark	1.01	1.73

GDP = gross domestic product.
Source: www.oecd.org/dac/images/ODA99amo.jpg.

Table 5.3 shows the net overseas development aid given by OECD countries as a percentage of gross domestic product in 1999, ranked from meanest to most generous. The meanest country, by far, was the United States. Only Denmark, Norway, the Netherlands, Sweden and Luxemburg gave anywhere near the United Nations target of 0.7% of gross national product.[21]

There is little doubt that had all the OECD countries contributed 0.7% of their GDP to fight poverty in the Third World, many lives could have been saved and much misery could have been prevented. That poverty causes death is a fact known to all the OECD countries, and yet only Luxemburg, Sweden, the Netherlands, Norway and Denmark are prepared to fulfil the obligations they agreed on. The fact that the other OECD countries did not intend to kill millions of starving people in remote corners of the world does not mean that violence is not taking place. The effects of the downfall on their contributions is both foreseeable and avoidable, therefore the omission of not giving the full 0.7 % of their GDP to international aid is an act of unintended but foreseeable violence by omission.

Part IV: Conclusion

In this chapter it was argued that violence, including political violence, has four main distinctive faces: violence by intentional acts; violence by intentional omission; actions that cause foreseeable violence and omission that cause foreseeable violence. The point of this exercise was simply to expand on the definition of the concept of violence, by break down the complexity of this concept into its main components, in order to have a more clear understanding of what violence is and when it occurs.

When analysing violence, it is important to remember that the moral assessment of an act of violence, political or non-political, cannot be derived from the definition of violence itself. Although the idea of a violation usually carries a negative connotation, it is not wrong by definition. As Runkle (1976, 368–369) rightly points out, if violence is wrong by definition, there is little point in talking about violence: 'Would it not be better to scrutinize objectively a type of action, then proceed to the ethical issues concerning its use? That is what we ordinarily do with such actions as promise-keeping, sexual intercourse, and killing. Can we not do the same with such apparently violent actions as bomb attacks, knifings, and kicks in the head?'.

There is an important difference between saying that violence is prima facie wrong, and saying that violence is wrong by definition, since not all violations of integrity are necessarily bad or wrong. Violating the physical space of another person is usually considered inappropriate, although in cases of self-defence the violation is legally and morally acceptable. An act of political violence against a totalitarian oppressive regime is, within certain limits, morally commendable. At the same time terrorism is beyond the pale of morality,[22] if by terrorism we understand the indiscriminate random killing of innocent people.[23]

With this chapter terminates the first stage of our analysis of violence, based on the definition of the concept of violence. Starting from the next chapter, and for all the subsequent chapters, we will leave behind us the debate on the appropriate definition of violence. Having defined the idea of violence as the violation of integrity, and having highlighted its four main faces, the second stage will seek answers to normative questions regarding the ethics of violence.

Notes

1. For a philosophical analysis of a very similar act of sexual violence, analysed from the point of view of the victim, see Brison (2002). This is possibly the most philosophically sophisticated and informative book on violence to be found.
2. For a lucid but shocking account of systematic rape during the wars in Bosnia-Herzegovina and Croatia, see Allen (1996). The International Criminal Court now considers rape during wartime a 'crime against humanity'.
3. Source: *The Guardian*, Saturday 13 January 2001.
4. Source: 'Drinking and Driving', *Institute of Alcohol Studies*, 5 November 2004.
5. Source: *A Cry in the Night: The Kitty Genovese Murder*, by Mark Gado: *http://www.crimelibrary.com/serial_killers/predators/kitty_genovese/*.
6. For a useful overview of how feminism forced us to rethink the essence of politics, see Carroll and Zerilli (1999).
7. Weber postulated that an association should be called political 'if and in so far as the enforcement of its order is carried out continually within a given territorial area by the application and threat of physical force on the part of the administrative staff'. Quoted in Dahl (1999, p.14).
8. Honderich (1989, 8).
9. For a detailed analysis of the politics of domestic violence, see Breines and Gordon (1983).
10. See for example Fullinwider (1988).
11. The literature on civil disobedience is divided on the question whether civil disobedience is by definition nonviolent, or whether some violence is legitimate. In suggesting that there is scope for violence in civil disobedience, I am following Murphy (1971).
12. For a consequentialist argument against torture interrogation of terrorists, see Arrigo (2004); Bufacchi and Arrigo (2006).
13. Source: *The Independent*, 15 October 1998.
14. For a detailed analysis on economic sanctions on Iraq, the intent to cause wide-spread suffering, and the accusation of genocide, see Gordon (2002).

15. The following letter by an Iraqi refugee living in England, Haifa Zangana, appeared in *The Guardian*, September 17, 2002: 'On December 6 1995, I sent an A4 padded envelope to my nieces and nephews in Mosul. It contained one pencil case, three erasers, three sharpeners, six fountain pens, two markers, one glue-stick and two Biros. It was marked "gift for children". The envelope was returned, stamped: "Due to international sanctions against Iraq, we are not able to forward your packet." ' . . . . Here are some paragraphs from [a personal letter] from a friend: 'Let me share a laugh with you. As Selma, my wife, was being wheeled out of the operating theatre, the doctor handed me two things: a long prescription and, what else, do you think? Selma's uterus! I had to go find the medicine as soon as possible, and also to take the uterus to a private lab for a biopsy. It was the start of a 20-hour madman's journey around Baghdad'.

16. See Gordon (2002)

17. Source: *www.globalissues.org.*

18. See O'Leary (2002).

19. Source: *The Guardian*, 13 April 2002.

20. Source: Tessa Richards 'New Global Health Fund', *British Medical Journal* 2001; 322: 1321–1322 (2 June).

21. Source: Frank Shann 'Few Rich Countries Attain UN's Aid Target for Poor Countries', *British Medical Journal*, 2001; 323: 634 (15 September):

22. See Walzer (2002).

23. As Fullinwider (1988) argues, this is not necessarily the only or best way to define an act of terrorism, in which case our moral assessment of terrorism may change.

6
Why is Violence Bad?

Violence is not wrong by definition, but it is prima facie wrong. That means when violence occurs we must suspend moral judgement on the event until the perpetrator justifies his or her actions. The act of violence of rape is wrong, but the act of violence of fighting off a rapist is not wrong. It is only if no justification comes forth, or the justification given is inadequate, that we can say that the violence was wrong. Of course this raises the question 'why is violence wrong'?. If violence is defined as a violation of integrity, why is it wrong to violate someone's integrity?

This chapter suggests that the wrongness of violence is essentially related to the badness of violence. That is to say, in order to understand why violence is wrong, we must first explain why violence is bad. Of course this does not mean that everything that is bad is automatically wrong – we all know that it is bad to be incapacitated by flu or a nasty cold, but we would not say that it is wrong to be feeling ill. But when it comes to violence, the wrongness of violence is derived from the badness of violence. It follows that if we want to know why violence is wrong, we must first ask ourselves: 'why is violence bad?'.

With the possible exception of Nietzsche, no one would seriously argue that violence is good for its victims.[1] Most people naturally think that violence is bad for the person who suffers the violence, and some even suggest that violence is bad for those doing the violence.[2] But why? What is it about violence that makes it bad? In an attempt to shed light on the badness of violence, this chapter will approach the problem by way of a tangentially related question, namely 'why is death bad?' Violence is not synonymous with death, therefore 'why is violence bad' and 'why is death bad' are different questions, and the answer to the latter question does not present a perfect fit when applied to the former question. Nevertheless, understanding why death is bad will be a good starting point for an inquiry into the badness of violence. Part I will explore the similarities and differences between the concepts of violence and death. Part II will survey the literature on the badness of death, focussing in particular on its comparative or extrinsic evil (Thomas Nagel) and its intrinsic evil (F.M. Kamm). Part III will argue that the badness of violence cannot be fully understood simply by looking at the reasons why death is bad, and Parts IV and V will focus on the aspects of violence that make it distinctively bad. Part VI will explain why violence (unlike death) is both bad and wrong, and in certain cases worse than death, even when violence does not result in death.

Part I: Violence and death

The similitude and affinity between the concepts of violence and death cannot be denied. It is the physical nature of injury and harm caused by an act of violence that brings this concept within the orbit of the concept of death. Clearly the worst kind of violence is that which leads to death, therefore it is only to be expected that when forming an opinion on violence, we almost inevitably think of the evil of death. Genocides, wars, homicides, massacres, executions, are acts of violence we deplore exactly because they cause deaths, and even when an act of violence does not cause death, as in the case of rape, maiming or mutilating, death still remains the point of reference for all lesser forms of abusive physical force. In other words all physical violence short of causing death is considered bad either because it takes the victim closer to death, or because the victim is threatened (implicitly or explicitly) with the ultimate evil, namely death.

This popular story about how violence and death are related is widely shared, even persuasive, but ultimately flawed. The major problem with this line of reasoning is that it fails to appreciate the complexity of violence. Violence cannot be reduced to *physical* injury and suffering. First of all not all violence is physical. Psychological cruelty is as much part of violence as the use of physical force against a person, and to reduce psychological violence to intermediate points on the scale of violence leading to death is to miss the point about the badness of violence. What is appalling about hate crime, domestic violence and rape has very little to do with the prospect of death. If that was the case, we could not explain why some victims of violence (torture or rape for example) are suicidal after surviving the ordeal. This point will come under closer scrutiny in Part V below.

The idea of violence is much more complex than death, therefore we should not expect the concept of death to tell us why violence is bad, and wrong. With death, it is an all-or-nothing affair. There are no degrees of death. On the other hand there are degrees of injury and suffering, and therefore different levels of violence. Physical and psychological injury or suffering may be more or less intense, more or less severe, more or less aggressive, more or less sustained. Violence is bad, but there are different degrees of badness.[3]

Finally, the concepts of violence and death capture two fundamentally diverse phenomena: violence defines a social relationship, while death describes an event. As suggested in Chapter Two, an act of violence is a social act involving minimally two social agents, the perpetrator and the victim, or even three social agents if we include the spectator or witness. An extreme act of violence, such as murder, also involves a social relationship between the killer and the victim. But the act of murder should not be confused with the event of death. Murder is the unlawful killing of one human by another, whereas death is fundamentally an event of a physiological nature. Veatch (1978) explains how death symbolizes the loss of vital functions, of the brain's functions and of neocortical functions. Such losses represent physical changes in the status of a living entity. Kamm (1993, 39) refers to death as involving 'the destruction of the person', where 'destruction' describes a physical event. Even Glover (1977, 43), who prefers to define death in terms of 'the irreversible loss of consciousness', goes on to explain that our best evidence of this is the continued absence of electrical activity in the brain, hence once again the tendency to reduce death to a physical state.[4]

All this suggests that the reasons why violence is bad cannot be reduced to the badness of death, even if violence were to cause death. But if violence is bad for reasons independent of the badness of death, what are these reasons? In order to capture what makes violence distinctively bad, in what follows the different arguments for the badness of death will be analysed from the point of view of violence. The aim is not to force the solution to one problem (why is death bad) to fit another problem (why is violence bad). On the contrary, it is the nature of the misfit between the badness of death and violence that is most revealing. From the comparison between the badness of death and violence, one distinctive aspect of the badness of violence will emerge, namely, that violence is bad because of the way it makes the victims of violence feel about themselves. In other words, what makes violence bad is not only the experience of injury and suffering per se, although that is certainly part of it, but also the social meaning of *being* violated. An act of violence is a social act, involving social actors. The badness of violence must be understood in terms of the logic of this social relationship.[5]

Part II: Why is death bad?

There are two dominant ways of understanding the badness of death, as an extrinsic or intrinsic evil. The best known and still most influential argument for the extrinsic evil of death is Nagel's (1979, 1–2) Deprivation Factor: 'If death is an evil at all, it cannot be because of its positive features, but only because of what it deprives us of.... death is an evil because it brings to an end all the goods that life contains'. The Deprivation Factor requires a direct comparison between what a person has experienced up to the moment of death and what the person would have gone on to experience, had death not interrupted the life process. Although the illegitimacy of this comparison has been questioned,[6] not least because of the hedonistic nature of experiences, there are many who are prepared to defend the Deprivation Factor. As Feldman (1991, 218) points out, what is required is to develop a rough system for quantifying an individual's welfare level in different possible worlds: 'my death would be bad for me not because it would cause me to suffer pain, and not because it would itself be intrinsically bad for me. Rather, it would be bad for me because it would deprive me of 600 units of pleasure that I would have had if it had not happened when it did. More precisely, it would be bad for me because my welfare level at the nearest world where it occurs is 600 points lower than my welfare level at the nearest world where it does not occur'.

There are some notable advantages to the Deprivation Factor, but also some major problems. The Deprivation Factor deserves credit for explaining why the premature death of a young person strikes us as being tragic in a way that is different compared to the death of someone who has had 'a full life'. Nagel uses the example of Keats who died at the age of 24 and Tolstoy who died at the age of 82.[7] Yet notwithstanding its virtues, the Deprivation Factor has severe limitations, the most serious of which is that it fails to plausibly distinguish death from prenatal non-existence.[8] This point has been raised by F.M. Kamm, who faults the Deprivation Factor on the asymmetry problem, namely the fact that death is worse for the person who dies than his non-existence prior to his creation. According to Kamm, what makes death bad is not fully captured by the fact that death deprives the person who dies of goods of life he would have had if he had lived. This suggests that there is more to death than an extrinsic evil.

There are two aspects to Kamm's suggestion that death may also be intrinsically bad: the Extinction Factor and the Insult Factors. The Extinction Factor is an attempt to shed light on the endlessness of the nothingness of death, the fact that death means everything for oneself is *all over*. Kamm (1993, 64) defines the Extinction Factor in the following terms: 'The Extinction Factor is that death ends permanently all significant periods of a person's life; there is no more possibility of significant periods of life'. Kamm explains that the Extinction Factor applies to death but not to prenatal non-existence, since the latter holds the possibility of life to come. Furthermore, it is the end of all possibilities of life, rather than the loss of goods of experience and action, that awakens terror in us. The Insult Factors expose a different dimension of death as an intrinsic evil. As Kamm (1993, 64) explains: 'The Insult Factors arises because death involves a loss of goods happening to a person who already exists . . . In confronting us when we already exist and undoing what we already are, death takes away what we think of as already ours and emphasizes our vulnerability'. Like in the case of the Extinction Factor, the Insult Factors have the advantage of applying to posthumous non-existence but not to prenatal non-existence, hence reinforcing the thesis of the badness of death as both an extrinsic and an intrinsic evil.

Part III: Why violence is bad: extrinsic reasons

In the next two sections the analysis will switch from the badness of death to the badness of violence. As already mentioned, the concepts of violence and death are not interchangeable, since violence has a much broader scope than death. Nevertheless, it may be informative to see to what extent the three dominant approaches to the badness of death also apply to the badness of violence. Of course we should not expect to find a perfect fit, but that should not worry us. In fact, it is precisely where the badness of violence fails to fit into the framework provided by the badness of death that the distinctive nature of the badness of violence is to be found.

Starting with the Deprivation Factor: does violence inflict deprivation on the victim, and if so could the badness of violence be understood along the lines of the Deprivation Factor? Assuming that the victim of an act of violence survives the attack, any deprivation they may experience would be of a different nature compared to the deprivation of someone who dies. The Deprivation Factor defines deprivation in terms of not getting more goods of life. In the case of violence, the victim does not suffer a deprivation as such, if by deprivation we mean an absolute and timeless withdrawal,[9] instead it is more accurate to say that the victim suffers a restriction in her choice set. Exactly what restrictions are being experienced by the victims of violence will depend on the nature of the act of violence, although some generalizations can be inferred. First of all, the victim of violence is restricted in their well-being for the duration of the injury. If a villain breaks your arm, you will be restricted in the use of the arm (and all the benefits that may bring you) for as long as it takes for the broken arm to heal. On the other hand, if the injury is so serious to be permanent, or even to necessitate the amputation of your arm, the violence has restricted you in the use of your arm from that moment in time until death. But whether your arm is in a sling for 10 weeks, or amputated, the injury inflicted by the villain's act of non-deadly violence is fundamentally a restriction on the victim's freedom, not a deprivation.[10] This can be referred to as the Restriction of Freedom Factor.

Of course physical restrictions are not the only deficits generated by violence. At a psychological level, violence (whether physical or psychological) may impair the victim's integrity and sense of security.

An act of violence may instil in the victim the fear that the same calamity may strike again. This sense of fear may be paralysing, it may undermine the victim's confidence, their ability to trust others, and it may even lead to other psychological dysfunctions such as paranoia or panic attacks. In the well-documented case of rape for example, the psychological effects may include depression, silent withdrawal, hypochondria, lack of self-confidence, feelings of shame or guilt, and self-destructive behaviour.[11] This will be referred to as the Psychological Damage Factor.

It is possible that something along the lines of the Restriction of Freedom Factor and the Psychological Damage Factor can account for the badness of violence. The badness of violence is, at least in part, an extrinsic evil. Yet, it would be wrong to suggest that violence is *only* an extrinsic evil. Part II shows how in the literature on the badness of death the Deprivation Factor gets into trouble for failing to account for the fact that death is worse than prenatal non-existence (the asymmetry problem). In terms of the badness of violence the Restriction of Freedom Factor and the Psychological Damage Factor also run into a problem, albeit of a different nature; namely, they fail to account for the fact that restriction of freedom and fear may be the result of accidents rather than violence, in which case the Restriction of Freedom Factor and the Psychological Damage Factor are not the exclusive domains of the badness of violence. This will be referred to as the equivocation problem.

Consider the following example. In scenario A you lose the use of your right arm after being tortured by a villain. In scenario B you lose the use of your right arm after being attacked by a shark. In both cases your freedom has been restricted, but only scenario A is a case of violence, which suggests that the Restriction of Freedom Factor fails to distinguish between an act of violence (scenario A) and a mere accident (scenario B). But that is not all. As a result of the torture that you have endured, you now suffer from psychological inhibitions. But you may suffer from similar psychological inhibitions after the shark attack, for example you panic anytime you get near the sea. This suggests that the Psychological Damage Factor also fails to distinguish between an act of violence and a mere accident.

It is because the Deprivation Factor fails to deal adequately with the asymmetry problem that Kamm argues for an intrinsic approach to the badness of death. Similarly the Restriction of Freedom Factor and the Psychological Damage Factor fail to deal adequately with the equivocation problem. This suggests that there are other reasons why violence is bad. In Part IV below, following Kamm's lead the intrinsic badness of violence will come under close scrutiny.

Part IV: Why violence is bad: intrinsic reasons

Just as in the case of death, there is also an intrinsic dimension to the evil of violence. The literature on the badness of death suggests two ways in which death can be an intrinsic evil: the Extinction Factor and the Insult Factors. In the case of murder or wars, the fact that violence is the cause of death is bad because for the victim it is all over, that is to say, violence ends permanently all significant periods of the victim's life. This is fine as far as it goes, but unfortunately it does not go far enough. The problem is that not all violences are deadly, therefore the Extinction Factor is only of limited value, since it fails to capture the badness of violence for all those cases (arguably the majority of cases) when violence does not lead to death. If violence in all its forms is an intrinsic evil, it must be for other reasons apart from the Extinction Factor.

The Insult Factors are more promising. Kamm emphasizes the fact that death takes away what we think of as already ours and therefore emphasizes our vulnerability. The idea of vulnerability is crucial to Kamm's (1993, 41) intuition: 'death exposes the vulnerability of what exists'. Another way of capturing this vulnerability is in terms of our powerlessness. Kamm's decision to refer to the Insult Factors as an instance of 'insult' is perplexing, considering that insults usefully refer to harmful judgements of a personal nature, although there is nothing personal about the timing of one's natural death. The insult refers to one's vulnerability, or as Kamm (1993, 56) puts it 'the *vulnerability* exhibited when something is destroyed'. By calling it the Insult Factors, Kamm is referring to a cluster of factors that exhibit a person's vulnerability, from destruction (a person is destroyed by death) to decline (death constitutes a declining state of affairs), which are not captured by the loss of goods of life the person would have had if the person had lived longer.

The example used by Kamm (1993, 42) to explain the nature of the Insult Factors is telling: 'So the person who never had an arm and the person who has lost an arm live equally hard lives. A court may say one is no worse off than the other. But one has suffered an insult the other has not suffered, and in this sense, something worse has happened to him'. The point of this example is to illustrate that death is a decline. Yet what is particularly interesting about this example is that losing an arm is not an issue of death, but it could be an issue of violence. In the account of the Restriction of Freedom Factor and Psychological Damage Factor, the example of a villain breaking your arm was used. The badness of this act of violence is not only that the villain has deprived you of a set of goods for the duration of your injury, but also that by breaking your arm the villain has violated your integrity by exposing your vulnerability and powerlessness. In many ways, the insult (the sense of vulnerability and powerlessness) hurts as much as the physical injury.

One could go as far as saying that what Kamm calls the Insult Factors apply much better to the badness of violence than to the badness of death. After all, it is not the general state of vulnerability per se that is problematic, since we are all aware that mortality is the essence of the human condition. It is being vulnerable *to* someone, or having our mortality being determined by another person, another mortal, that is the issue. Another way of stating this point is by saying that what is most troubling is not being powerless per se, but being powerless in relation to someone else who has power over us. There is a social dimension to vulnerability and powerlessness that is not fully captured by Kamm's account of the Insult Factors. This social dimension is prevalent in issues of violence, but lacking in issues of death.[12] The vulnerability and powerlessness experienced by the victim of violence is degrading and humiliating. It is this social dimension that is the worst part of our vulnerability: death as a result of an earthquake is undoubtedly bad, extrinsically and intrinsically, but death as a result of murder or genocide is even worse, being humiliating and degrading. In order to distinguish between the insult of death and the insult of violence, the latter will be referred to as the Humiliation Factor.

Part V: The Humiliation Factor

The concept of humiliation plays a crucial role here, therefore it needs to be defined with some precision. There are two different ways of understanding the idea of humiliation. The psychological sense refers to a feeling of embarrassment or shame or mortification. Psychologically I might feel humiliated if my ten-year-old niece beats me at a game of chess after I taught her how to play the game, and in turn she might feel humiliated if no one asks her to dance at a party, but this is not the kind of humiliation that is interesting to an account of violence. The problem with the psychological sense of humiliation is that these feelings may not be rational, in fact as Margalit (1996, 9) reminds us: 'the psychological sense of humiliation does not entail that the person who feels humiliated has a sound reason for this feeling'. Instead it is the normative sense of humiliation that interests us, where the emphasis is on reasons for feeling humiliation as a result of others' behaviour. In the normative sense, humiliation refers to the state of being reduced to lowliness or submission. Humiliation in this sense is captured by the notion of abasement, meaning to bring someone down.

Humiliation reduces one to be 'less', but less than what exactly? Of course the idea of 'being less' is comparative, hence it is crucial to specify in relation to what one is 'less of' as a result of humiliation. There are two possible answers here: humiliation can make one be 'less' in relation to oneself before the humiliation occurred, or one can be 'less' in relation to someone else, namely the humiliator or humiliators. I will explain both in turn. A person is humiliated when they are forced into a situation where they are reduced to less than they were before. As a result of this abasement, a person's sense of identity is damaged, and as one struggles to recognize oneself, a person loses their self-respect. Alternatively the act of humiliation may force someone to feel less than the person who is perpetrating the violence. In the latter case, humiliation is attached to a sense of social inequality in terms of power and vulnerability between the humiliator and the humiliated.

Needless to say, being humiliated to less in relation to oneself, and being humiliated to less in relation to another person, are often two sides of the same coin. Sexual violence brings out both aspects of humiliation in its normative sense, as the many cases of systematic rape during wartime indicate. Guatemala is a case in point, although the same would apply for any case of rape, anywhere in the world, during wartime or peace.

Sexual violence as humiliation

Perhaps more than any other group, women suffered the worst atrocities during the thirty-six years of civil war that devastated Guatemala between the 1960s and 1990s. Violence against women by the military was not accidental or exceptional, instead the rape of women was a systematic practice during military operations in rural areas. Rape was considered a way to subdue and humiliate communities and families.

After the signing of the Peace Accords in 1996, two comprehensive reports appeared which chronicle the human rights violations and acts of violence inflicted over this thirty-six year period: *Guatemala: Never Again!* by the Recovery of Historical Memory (REMHI) project of the Catholic Archbishop's Human Rights Office, and *Guatemala: Memory of Silence*, by the Historical Clarification Commission (CEH), commonly known as the Truth Commission, created under UN auspices in 1994.[13] The official CEH report found that acts of genocide were committed against specific Mayan communities. Both the CEH and the REHMI reports discuss in some detail the full extent of violence against women during these years. REHMI's testimonies include 149 victims reported in 92 accounts of sexual assault. These include rape as the cause of death and as a form of torture and sexual slavery with the repeated rape of the victim. Because of the guilt and shame associated with sexual assault, we can safely assume that violence against women is grossly under-reported compared to other forms of violence such as torture or murder.

Women giving testimonies repeatedly made the same comment: 'They treated us worse than animals'. This is one example taken from a testimony:

> One day I was able to escape and, while hidden, I saw a woman. They shot her and she fell. All the soldiers left their packs and dragged her like a dog to the riverbank. They raped and killed her. Also, a helicopter that was flying overhead landed, and they all did the same thing to her. Case 11,724 (perpetrator), Xecojom, Quiché, 1980. (REHMI 1999, 77).

The language used to describe these type of sexual violence, being treated 'worse than an animal', or being 'dragged like a dog', is a reflection of the humiliation experienced by the victims. In the systematic rape of women of all ages, the victim is degraded to less than a human being worthy of respect. The REHMI (1999) report goes on to explain sexual violence in the following terms:

> Terror, in this extremely violent context, included ridiculing the victim. The dehumanization of the perpetrators led them to devalue the humanity of their victims. (p.73)

> On the interminable list of abuses, humiliations, and torture that women endured, sexual assault stands out as one of the cruellest and most frequent. Its complexity lies in its nature as a show of power by the perpetrators and an experience of abuse and humiliation for the victim. (p.76)

> The purpose of such atrocities was to degrade women through their sexuality, to show the highest contempt for their dignity as people. (p.79)

The REHMI report gives the following reasons for sexual violence against women: a show of power; a show of victory over adversaries; a bartering tool; war plunder.

The rape of Maya women during the Guatemalan civil war, and sexual violence in general, reflect the full extent of the humiliation suffered by victims of violence. This suggests that perhaps more than any other idea, the Humiliation Factor captures the essence of what makes violence bad. The Humiliation Factor is distinctive of violence, hence it constitutes an essential part of the answer to the question: 'why is violence bad?' The Humiliation Factor underlines the fact that when their integrity is being violated, victims of violence are not only harmed but wronged, and their self-respect suffers as a result of it. Violence is degrading, more so than death. It destroys a person's self-confidence, it diminishes the sense of a person as a person, and it deprives a person of their self-esteem. John Rawls famously points out that self-respect is arguably the most important primary good (things that every rational person is presumed to want). He defines self-respect (self-esteem) as having two aspects: a person's sense of one's own value, and a confidence in one's ability. As Rawls (1971, 440) puts it: 'Without [self-respect (self-esteem)] nothing may seem worth doing, or if some things have value for us, we lack the will to strive for them. All desire and activity becomes empty and vain,

Table 6.1   Badness of death versus badness of violence

	Death	Violence
Extrinsic bad	Deprivation factor	Restriction of freedom factor
		Psychological damage factor
Problem with extrinsic bad	*Asymmetry problem*	*Equivocation problem*
Intrinsic bad	Extinction factor	Humiliation factor
	Insult factor	

and we sink into apathy and cynicism'. Unlike accidents, violence represents an assault on a person's self-respect (self-esteem). Such assault may be more difficult to perceive than an assault of a more physical nature, but it is not less real. The extensive literature on domestic and family violence is enlightening on this issue.[14]

Table 6.1 summarizes the arguments put forward in Parts II, III and IV above. Part V below will suggest why the Humiliation Factors make violence not only bad, but also wrong and worse than death.

Part VI: Why violence is wrong

Death is bad, but it is not necessarily wrong. Queen Elizabeth I died in 1603 from natural causes. Mary Queen of Scots, cousin of Queen Elizabeth I, was beheaded in 1587. Both deaths are bad, but only the latter is wrong. What makes it wrong (for the person who dies of course) is the fact that Mary Queen of Scots did not just die, but was murdered, by order of Queen Elizabeth I. Although Kamm (1993, 21) does not mention violence in her work, she discusses the nature of killing, and points out that what makes killing wrong is to some degree independent of what makes death bad: 'wrongness is not derivable from the badness of outcome'. Kamm is right, the wrongness of killing is not derivable from the badness of death, but it is derivable from the badness of violence. Killing is a form of violence, and knowing why violence is bad may shed some light on why killing is wrong.

Kamm (1993, 21) explains why killing is wrong in the following terms: 'The fact that one person determines the non-existence of another person against his will, even in his own interest (as in involuntary euthanasia), is a factor in making killing wrong'. This sentence is full of hidden meaning, therefore it needs to be carefully unpacked. First of all, in the act of killing there is a social relationship between two persons, the Killer (K) and the Victim (V). The wrongness of the act of killing has something to do with the power relationship between K and V. Kamm says that one person 'determines' the non-existence of another. This means that K not only has the power to determine the non-existence of V, but also acts upon this power. Kamm also says that the non-existence of V is determined by K against his will. This strengthens the thesis that wrongness has something to do with a relationship of power. Weber (1978) defined power as the ability of an actor within a social relationship to carry out his will *despite the resistance of others*. What makes K's act of killing V wrong is precisely the fact that killing V is against the will of V.[15]

The reason for emphasizing the power relationship between K and V is not to draw attention to the power of K, but to the powerlessness of V. Powerlessness leads to vulnerability, and vulnerability is an intrinsic evil. Kamm says that the awareness of our vulnerability is what makes death bad. She is probably right. But if that is true in the case of death (the Insult Factors), it is even more so in the case of violence (the Humiliation Factor). In fact, as mentioned in Part IV above, one could argue that Kamm's argument applies much better to the badness of violence than to the badness of death. Humiliation like violence is socially constructed, being one side of a power relationship. We are humiliated when our integrity is being violated.

One interesting aspect of Kamm's (1993, 21) analysis of the badness of death is that she does not think there is a difference between natural and human causes of death: 'Then anything, whether occurring naturally or by human intervention, that stops the process maintaining the person already present might be bad . . . it may be offensive for people or even for nature to stand in the relation of causing death to a person'. That may be the case for death, but it certainly does not apply to violence. In fact, it is the opposite in the case of violence. To suffer as a result of a shark attack is bad (for extrinsic reasons), but to suffer at the hand of another person is not only bad (for extrinsic and intrinsic reasons), it is also wrong. The wrongness is determined by the violation of integrity perpetrated by one social actor on another social actor, and by the unequal power relations between the perpetrator and the victim. These issues are intrinsic to the act of violence, whether it results in death or not.

It is important to remember that not all violences are deadly. If killing is wrong, not because of the badness of death but because of the badness of violence, it follows that all other non-lethal forms of violence are also wrong. In fact, with the possible exception of consensual violence,[16] all violence is prima facie wrong. What makes violence wrong is not only that the vulnerability of the victims of violence are being exposed, but also that the perpetrators of violence, in the process of violating the integrity of the victim, is taking advantage of the power they enjoy over the victims, and in violating their integrity the perpetrator is violating the personhood of the victim. As Scheper-Hughes and Bourgois (2004b, 1) rightly point out, to understand what is bad and wrong about violence we must go beyond the physicality of the act: 'violence can never be understood solely in terms of its physicality – force, assault, or the infliction of pain – alone. Violence also includes assaults on the personhood, dignity, sense of worth or value of the victim'.

The reasons why violence is wrong are different from the reasons why death is wrong. The violation of integrity that is the essence of what makes violence bad also makes violence wrong, whereas the wrongness of death cannot be derived from the badness of death. At this point there is one last question that needs to be addressed: is violence worse than death? This is a complex question, but it is worth exploring the idea that perhaps some types of non-lethal violence may be worse than death. The assertion that violence is worse than death is counter-intuitive, since as the Extinction Factor suggests, death is arguably the worst thing that could happen to us. Nevertheless, the fact that the wrongness of violence is derived from the badness of violence, suggests that there may be something about the Humiliation Factor that could make it even worse than the Extinction Factor.

Apart from the actual pain and suffering, what makes violence bad is the awareness of one's vulnerability, and the knowledge that one's integrity has been violated. One can only be aware of one's vulnerability or integrity if one is alive, which is why non-lethal violence is not only bad and wrong, but worse than deadly violence. In the last analysis, from the victim's point of view, one of the worst aspects of violence is that he or she has to live with the violence, that is to say the victims have to live with the awareness of their vulnerability and knowledge that their integrity has been violated. Once again, the literature on domestic violence is revealing on this point. Living with the trauma of violence can be an on-going torment. The fact that some victims of violence seek refuge in the act of suicide suggests that death is not the worst thing that can happen to a person. The assumed suicide of Primo Levi on 11 April 1987, forty years after he survived Auschwitz is a testimony to the pervasive evil of violence.[17]

Part VII: Conclusion

There are extrinsic and intrinsic reasons why violence is bad. Violence is extrinsically bad because of the Restriction of Freedom Factor and the Psychological Damage Factor, and intrinsically bad because of the Humiliation Factor. The Restriction of Freedom and Psychological Damage Factors refer to the experience of injury and suffering, which is certainly part of the evil of violence, although its importance has perhaps been exaggerated in the literature. Apart from the harm of experiencing violence, the Humiliation Factor suggests that violence is also bad because of the way it makes the victim feel *before* the act of violence (being threatened with violence, even if the threat never materializes), *during* the act of violence (the feeling of powerlessness and subordination), and *after* the violence has occurred (memories of violence). These feelings cannot be reduced solely to the anticipation or recurrence of a certain unpleasant experience, although this is certainly part of it, as any victim of torture will testify. Instead, these feelings are bad also because they make the victim feel vulnerable, violated, degraded and inferior to the perpetrator of violence. Being violated can undermine a victim's self-respect and self-esteem.

The Humiliation Factor states that violence exposes the powerlessness of the victim, making the victim vulnerable to the perpetrator of violence. The Humiliation Factor is similar (but not identical) to Kamm's Insult Factors on the badness of death. The difference is that the Humiliation Factor emphasizes the power relationship between two social actors: the person who performs the act of violence, and the victim who suffers from it. The Humiliation Factor makes violence both bad and wrong, therefore unlike in the case of death, the wrongness of violence is derivable from the badness of violence. Finally, because not all acts of violence lead to death, and violence captures the unequal relationship of power between perpetrators and victims, violence can be even worse than death: as a victim of non-lethal violence, living with the awareness of the Humiliation Factor can be even worse than the eternal peace that comes from non-existence.

Notes

1. Nietzsche (1977, 100–101) says: 'Examine the lives of the best and most fruitful men and people, and ask yourselves whether a tree, if it is to grow proudly into the sky, can do without bad weather and storms: whether unkindness and opposition from without, whether some sort of hatred, envy, obstinacy, mistrust, severity, greed and violence do not belong to the *favouring* circumstances without which a great increase even in virtue is hardly possible'.
2. Gandhi (1997) famously argued that violence is detrimental to its perpetrators, as it corrupts their soul. This chapter will be dealing exclusively with the badness of violence for those who are the victims of violence, not its perpetrators.
3. While there are obviously no degrees of death, there are different ways of dying, and some at least do not invite being called 'bad' as such, as in the case of euthanasia. Yet death and dying are not the same thing. Dying is the last stage in the process of living, therefore it is still part of life, not part of death.
4. The reason Glover distinguishes between the irreversible loss of consciousness and the loss of all brain activity is because while loss of all brain activity guarantees loss of consciousness, the converse does not hold. People in a vegetable state have no consciousness even though there may be some electrical activity in some parts of the brain.
5. This points to another important difference between the badness of death, and the badness of deadly violence. Death is bad even if it occurs naturally at the end of a full life-cycle. Deadly violence is bad not only because of the badness of death, but because the action of the perpetrator has interfered with the victim's natural life-cycle.
6. See for example Silverstein (1980).
7. Nagel says that *only* the death of Keats is generally regarded as tragic, but not the death of Tolstoy. This is debatable. The death of John Rawls on 22 November 2002, at the age of 81 is tragic, even though one could argue that he lived a full life. The point is not whether one death is tragic as supposed to another that is not tragic, but why one tragedy is different from the other tragedy. One could even argue that the death of Rawls at the age of 81 is in some ways more tragic than the death of a baby born with AIDS in Africa, whose short life is destined to be one of suffering.
8. Is interesting to point out that something like the Deprivation Factor is used by pro-life advocates. See for example Marquis (1997), who

argues that the termination of life of the foetus deprives it of its future experiences, and it is for this reason that abortion is not only bad but also wrong.

9. One important exception is when A is deprived of B when B is murdered by C (for example, A is the child and B is the mother). Here A and B are both victims of C's violence.

10. Freedom is defined here along the lines suggested by Steiner (1994, 8): 'a person is unfree to do an action if, and only if, his doing that action is rendered impossible by the action of another person'.

11. See McCluskey and Hooper (2000); Brison (2002).

12. Killing is violence that results in death; it is not about being dead as such.

13. *Guatemala: Never Again!* (REHMI 1999) is an abridged English translation of *Guatemala: Nunca Más* (4 Vols.), Oficina de Derechos Humanos del Arzobispado de Guatemala, 1998. The CEH report assigns blame for 93 per cent of the atrocities to the government forces and their allied paramilitary bands, and only 3 per cent to the guerrillas. More than 300 mass graves across the country have been identified. A recent UNICEF report says that some 20 per cent of the 200,000 victims of Guatemala's long civil war were children.

14. See Vincent and Jouriles (2000); Hester *et al.* (1996); Mullen *et al.* (1996).

15. If killing is not against the will of the victim, as in the case of voluntary euthanasia, then killing is not wrong. In the case of euthanasia, killing is not only not against the will of V, but it is not even against the interest of V.

16. Sado-masochism and assisted suicide come to mind here. On the former see Archard (1998).

17. There is no conclusive evidence that Primo Levi committed suicide, or that Auschwitz was on his mind as he did so, since he did not leave a suicide note. For a sceptical view on Levi's suicide thesis, see Gambetta (1999).

7
Violence and Social Justice

One of the most remarkable claims Rawls (1971, 343) makes in *A Theory of Justice* is when he refers to unjust social arrangements as a kind of violence: 'Unjust social arrangements are themselves a kind of extortion, even violence, and consent to them does not bind'. This is also one of his least celebrated claims, which explains why it has gone almost totally unnoticed. By comparing unjust social arrangements to a kind of violence, Rawls combines in one sentence the major moral, social and political concern of the time, with the new paradigm that was to take its place, respectively political violence and social justice. It is now widely recognized that it is because of Rawls's seminal work that the question of social justice has taken centre stage in political philosophy. As Barry (1990) poignantly remarks, in political philosophy there is a pre-Rawlsian and a post-Rawlsian world, and *A Theory of Justice* marks the watershed between the past and the present. Almost forty years after *A Theory of Justice* was first published, we are still living in a post-Rawlsian era. Formulating, defending and promoting principles of justice that mould the basic structure of society remain the major preoccupation for most political philosophers, and rightly so. But in 1971 things were different.

Between the end of the 1960s and the start of the 1970s, the hottest issue on the political philosophers' agenda was not social justice but political violence. The civil rights movement, the cold war, The Vietnam-War and the anti Vietnam-War protests propelled the issues of civil disobedience and state violence at the forefront of social, political and moral discourse. The concept of violence enjoyed more attention between 1968 and 1974 than it has received since. But as social and political philosophers switched their attention from political violence to the idea of social justice, interest in the concept of violence waned. Even Rawls's surprising claim that unjust social arrangements are a kind of violence passed unnoticed.[1]

The aim of this chapter is to investigate the elusive relationship between the concepts of violence, injustice and social justice. The focus of attention will not be whether it is legitimate for justice to be promoted through violence, a question that will be dealt with later in Chapter Nine. Important as it is, especially during the present times of war, this question will have to be put on the back burner until we have a better understanding of what social justice is, and how social justice is related to violence. In particular, given that the aim of social justice is to overcome injustice, this chapter argues that we need a theory of violence in order to understand the nature of injustice.

Part I will call attention to the conceptual overlap between the phenomenon of violence and our concerns for injustice. Part II will account for the widely held view, expounded by many social and political theorists at the radical end of the ideological spectrum, suggesting that social injustice is simply another type of violence, and that these two terms are conceptually identical. Although still very popular and appealing, Part III will argue that there is a problem with this strategy. While strictly speaking it is not incorrect to think of an injustice as an act of violence, which in part explains why the extensive literature on exploitation tends to use the terminology of violence to describe a case of injustice,[2] simply collapsing the idea of injustice into the concept of violence does not add anything to our understanding of injustice. In an effort to re-conceptualize the relationship between injustice and violence, Part IV will argue that we should reverse the relationship between injustice and violence. Instead of saying that all injustice is a type of violence, we should start from a theory of violence, and ask ourselves what a theory of violence can teach us about injustice. It will be suggested that by starting with a conceptual analysis of the idea of violence, we are in a position to have a better understanding of what an injustice is, why it is bad, and what makes it wrong.

Part I: Violence, injustice and integrity

In Chapter One I argued that one popular way of understanding the meaning of violence is in terms of a violation of rights. Thinking of violence in terms of a violation of rights has the potential advantage of catapulting the idea of violence at the forefront of all discussions on social justice. After all, if we start from the assumption that the protection and promotion of rights is a widely-shared aim for most theories of social justice, by defining violence as the violation of rights we are necessarily implying that violence is by definition a central concern for social justice.

The fundamental premise of this argument cannot be faulted. Mill (1991, 195) is one of the first liberal philosophers to define justice in terms of individual rights. In his essay on *Utilitarianism*, in the last chapter 'Of the Connection between Justice and Utility', Mill writes that 'the notion which we have found to be of the essence of the idea of justice, that of a right residing in an individual, implies and testifies to this more binding obligation'. One hundred and fifty years later contemporary liberal theorists of social justice still share Mill's intuition, even if many would reject Mill's utilitarian outlook. Thus Rawls (1971) famously calls for equal civil and political rights in his first principle of social justice, while Steiner (1994, 2) makes the correlation between justice and rights forcefully clear: 'The elementary particles of justice are rights. Rights are the items which are created and parcelled out by justice principles'. Steiner goes on to say that we learn something about justice by examining the formal or characteristic features of rights.

Logically, it follows that if the elementary particles of justice are rights, then the elementary particles of *injustice* must be rights violations. Not surprising this is exactly the way many scholars think about injustice. Thus Shapiro (1999) defines injustice in terms of the violation of people's basic interests,[3] and Levy and Sidel (2005, 6) base their work on social injustice and public health on the assumption that social injustice violates fundamental human rights, defining injustice as follows: 'the denial or violation of economic, sociocultural, political, civil, or human rights of specific populations or groups in the society based on the perception of their inferiority by those with more power or influence'.

At this point, in order to make violence central to the concerns of social justice, all we need to do is to define violence as a violation of rights. Unfortunately, it is exactly this next step that is not legitimate, since defining the idea of violence as a violation of rights is profoundly problematic, for all the reasons already mentioned in Chapter One. Basically, if violence is to be understood as the violation of rights, then one ought to say something about the nature of rights that are being violated. This is not as simple as may appear, since this question raises a number of philosophical conundrums: What is the nature of the rights that are being violated? Are we dealing with moral rights, legal rights or human rights? In defining violence as the violation of rights, do we restrict the violation to basic rights or do we include secondary rights? Are we concerned exclusively with negative rights or do we include positive rights? These are difficult and contentious questions,[4] but the bottom line is that all attempts to defend the idea of violence as a violation of rights suffer from the same predicament, namely, that violence becomes so common, so widespread, so pervasive, to be virtually unavoidable. If violence is the violation of economic, sociocultural, political, civil or human rights, then it becomes virtually impossible to escape violence, either as a victim or as a perpetrator. From an analytical point of view, to be over-inclusive has serious drawbacks.

The problems dogging the notion of violence as a violation of rights can be circumvented by rethinking the nature of the violation taking place. In Chapter Two, I suggested a definition of violence along the lines of a violation of integrity, and in Chapter Six I argued that what makes violence bad, and prima facie wrong, is having one's personal integrity violated, since this involves being degraded or humiliated by another person, which in turn damages one's sense of self-respect and perhaps even self-esteem. The concept of humiliation is doing some crucial work here, therefore it needs closer analysis.

Margalit (1996, 9) argues that the notion of humiliation should be at the centre of our moral concerns, indeed Margalit defines a decent society as one whose institutions do not humiliate the people under their authority.[5] He defines humiliation as 'any sort of behaviour or condition that constitutes a sound reason for a person to consider his or her self-respect injured', which suggests that his concept of humiliation rests on that of self-respect.[6] Self-respect is in turn defined as the honour a person grants him/herself solely on the basis of the awareness that he/she is human. Margalit's account of humiliation and self-respect may be problematic on a number of levels, as many commentators have pointed out.[7] Yet leaving aside the correct definition of the concepts of humiliation and self-respect, or indeed whether it is an essential or even simply a typical feature of humiliation that it injures self-respect, these two concepts go some way in shedding light on the issue of why violence is bad, and prima facie wrong.

We can improve on Margalit's generic idea of humiliation having a damaging effect on our self-respect, by taking on board Lukes' (1997) suggestion that these concepts are related by way of the more accurate idea of *ascriptive* humiliation: 'By this I intend a kind of maltreatment that consists in domination that results in distinctive kinds of injustice. By "domination" I mean to refer to the systematic use of power in a social context of unequal power relations. In such a context ascriptive humiliation consists in mistreating people by means of ascription, in the classical sociological sense of the term: that is, by reference to statuses that are assigned to individuals, identifying what individuals are, not what they do'. With the help of Lukes' idea of ascriptive humiliation as maltreatment, based on unequal power relations, consisting in domination, and resulting in injustice, the notion of violence as violation of integrity comes full-circle. The act of violence is an act of ascriptive humiliation, and to be humiliated becomes an issue of injustice.

There is of course some overlap between the ideas of violation of rights and violation of integrity. Only the most extreme forms of violations of economic, sociocultural, political, civil, or even human rights are humiliating, if by humiliation we understand ascriptive humiliation. It follows that only the most severe instances of economic, sociocultural, political, civil, and human rights constitute a violation of integrity. By introducing the ideas of ascriptive humiliation and violation of integrity, we are able to considerably reduce and confine the scope of violence, avoiding the charge of over-pervasiveness and over-inclusiveness, which threatens to stretch the meaning of violence beyond recognition. It is precisely this notion of violence as violation of integrity which will be assumed throughout the rest of this chapter.

Part II: Injustice as violence

A prevalent stance on the relationship between social justice and violence is offered by those who see a direct correlation between an injustice and an act of violence. The two most influential authors within this body of literature are still Newton Garver and Johan Galtung, whose work came to light in the late 1960s, although many have followed in their footsteps. After a brief overview of the ground-breaking arguments put forward by Garver and Galtung, the accounts of more contemporary authors who are still strongly influenced by Garver and Galtung will come under closer scrutiny.

In an essay originally published in 1968 in *The Nation*, later revised in 1973, Garver (1973, 257–258) argues that what is fundamental about violence in human affairs is that a person's fundamental rights are being violated: 'If it makes sense to talk about violating a person, that just is because a person has certain rights which are undeniably, indissolubly, connected with his being a person. The very idea of natural rights is controversial since it is redolent of Scholasticism, but I find myself forced to accept natural rights in order to understand the moral dimension of violence'. Garver goes on to specify that the right to one's body and the right to autonomy (dignity) are the most fundamental natural rights of persons. According to Garver the violation of a person can be classified into four different kinds based on two criteria, whether the violence is personal or institutional, overt or covert (quiet). Of these, the type of violence that is of most interest to us here is institutional covert violence.

Garver uses the example of a well established system of slavery or colonial oppression, or the life of contemporary ghettos, to highlight the reality of institutional covert violence. As he points out, once established such a system may require relatively little overt violence to maintain it. The Harlem riots in 1964 and the Watts riots in 1965 are singled out by Garver (1973, 264), who suggests that 'there is a black ghetto in most American cities which operates very like any system of slavery'. The violence lies in the violation of dignity as autonomy, since people are systematically denied the options that are available to others in our society. As Garver (1973, 265) explains: 'By suppressing options you deprive a person of the opportunity to be somebody because you deprive him of choices. The institutional form of quiet violence operates when people are deprived of choices in a systematic way by the very manner in which transactions normally take place, without any individual act being violent in itself or any individual decision being responsible for the system'.[8]

Garver's account of the injustice of the status quo in terms of institutional, covert violence finds in Galtung a powerful ally. Galtung distinguishes between 'direct violence', where the instigator of an act of violence can be traced to a person or persons, and 'structural violence', where there may not be any person who directly harms another person. Famously Galtung (1969, 168) defines 'structural violence' in the following terms: 'Violence is present when human beings are being influenced so that their actual somatic and mental realizations are below their potential realizations'.

Structural violence refers to institutional interferences that impede human self-realization, including the deprivation of one's needs. In structural violence the violence is built into the structure, and shows up as unequal power and consequently as unequal life chances. For example, if people are starving when this is objectively avoidable, then violence is occurring, regardless of whether there is a clear subject-action-object relation. As Galtung reminds us, structural violence is more deadly and destructive than direct violence.[9]

Garver and Galtung have their fair share of critics, nevertheless their theories are still very influential, and many contemporary radical social theorists still maintain the view that there is no difference between the injustice of the status quo and an act of violence. Salmi (1993) echoes Galtung when he argues that violence amounts to an avoidable action that constitutes a violation of a human right, understood in its widest meaning, or which prevents the fulfilment of a basic human need. Like Galtung, Salmi also emphasizes the impact of structural (indirect) violence, or the category of harmful or deadly situations or actions which do not necessarily involve a direct relationship between the victims and the institution, person or people responsible for the plight. Salmi (1993, 18) suggests that the hunger issue may serve as an illustration of indirect violence: 'Each time human beings starve or are undernourished, not because of an absolute lack of food after a natural disaster but simply because food is not available for social or political reasons.... it is legitimate to consider these people as the victims of a form of social violence for which readily identifiable people or institutions are responsible'.

Lee (1996; 1999) also focuses on the poverty caused by the unjust international social order. By defining poverty as an institutional injustice causing significant harm, Lee defends the thesis that someone's being poor, when this is a harmful injustice, is the result of violence. Like the other authors in this tradition, Lee also claims that the primary sources of poverty are the institutional structures determining distribution. In redefining social injustice as a type of violence, Salmi and Lee are making the point that misery and destitution is not only an issue of injustice, it is much more serious than that, it is an act of violence.

The works by Garver and Galtung in the 1960s, and by Salmi and Lee in the 1990s, are a clear indication that the marriage between violence and injustice has taken the form of a direct exchange, whereby any gross social injustice is reclassified under the heading of institutional or structural violence. From an ideological and political point of view, this approach still serves an important function, and it is to be hoped that this literature will continue. But from a philosophical or analytical point of view, there are some serious reservations to be accounted for.

Part III: Injustice as violence: a misleading equation

It cannot be denied that equating issues of social injustice with acts of violence adds some force to arguments aimed at accentuating the plight of exploitation, oppression, and systematic discrimination. When for example Perry (1970, 9) tells us that injustice depends on violence, and that violence is evil, he is invoking the language of violence to condemn the evil of injustice: 'Because coercion, exploitation, infringement of liberty, and maintenance of injustice depend on violence – on the unjustified use of force – violence may be viewed plausibly as the root source of all social evils'.

Arguments of this nature may perform a useful political or ideological function, even though one is left wondering whether there is any substance behind the rhetorical points being scored. It is not clear what, if anything, the term 'violence' adds to our understanding of injustice. Even Galtung (1969, 171) is aware of this problem, although he continues to use the two terms interchangeably: 'In order not to overwork the word violence we shall sometimes refer to the condition of structural violence as *social injustice*'. Why Galtung feels that he needs two terms, structural violence and social injustice, to perform the same function, remains a mystery.

In an effort to defend this strategy of raising our awareness of the evils of injustice by invoking the terminology of violence, Lee (1996, 78) argues that we need to employ terms like 'violence' when describing issues of social injustice exactly because it is important to stress the moral seriousness of the unjust status quo: 'The term "violence" is a very important term of moral evaluation, specifically, or moral condemnation, so to fail to extend it to the harms of social order would be to fail to recognize their moral seriousness, their moral continuity with the harms of social disorder'. Lee (1996, 79–80) goes on to say that there is no difference between the actions of a criminal, and those of an unjust social order: 'Both the outlaw and the maintainer of an unjust status quo are capable of great moral wrongs, and we should not let this point be obscured by reserving the strongest condemnatory language for only one of them'.

The problem with this strategy is that it is rhetorically rich but conceptually or analytically barren. It is true that violence is a term of moral evaluation, perhaps even moral condemnation, but it is not the only term at our disposal. 'Injustice', 'unfairness', 'favouritism', 'prejudice', 'discrimination', 'bigotry', are all terms of moral evaluation, each referring to a specific phenomenon. The rhetorical move of classifying an injustice as an act of violence carries the handicap of being a strategy open to anyone who wants to defend a particular theory of justice. We have already seen how Rawls uses the language of violence to make a point about what he considers to be unjust social arrangements. A similar move can be found in Nozick's (1974) defence of libertarian social arrangements. Nozick (1974, 169) famously argues that rights are being violated every time people are unjustly taxed, and he uses the language of violence to get his message across: 'Taxation of earnings from labour is on a par with forced labour', therefore any taxation for the sake of policies beyond the minimal state will violate persons' rights not to be forced to do certain things, and is unjustified. The point here is that although injustice and violence share a common core, identified in the violation of rights, the rhetorical move from injustice to violence can be applied to any conception of justice, therefore simply by redefining an injustice as an act of violence does not add anything to our understanding of the nature of injustice, or why an injustice is wrong.

The inappropriate use of the term 'violence' to describe an injustice may give rise to conceptual confusion, which may prove to be counterproductive to the cause of fighting injustice. In fact there are three risks associated with using the term violence to condemn an injustice. First, the conceptual confusion borne from using the emotively loaded word 'violence' when the grievance can be better described and treated under another name, for example 'injustice', may lead to the accusations being dismissed as unfounded. As Audi (1974, 38) points out: 'misnaming the disease can lead to the use of the wrong medicine – or none at all'.

Secondly, as the range of things denoted by a term expands, its descriptive force contracts. Platt (1992, 188) points out that the risk here is that the moral condemnation of violence becomes meaningless: 'as the term violence is applied to an ever-expanding range of behaviours the moral judgement "violence is morally wrong" becomes ever less informative'.

There is also a third risk, arguably the most hazardous, associated with the conceptual confusion which arises when an injustice is redefined as an act of violence. Rightly or wrongly, many people think of violence as intrinsic to human behaviour. This neo-Darwinian school of thought, popular in some universities and in most bars, likes to think of *homo sapiens* as animals driven by urges and desires, which may be uncontrollably violent. The recent literature on the genetic causes of criminal behaviour has added a scientific backbone to this controversial thesis.[10] If an injustice is reclassified as an act of violence, there is the potential risk that injustice will also be seen as inevitable. This would be extremely detrimental to the cause of justice, if not tragic. Not surprisingly a growing number of moral philosophers have entered the debate on the genetics of violent behaviour, arguing that explaining violence in terms of genetic factors may have implications for the moral responsibility we assign to the agent.[11] The risk that a genetic explanation for violence turns into a justification for injustice is too great to even contemplate. Fortunately this debate between geneticists and philosophers can conveniently be by-passed if we rethink the relationship between injustice and violence: instead of starting with a claim about injustice and simply rephrase it using the stronger language of violence, we should start with a theory of violence, and ask ourselves how this helps us to understand the evil of injustice.

Part IV: From violence to injustice

The tendency to equate an injustice with an act of violence may have a lot to do with the fact that there are victims of justice and victims of violence, and it is not always easy to distinguish one from the other. For example Simon (1995, 30) says that social injustice 'consists of an infliction of social harm upon relatively harmless individuals', and of course violence is also usually described in terms of inflicted harm, as suggested by Geras (1990, 22): '[violence is] the exercise of physical force so as to kill or injure, inflict direct harm or pain on, human beings', or Harris (1980, 19): 'An act of violence occurs when injury or suffering is inflicted upon a person or persons'. But just because there are victims of injustice and victims of violence it does not mean that an injustice is simply another word for an act of violence.

The problem with equating an injustice with an act of violence is that we lose out many things that a theory of violence has to offer to a theory of justice. I believe there are some important benefits to be drawn from comparing the literature on violence with the literature on justice, but we become aware of these benefits only if we take a theory of violence as our starting point, and only subsequently proceed to analyse issues of injustice from the point of view of violence, not vice-versa as is the custom within the literature on social justice. In particular, it may be useful to appeal to the notion of victim (of violence) in order to understand the idea of being a victim (of injustice), therefore understanding why violence is bad makes us aware of why injustice is bad. For anyone interested in social justice, it is imperative to fully understand why injustice is bad, and a theory of violence enables us to understand this. But the starting point of our inquiry must be a theory of violence. Substituting the term 'violence' for 'injustice' is nothing more than a rhetorical move that fails to add anything substantive to a theory of justice poised to uproot injustice.

Considering the vast literature on virtually every aspect of social justice, it is surprising how little has been written on the concept of injustice. Shklar's (1990) *The Faces of Injustice* is one notable exception. While some of the ideas Shklar articulates in her book are preposterous, for example her claim that injustice is desirable because it brings peace and quiet,[12] she is probably right in her assessment that victims of injustice often choose not to recognize the injustice of the situation. Shklar (1990, 38) explains this puzzle by pointing to the degrading nature of being a victim: 'Most people hate to think of themselves as victims; after all, nothing could be more degrading. Most of us would rather reorder reality than admit that we are the helpless objects of injustice'.

Shklar's account of what is objectionable about being a victim is informative, and can be put to good use. Perhaps what is most disturbing about injustice is the sense of helplessness experienced by the victims, which is indicative of their vulnerability and powerlessness. This suggests that what makes social injustice bad and wrong has something to do with the dominant/subordinate relations of power within society.[13] It is interesting to note that powerlessness and vulnerability also define the experience of victims of violence, and although an injustice should not be confused with an act of violence, their similarity on this issue can be revealing. In fact, it may be possible to understand what is bad and wrong about injustice by exploring the phenomenon of violence, in particular why violence is bad. From the literature on violence we learn not only why violence is bad, and prima-facie wrong, but we also get a glimpse of why we consider injustice to be bad and wrong.

The concept of violence is evaluative, and perhaps even normative. We assume that violence is bad, even though the fact that violence is bad does not make violence wrong by definition. There are times when some violence, albeit bad, can be justified as the lesser or two evils, for example when the risks to human life of undertaking violence are not as great as the risks to human life of abstaining from violence.[14] But when violence is not or cannot be justified, violence is not only bad, it is also wrong.

The reason why violence is bad and wrong were explained in Chapter Six in terms of the Humiliation Factor, namely the sense of humiliation, vulnerability and powerlessness that goes with having one's integrity violated. It is being vulnerable *to* another being, or being humiliated by having our humanity being determined by another person, or being powerless in relation to someone else who exercises power over us, that is the real issue. There is a social dimension to humiliation, vulnerability and powerlessness that is prevalent in issues of violence, but lacking in issues of death. Furthermore it is this social dimension that is the worse part of being the victim of violence.

The Humiliation Factor explains what the worse part of violence is, and why violence is both bad and wrong. The Humiliation Factor underlines the fact that victims of violence are not only harmed but also wronged, and their self-respect and self-esteem suffers as a result. Violence is degrading. It destroys a person's self-confidence, it diminishes the sense of a person as a person, and it deprives a person of their self-respect and self-esteem. As pointed out in Part II above, John Rawls famously argued that self-respect (self-esteem) is arguably the most important primary good. Violence represents an assault on a person's sense of himself or herself as a moral agent deserving concern and respect.

Violence is not only bad, it is also *prima facie* wrong. In an article written in 1970, but published only posthumously in 1993, Gerald MacCallum Jr. suggests that what makes violence wrong is that fact that the integrity of something has been changed, destroyed or violated, although MacCallum remains unsure whether there is anything wrong per se with damage to or destruction or violation of the integrities of things.[15] Following the analysis in Part II above of violence as a violation of our integrity, given that humiliation undermines our self-respect, we can say that what makes violence not only bad but also wrong can be traced to the inequality between the perpetrator and the victim of violence, where the former has the power to determine the fate of the latter, against her will. MacCallum is right when he says that violence is a violation of a person's integrity, but what is missing from his account of violence is the idea of humiliation. Having one's integrity violated is humiliating and degrading. Violence undercuts self-respect, and it undermines a person's sense of their own value, and a confidence in their ability. Between Margalit and MacCallum, the reason why violence is wrong becomes intelligible.

The concept of victim is socially constructed, since victims are only one side of a power relationship. Victims become aware of their vulnerability when they are forced by the perpetrators into a power relationship where they are humiliated in their submission.

What makes violence bad and wrong is not only the fact that the vulnerability of the victim is being exposed, but also that the perpetrator of violence is in a position to take advantage of the power they enjoy over their victim. Litke (1992, 176) is absolutely right when he points out that 'violence can be considered the disempowerment of persons', but what of injustice? Can injustice be understood along the same lines?

So far the reason why violence is bad, and prima facie wrong, has been explained in terms of the humiliation, vulnerability and powerlessness associated with being a victim of violence. The same analysis applies in the case of injustice. Understanding the badness of violence in terms of humiliation and undermining self-respect helps us to see more clearly the nature of injustice, as well as define the aims of a just society. Like violence, injustice is also prima facie bad and wrong, therefore the concept of injustice is also evaluative and normative. This does not mean that the terms 'violence' and 'injustice' are interchangeable, or that the term 'violence' ought to be used polemically when describing an injustice. Yet at a fundamental level the concepts of violence and injustice have something in common, since both injustice and violence are defined from the point of view of the victim.

There are two possible ways of explaining what is bad and wrong about an injustice. The first is to say that an injustice is bad because of the detrimental material impact the injustice will have on the injured party. When a less deserving candidate is offered a job, or a promotion, before a more deserving candidate, the injustice suffered by the second candidate can be measured in monetary terms. This explanation, which echoes the great deal of attention economic justice has attracted in the literature on distributive justice, has some merits, but it is ultimately unsatisfactory. To account for the badness of injustice in terms of the unjustified loss of material goods that were rightly due to someone is not simply to misunderstand the tragedy of an injustice, but also to trivialize it.

The true nature of injustice can perhaps be seen by way of examining the case of Coleman Silk, the fictional character in Roth's (2001) novel *The Human Stain*. Coleman Silk is a light-skinned African American born in New Jersey. His father was discriminated against because of his race, the way that all African Americans were being systematically discriminated against in the first half of the twentieth century. This discrimination had an economic dimension, which means that the injustice could possibly be measured in terms of the restricted job opportunities open to African Americans. From a purely economic point of view, because injustice has an impact on the victim's income potential, injustice could be compared to an extra, unfair tax.

The problem with the economic analysis of the badness of injustice is not that it is false, but that it gives too much importance to a feature of injustice that is secondary. The core reason why injustice is bad lies elsewhere. Coleman Silk escapes the institutional injustice his father suffered by faking a new identity for himself. After breaking all ties with his family, and his roots, he reinvents himself as a Jew, on his way to becoming a successful classics professor. To Coleman Silk the advantage of being a Jew, or the disadvantage of being an African American, has nothing to do with income potential. That is not the reason why Coleman Silk kept a secret hidden from everyone for fifty years, until his death. What led Coleman Silk to reinvent himself can be attributed to the sense of powerlessness and vulnerability he felt as a young African American growing up in the United States after the war.

For Coleman Silk what was much worse than the potential loss of income was the fact that he was made to feel powerless in front of such injustice, and that his socially constructed vulnerability was exposed and regularly being taken advantage of. In the last analysis, what is bad about injustice can be expressed in terms of the same Humiliation Factor that accounts for the badness of violence. Like victims of violence, victims of injustice are made to feel powerless and vulnerable. That is ultimately why injustice is both bad and wrong.

Part V: Conclusion

In 1971 Rawls changed political philosophy forever. Not only he placed questions of justice at the heart of the concerns of contemporary political philosophers, but by focussing on the moral arbitrariness of luck he set the agenda for the present generation of political philosophers. The overwhelming emphasis on economic justice that has followed the publication of Rawls's *A Theory of Justice* may say more about his commentators than Rawls's own concerns, yet apart from passing remarks on injustice being a form of violence, the problem of violence is almost totally absent from Rawls's work.

This lacuna in Rawls's work has not gone totally unnoticed. Amongst contemporary theorists of justice Iris Young (1990) is arguably the best known advocate of a theory of justice finely tuned on concerns of oppression and violence. She argues that oppression denies people of their basic human right to be free, furthermore oppression is socially and structurally constructed and sanctioned. According to Young, the eradication of oppression is ultimately what a theory of social justice should be about. Young finds a sympathetic ear in Anderson (1999), who champions a theory of 'democratic equality' that aims to abolish socially created oppression.

Young's theory of justice ought to be praised not only for reintroducing the problem of violence within the orbit of injustice, but also for prioritizing the elimination of violence and oppression as the defining quality of a just society. At the same time one feels that in her effort to reinstate political oppression as the main concern of a theory of justice, the correspondence between injustice and violence is too stark, and as a result Young seems to be opting for a simple equation between injustice and violence that echoes the strategy expounded in Part II, but ultimately rejected in Part III above.

This chapter suggests that the principal aim of a theory of justice is the eradication of injustice, but we don't learn anything new about injustice by simply calling an injustice by another name, like 'crime' or 'violence'. What we need to do is inverse the roles, start from a theory of violence, and analyse injustice in terms of violence. If we do this, we learn that an injustice is bad and wrong for the same reasons that violence is bad and wrong, namely, because those who suffer an injustice are humiliated into feeling powerless and vulnerable, just like the victims of violence. Reading the literature on violence reminds us why we must fight injustice. To make a direct equation between violence and injustice is simplistic and misleading, which is why such reductivism should be avoided. More modestly, this chapter simply suggests that if the aim and scope of a theory of justice is to eradicate injustice, it is crucial to understand exactly why injustice is bad and wrong. This is where the literature on violence, and why violence is bad in particular, is enlightening. A theory of violence should be the starting point for any theory of justice. Knowing why violence is bad helps theorists of justice understand the true nature of injustice. In the next chapter, it will be argued that analysing the injustice of exploitation through the lenses of violence adds a whole new perspective on exploitation, and therefore to the aims of a theory of justice.

Notes

1. Of course Rawls was always very interested in the ethics of violence. In 1969 he published his views on civil disobedience, which he characterized as non-violent acts, (Rawls 1969). This article found its way in Part 2, Chapter 6 of *A Theory of Justice*. Since then Rawls returned to the question of violence only on one occasion, when he published his views on the bombing of Hiroshima and Nagasaki (Rawls 1995).
2. The complex question of exploitation will be the focus of Chapter Eight.
3. According to the interest-theory of rights, this is equivalent to saying that violence is the violation of people's rights.
4. Nickel (2007) provides a good introduction to these problems.
5. Margalit distinguishes between a decent society and a civilized society. The latter is where citizens do not humiliate one another.
6. In an attempt to be more specific about the concept of humiliation, Margalit goes on to say that there are three elements that constitute humiliation: treating human beings as if they were not human; performing actions that manifest or lead to loss of basic control; rejecting a human being from the 'Family of Man'. This is in fact more confusing than enlightening, and especially the second and third elements can be seriously questioned.
7. See Lukes (1997); Quinton (1997); Schick (1997).
8. Garver has not changed his views on any of these issues; see Garver (2003).
9. See also Galtung (1996).
10. See Taylor (1984).
11. See Glover (1995); Wasserman and Wachbroit (2001).
12. Shklar (1990, 45) explains her claim that injustice brings peace and quiet as follows: 'One of the reasons why there is no cure for injustice is that even reasonably upright citizens do not want one. This is not due to disagreements about what is unjust but to an unwillingness to give up the peace and quiet that injustice can and does offer. In this they may well be right'.
13. On this point see Kallen (2004).
14. See Audi (1971, p. 92).
15. In publishing for the first time MacCallum's essay 'What is Wrong with Violence?', the editors also published MacCallum's 'Notes for "What is Wrong with Violence?"', where MacCallum (1993, p.256) admits that on the question whether there is anything wrong per se with damage to or destruction or violation of the integrities of things, there is still more work to be done here: 'I touch on this issue (with special reference to the notion of autonomy and, incidentally, freedom), but hardly pursue it'.

8
Exploitation, Injustice and Violence

The principal aim of this chapter is to put to test the theory offered in the previous chapter, where the need to rethink the relationship between injustice and violence was elaborated. To sum up, the orthodox view defends a direct approach, where an injustice is simply but controversially renamed or redefined in terms of an act of violence. Because violence is morally abhorrent, it is tempting to rename acts of injustice as acts of violence; indeed this polemical move is popular amongst those who want to emphasize the brutality and immorality of injustice. And yet, although it is true that often an injustice cannot be distinguished from an act of violence, ultimately there is no benefit in simply replacing one term for the other. For sure, words count, but is claiming synonymy between injustice and violence enough? Is there more to the relationship between injustice and violence than a verbal dispute? These issues cannot be settled in abstract, which is why the focus of this chapter will be on a specific illustration of injustice, namely, exploitation.

In the previous chapter I suggested rethinking the relationship between injustice and violence along the following lines. Instead of starting with an injustice, only to proceed to rename this using the terminology of violence, the relationship between injustice and violence needs to be reassessed. The starting point should be a comprehensive theory of violence: we appeal to our understanding of why violence is bad and prima facie wrong in order to gain an insight into the badness and wrongness of injustice. In Chapter 6 I argued that what makes violence bad can be explained in terms of the Humiliation Factor, which states that an act of violence is bad because it is insulting and humiliating to the victim. Victims of violence not only experience powerlessness, but their integrity comes under attack. The question is whether the same analysis can be applied to the victims of injustice, and if so, whether we learn something new about injustice by analysing this concept through the lenses of violence. Does this new approach to questions of injustice deliver what it promises? The proof, as they say, is in the pudding. That is why this chapter will focus on one illustration of injustice, namely, the injustice of exploitation. More specifically, it will focus on one case study of exploitation, namely, the exploitation of indigenous Mayas in Guatemala in the last 500 years, from the Spanish *conquistadores* to today's *ladino* ethnic group. But before we get entangled in theoretical and empirical issues regarding exploitation, it is necessary to delineate the idea of exploitation.

Part I: The concept of exploitation

Exploitation is a slippery concept, which can be legitimately applied in a variety of contexts.[1] In what follows I suggest we restrict our analysis to exploitation as a social and political act. Thus it is not the exploitation of natural resources (exploiting a coal mine) or certain situation (exploiting the weakness of my chess opponent to win a game) that is at issue, but the exploitation of one person by another person. The exploitation of people can take different forms: sometimes it is their weaknesses or vulnerabilities that are being exploited (as in the case of weaker bargaining position), while other times it is their strengths that are being exploited (a talented musician may end up being burned out by a gruelling schedule of concerts), and of course most often people are exploited for both their weaknesses and strengths. In terms of understanding the nature of social injustice, it is the issue of weaknesses and vulnerability that is our primary concern. It may be important to remember that human vulnerability can take many different forms, being both physical (child abuse or even child labour) and metaphysical (desires and emotional needs), although vulnerability always arises in a social context characterized by an unequal power relationship.

According to the Oxford English Dictionary (OED), to exploit is 'to employ to the greatest possible advantage' or simply 'to make use of', therefore when A exploits B, A is using B to the greatest possible advantage. The OED is right of course: to 'exploit' is essentially to 'use', although these two terms are not synonymous. I can say that 'I'm using a computer to write this book', but it would sound odd to say that 'I'm exploiting a computer to write this book'; this suggests that there must be more to exploitation than simply using someone. After all, we use people all the time, without doing anything wrong. I 'use' the driving skills of a bus driver to get me to work; I 'use' the culinary skill of a chef whenever I go out to a restaurant; I 'use' the expertise of my colleagues when I discuss philosophy with them; and so on. But in none of these cases would it be appropriate to say that exploitation is taking place.

Furthermore the difference between 'exploiting' and 'using' is not simply quantitative or a question of degree, where *to exploit* refers to using more fully or more extensively. To exploit someone is to use someone in a special way. There is a qualitative difference between the acts of 'exploiting' and 'using' someone. Appreciating this qualitative difference between 'exploiting' and 'using' is crucial in terms of understanding certain normative issues about exploitations, including why exploitation is bad and wrong. This analysis of exploitation has the advantage of adding a new dimension to our understanding of the phenomenon that goes beyond the standard account of exploitation.

In Parts II and III, the limits of the standard account of exploitation will be highlighted. The standard view on exploitation is that it is the injustice of certain institutionalized practices that makes exploitation possible. It follows that in order to eradicate exploitation we must change the structural conditions that engender exploitative relations. The injustice of this institutional framework is then articulated by invoking the idea of structural violence or institutional violence, a case of the term 'violence' substituting the term 'injustice' for heightened rhetorical effects. But apart from scoring polemical points, it is not clear whether we learn anything new about exploitation simply by calling it by another name. Understanding the institutional reasons why exploitation occurs is obviously important, but it is not the only important question. We also need to ask ourselves why people exploit one another, and what makes exploitation bad, and above all, why exploitation is wrong.

Thus, in Parts IV–VI a different analysis of exploitation will be put forward. This will consist of two separate stages. First, in order to understand why exploitation is wrong we first need to know why exploitation is bad, since the wrongness of exploitation is derived from its badness. It is here that the literature on violence, and why violence is bad in particular, becomes particularly useful. This takes us to our second stage, that the answer to the question 'why is exploitation bad?' is not dissimilar to the answer to the question 'why is violence bad?'. The Humiliation Factor applies as much to exploitation as it applies to violence. Exploitation is bad and wrong for the same reasons that violence is bad and wrong. In the last analysis, a theory of justice has much to learn from a theory of violence.

Part II: The circumstances of exploitation

The literature on exploitation tends to focus on what makes exploitation unjust, and the injustice is sought in the circumstances that make exploitation possible. This type of explanation has a long and distinguished tradition, which includes the vast majority of Marxists as well as some left-libertarians.[2] The classical Marxist doctrine on the nature of exploitation, based on the unequal exchange of labour, is therefore the natural starting point of our analysis.

Mandel (1970, 23–24), an influential Marxist luminary writing in the 1960s and 1970s, explains the concept of exploitation or surplus value, in the following terms: 'Surplus-value is simply *the monetary form of the social surplus product,* that is to say, it is the monetary form of that part of the worker's production which he surrenders to the owner of the means of production without receiving anything in return'.[3] Suffice it to say that according to this model, it is the structure of capitalism (defined in terms of private property, capital accumulation and social classes) that encourages the unequal exchange of labour, making exploitation both a reality and an injustice.

Contemporary scholars of exploitation, even those who come from a Marxist tradition, tend to be critical of the old-fashioned Marxist model. John Roemer (1994, 96) suggests we abandon the classic Marxist definition of exploitation as the unequal exchange of labour and replace it with a different conception, where exploitation is 'conceived of as the distributional consequences of an unjust inequality in the distribution of productive assets and resources'. According to Roemer, and contrary to what classical Marxists like

Mandel have hitherto argued, exploitation is not in itself a fundamental theory of (in)justice, if by exploitation we mean the extraction of surplus labour at the point of production. In order to perceive its injustice, we need a deeper theory of exploitation, one that gives priority to property relations. Roemer suggests that injustice is essentially a question of unfair or unequal distribution of productive assets and resources. It follows that the injustice of exploitation is the product of the large inequality in access to the means of production.[4]

Steiner (1984), a left-libertarian, endorses a similar conclusion to Roemer, although he arrives at it via a different route.[5] Steiner holds what he calls a liberal conception of justice, and therefore he offers a liberal reading of exploitation. According to Steiner, injustice is essentially a question of violation of rights. But whose rights are being exploited? Counter-intuitively Steiner tells us that it is not 'the exploited' whose rights are being violated. Instead it is all the third parties that are prevented from interfering in the relations of exploitation between the exploiter and the exploited. The key to Steiner's analysis is that we should think of exploitation as a trilateral relation among the exploiter, the exploited and all the other parties who suffer rights violations: A (the exploited party) exchanges his 5X for B's 3X (the exploiter). While this exchange is voluntary, A is unhappy with the terms of exchange. He would have preferred to exchange his 5X for someone else's 5X (say, C's 5X), but the possibility of exchange between A and C was not present, due to the interference of B. That is because B prevented the trade between A and C, perhaps by forcibly preventing C from offering A 5X or even 4X. A is the one who is being exploited, but it is C's rights that are being violated.

Notwithstanding their differences, there are important similarities between Roemer and Steiner on the question of exploitation, especially on the issue of the unequal distribution of natural resources. Roemer sees injustice in the basic structures of capitalist society, for example in the inequality in the access to the means of production. Exploitation is for Roemer merely a consequence of this fundamental injustice. Similarly Steiner refers to the property system of a society in terms of the institutional circumstances of exploitation, whereby exploitation occurs when some persons do not own natural resources. For example, a person's monopoly ownership of natural resources can constitute a circumstance of exploitation.

Steiner suggests land nationalization as a possible solution to the problem of exploitation. Thus, although Roemer and Steiner focus on different aspects of injustice, they both approach exploitation in terms of the structural circumstances responsible for generating this phenomenon.

To summarize this first position, we can say that exploitation is unjust to the extent that exploitation is the product of an initial inequality in the basic distribution of resources, and in turn this inequality is reinforced by the reality of ongoing exploitation. While this model of explanation is laudable, being fundamentally correct in its assessment, it has the drawback of being incomplete. Concentrating on the circumstances of exploitation has the possible shortcoming of blaming this immoral act on the basic structure of society rather than on the will or volition of the exploiter. The moral responsibility of the exploiter is diminished when exploitation is explained in terms of structural circumstances. Nevertheless the focus on the circumstances of exploitation strikes a cord with many critics of neoliberal economic policies currently enjoying hegemonic standing in world affairs.

Part III: Exploitation as structural violence

By putting all the emphasis on the circumstances of exploitation, it is only to be expected that the injustice of exploitation is often construed as a type of violence, to be precise as structural violence.[6] We have come across Galtung's famous account of structural violence in a few occasions throughout this book. Galtung tells us that unlike in the case of direct violence, structural violence is built into the structure and shows up as unequal power and consequently as unequal life chances. Galtung includes under this concept three categories: indirect violence, repressive violence and alienating violence. While it's over four decades since he developed and perfected his theory of structural violence, Galtung still believes that exploitation is at the core of everything structural violence stands for. Exploitation results in millions of people dying of starvation or living in a permanent involuntary state of poverty, which usually encompasses malnutrition and illness. Galtung likes to compare exploitation to a cancer in that one part of the social and human organism lives at the expense of the rest. There is also what Galtung terms 'cultural violence', the acceptance and legitimization of violence as a necessary or inevitable aspect of human society.[7]

It is hard to disagree with the spirit of Galtung's arguments. In Chapter 4 the exploitation of Chinese workers during the construction of the Transcontinental Railroads in the United States in the 1860s and 1870s was introduced as an example of foreseeable but unintended violence. In what follows I want to consider another disturbing example, namely the exploitation of Mayan peasants in Guatemala over the last 500 years. Needless to say the case of the Maya peasants is representative of the exploitation of millions of people not only in Latin America, but all over the world. The exploitation suffered by Mayan Indians is a perfect example of structural violence.

Exploitation has been part of life for the Mayan Indians in Guatemala at least since the starting of campaigns of Spanish conquests 500 years ago. Looking back to the sixteenth century, exploitation in Guatemala can easily be traced back to the expropriation of land by the colonial government. The new landowners needed a limitless amount of labourers to work their holdings, which was conveniently provided by the landless Indian population. Different forms of forced labour were put in place, from the *encomienda* (which reduced entire communities to serfdom), to the *mandiamiento* (whereby all Indians were obliged to work a set number of weeks each year for the big landowners) to the *repartimiento* (whereby colonial landowners made requests to governmental officials for specific numbers of labourers from the Indian community). Debt slavery, through which Indians were tied to particular plantations by advances of wages and accumulated indebtedness, became common later in the seventeenth century. By accepting advanced money, individual Indians were obligated to migrate to plantations in order to work off debts at very low wages. In the 1930s, General Jorge Ubico introduced vagrancy laws, which meant that Indians (*jornaleros*) had to work between 100 and 150 days a year for large landowners, whether or not they were in debt.[8]

All the historical evidence is pointing to inequality in land ownership as the crucial circumstance that made exploitation possible, vindicating the theories of exploitation expounded by Mandel, Roemer and Steiner. It also points to the desire to secure an economic benefit as the motivation for exploiting the labour of indigenous Indians. Indeed this analytical framework can still be used to explain exploitation in contemporary Guatemala. Inequality in land holding is one of the most distinctive features of life in Guatemala today. The United Nations human development report estimates that 65% of productive land is in the hands of 3% of the population, a situation which has not changed in the last 30 years.[9] As a result, poverty and exploitation are rampant in Guatemala today: 85% of Guatemalans live in poverty, with 60% illiteracy and 46.6% unemployment rate. The 80,000 Guatemalans who toil in sweatshops (*maquilas*) earn a daily wage of $2.50, while suffering dehumanizing conditions: they are forced to work overtime without pay; female employees are prohibited from becoming pregnant; workers are denied medical visits; female workers are constantly subjected to sexual harassment.[10]

The misery, poverty and death caused by centuries of blatant exploitation in Guatemala fits in perfectly with Galtung's notion of structural violence, where the violence is built into the structure (in the case of Guatemala in the form of international market forces and neo-liberal policies) and shows up as unequal power (the subordination of Mayans in Guatemalan society) and consequently as unequal life chances (the poverty and misery of contemporary Mayans). It is very tempting to make the short step from the injustice of exploitation to exploitation as structural violence, but I believe it is best to resist this temptation, even though this is not an inaccurate assessment of the situation. As explained in the previous chapter, there is a concern that nothing is gained by simply replacing one term of moral condemnation for another. If we acknowledge the injustice of exploitation, then that is more than sufficient to do something about it, whether or not we call this injustice an act of violence. Referring to the injustice of exploitation as structural violence does not make exploitation any worse or a more pressing issue. What we should do instead is to draw on a theory of violence in order to assess why exploitation is not only unjust, but wrong. In other words, the relationship between exploitation and violence should be reversed: it is not simply a question of exploitation being violence, but violence explaining the nature of exploitation.

Part IV: Why exploitation is wrong

In a powerful and original analysis of exploitation, Wood (1995) argues for a distinction between badness and injustice. Exploitation is nearly always a bad thing, but its badness does not always consist in exploitation being unjust. In fact a society can be pervasively exploitative while remaining fundamentally just. After all, as Wood reminds us, exploitation may benefit the exploited, indeed it may occur with the exploited person's fully voluntary consent. So what is wrong with exploitation? Wood (1995, 150–151) tells us that the real reason that makes exploitation objectionable is the following: 'proper respect for others is violated when we treat their vulnerabilities as opportunities to advance our own interests or projects. It is degrading to have your weaknesses taken advantage of, and dishonorable to use the weaknesses of others for your ends'.

Wood's analysis of exploitation represents a radical departure from Mandel's or Roemer's or Steiner's theories, to the extent that it accounts for badness even where the exploitation involves no unfairness, injustice or violation of rights. Furthermore by emphasizing that exploitation is bad because it is an affront on people's human dignity to have their weaknesses used, Wood is pointing to a dimension of exploitation which goes beyond the juridical-economic structuralism of property rights, distribution of resources and rights violation. I suggest we refer to this other dimension of exploitation as the 'motivations of exploitation'.[11] This motivational dimension is particularly important in order to understand why exploitation is wrong.

The best way to fully understand why exploitation is wrong is by way of a theory of violence. Violence is bad and prima facie wrong because it is humiliating to have one's integrity violated, making one feel vulnerable and powerless. Violence weakens a victim's perception of himself/herself as a person worthy of respect, therefore undermining their self-respect. We find all these issues present in the act of exploitation. Exploiting another person means violating the integrity of the person being exploited, which makes exploitation both humiliating and degrading. To exploit someone is to use them in a particular way which degrades or humiliates them. There is a motivational dimension to the reality of exploitation that is neglected by the standard approach based on a set of unjust circumstances. Switching our attention away from the circumstances of exploitation, to its motives, opens a whole new perspective on the nature and immorality of exploitation.

Part V: Why people are exploited

There are two sides to social justice: structural concerns and motivational concerns.[12] The same can be said for exploitation. We can think of exploitation in terms of not only structural circumstances, but also motivational drives. Switching the focus of analysis from circumstances to motives goes a long way towards shedding new light on the concept of exploitation and why it is wrong.

Earlier I argued that the most popular accounts of exploitation tend to focus on the structural circumstances within which exploitation occurs. This is true of classical Marxist theories (Mandel), as well as contemporary models inspired by the Marxist literature (Roemer and Steiner). Of course these theories are not silent about motives, although the motives are usually explained in terms of the structural circumstances. Thus, according to classical Marxist accounts of exploitation, in the last analysis we can explain what motivates some people (or classes) to exploit other people (or classes) purely in economic terms, namely, to extract surplus value from their labour. What is motivating the exploiter is the desire to accumulate more profit, and exploitation is simply a means to this economic end.

Even Roemer, whose accounts of exploitation steers away from the classic Marxist line, endorses the same motivational assumption. According to Roemer's property relations definition of exploitation, the technical meaning of 'exploit' still remains the unequal exchange of labour, which suggests that the motive of the exploiter is still the same, namely, to extract a profit from the exploited. Similarly Steiner (1984, 226) tells us that in an exploitative relation 'the items transferred are held to be of unequal and greater-than-zero value'. The terminology used by Steiner is unambiguously economic, which suggests that the motive is also essentially economic: to force an advantageous exchange whereby the exploiter makes a gain at the expense of the exploited.

Clearly motives of an economic nature are present in an exploitative exchange and need to be acknowledged. Yet there is more to exploitation than the desire to secure an economic gain. Many writers have made this point, arguing that as it is generally defined, especially within the Marxist tradition, the concept of exploitation is much too narrow.[13] Exploitation, I want to propose, is motivated by two separate reasons. The first is a motive by the exploiter to gain an advantage at the cost of the exploited. This is basically what Marx had in mind when he wrote about capitalist exploitation and surplus value, and it also seems to find confirmation in Roemer's and Steiner's theories of exploitation. I will call this set of *Economic Motives* the EM model.

But apart from economic reasons, there may be another type of motive behind the desire to exploit others, namely, exploitation may arise from the desire by the exploiter to degrade, humiliate or inflict a moral injury on the exploited party. I will call this set of *Humiliating Motives* the HM model. Humiliating motives HM are not as straightforward as economic motives EM, which probably accounts for their neglecting and misunderstanding.

A common mistake is to associate the desire to degrade or humiliate others with 'being evil', where evil is defined as an irrational impulse.[14] I am not denying that evil exists, but I think there are good reasons why we should resist appealing to the idea of evil, understood as an irrational impulse, to explain the phenomenon of exploitation. First of all, appealing to the irrationality of evil is essentially equivalent to giving up on the search for a rational explanation for exploitation: irrationality cannot be explained rationally, therefore one cannot give a rational account of exploitation by appealing to the irrationality of evil. Secondly, assuming that one is responsible for one's actions only if they were within one's rational control, seeing evil as an irrational craving may lead to the view that an evil person is not responsible for their evil actions. For these reasons I will assume that the desire to humiliate or degrade others is not irrational.

Another mistake is to reject the claim that the humiliating motive has anything to do with exploitations, instead dismissing the desire to degrade or humiliate others as simply reflecting a negative prejudice, which turns into 'racism' if the bias is directed against another race or 'snobbism' if directed against another social class or 'sexism' if directed against the opposite sex, etc. I believe this is wrong, and that humiliation has everything to do with exploitation. The point to remember is that exploitation is about using another person, albeit in a special way. The question we need to ask ourselves is what benefit can be extracted by humiliating someone because of their race, social class, sex, etc. Or in other words, in what sense are the people being humiliated being 'used' by those doing the humiliating. I believe there may be considerable benefits, of a non-material nature, to the exploiter in degrading or humiliating the exploited, which are related to the process of identity formation.

Following Hegel and Sartre, Elster (1984) points to the mental process whereby a mode of consciousness is defined through the negation of another object. This is the case of the master–slave dialectic, where masters paradoxically treat their slaves as less than human while at the same time they need the gratitude of their slaves in order to define themselves as moral human beings. I want to suggest that something along similar lines can explain the reasons for wanting to humiliate or degrade others: it is not simply to identify with a moral human being, but more specifically (and problematically from a moral point of view) to identify with power and therefore establish one's superiority.

This idea of 'identifying with power' needs to be unpacked. The key to it lies in the concept of identity in general, and the process of identity formation in particular. Identity being a complex and debated concept, suffice to say that identity is based on differentiation, and differentiation upon disgust, which explains the act of degrading and humiliating. Stallybrass and White (1987, 191) provide us with a powerful account of the way identity relates to what is being rejected via the process of differentiation:

> The division of the social into high and low, the polite and the vulgar, simultaneously maps out divisions between the civilized and the grotesque body, between author and hack, between social purity and social hybridization. These divisions, as we have argued, cut across the social formation, topography and the body, in such a way that subject identity cannot be considered independently of these domains. The bourgeois subject continuously defined and re-defined itself through the exclusion of what it marked out as 'low' – as dirty, repulsive, noisy, contaminating. Yet that very act of exclusion was constitutive of its identity. The low was internalized under the sign of negation and disgust. But disgust always bears the imprint of desire.[15]

Stallybrass and White's account can be used to add another dimension to the master–slave dialectic. According to Elster, masters are moved by a desire to identify with a moral human being, instead following Stallybrass and White we may want to say that masters more specifically want to identify with power. Therefore the act of degrading and humiliating a vulnerable person is the exploiter's way of identifying with power. In the act of causing humiliation, a person is using another person to establish or reinforce their identity with power. This is a case of 'using' in a special way, hence it is not inaccurate to refer to this relationship as one of exploitation.

To recap:

(EM) Model: Economic Motive

Taking advantage of another person's vulnerability for the sake of securing an economic gain or benefit

(HM) Model: Humiliating Motive

Degrading or humiliating another person, as a way of differentiating oneself from them, and therefore in the process identifying with power.

The relationship between EM and HM is complex. Usually these two sets of motives work in tandem. In fact I suspect that the reason why these two motives have not been distinguished in the literature on exploitation so far is exactly because they are so tightly intermingled: A may extract an economic advantage by exploiting B, while also degrading and humiliating B in the process.

While EM and HM usually apply simultaneously, these two sets of motives can also act autonomously. As autonomous motives, EM and HM are self-sufficient. According to the logic of the EM model, A can exploit B exclusively for the sake of extracting an economic advantage from the relation, but without wishing to degrade or humiliate B. Alternatively, according to the logic of the HM model, A can have the desire to degrade or humiliate B, even if this fails to result in an obvious economic advantage. In fact in the most extreme cases, A will want to degrade or humiliate B, even if this involves an extra economic cost to A.

The problem with the classic Marxist conception of exploitation is essentially that it accounts only for economic motives, while neglecting the other sets of motives, such as the desire to morally degrade or humiliate others. Apart from the motive to take advantage of someone's vulnerability for economic reasons, exploitation may also derive from a motive to morally injure others. This is in line with Wood's argument that exploitation is 'insulting and degrading' to the exploited. What makes exploitation insulting and degrading is the fact that the integrity of the exploited party is being violated. In the last analysis, a comprehensive understanding of the phenomenon of exploitation must allow for both sets of motives, economic (the desire to secure an economic gain) and non-economic (degrading or humiliating another person, as a way of differentiating oneself from those considered one's inferior and therefore identifying with power).

Part VI: Exploitation as humiliation in Guatemala

In Part III the exploitation of Mayan Indians was introduced as a case study of exploitation as structural violence. A closer analysis of this case study suggests that in fact things are more complex than may appear. There is more to exploitation in Guatemala than the desire of *Ladinos* to secure an economic benefit by taking advantage of Mayan Indians' unequal bargaining powers, as suggested by the EM Model of exploitation. In particular, there is evidence to suggest that exploitation also emanates from the motive to humiliate and degrade the Indian population.

In Guatemala, the desire to humiliate and morally degrade the Mayan Indian population is as much a reason for exploiting them as the desire to secure an economic advantage, and yet the former motive often goes undetected. Tumin's (1952) famous anthropological study of a Mayan peasant community, which documents the open discrimination between *Ladinos* and Indians, is informative on this issue. Tumin tells us that the average *Ladino* family earns about $150 a year, including the value of the food products raised, while the average Indian family earns about $75 a year. Hired farm hands (*jornaleros*) receive 15 cents a day and food if *Ladino*, but only 10 cents a day if Indian.[16] From our point of view, what is most curious about this form of exploitation is that, as Tumin points out, Indian workers are generally more skilled and productive than *Ladino* employees. According to the logic of modern economics, one would expect the more productive and skilful workers to be remunerated accordingly, since it is in the interest of the employer to provide good workers with the right incentives to keep productivity levels high. But exploitation in Guatemala goes beyond the logic of economics. As Tumin (1952, 115–116) explains

> No Ladino employee of a Ladino employer is treated with the same disrespect and harshness as that accorded the most ill-treated Indian. . . . As a general rule, it is also true that most Ladino workers get better treatment than do Indians in the same status, Indians are reprimanded more harshly, expected to do harder and longer work, and are more peremptorily ordered about.

The above analysis suggests that while exploitation of a more familiar economic type is predominant, there is also evidence of a more perverse, mischievous motivation behind the exploitation of Mayan Indians.

Guatemalan Indians have always been, and still are, treated as inferior beings. In fact the most common complaint by Mayan Indians of *Ladinos* is that they treat them 'as animals'.[17] In her autobiography Rigoberta Menchú, a Guatemalan Indian who was awarded the Nobel Peace prize in 1992, often refers to the imagery of being treated as an animal. The description of the trips to the plantations on the south coast with her family when she was a little girl is revealing:

> The lorry holds about forty people. But in with the people, go the animals. . . . It sometimes took two nights and a day from my village to the coast. During the trip the animals and the small children used to dirty the lorry and you'd get people vomiting and wetting themselves. By the end of the journey, the smell – the filth of people and animals – was unbearable. (Menchú 1984, 21)

A few years later, as a young woman, Rigoberta Menchú went to work as a maid in the capital for a rich *Ladino* family:

> The food they gave me was a few beans with some very hard tortillas. There was a dog in the house, a pretty, white, fat dog. When I saw the maid bring out the dog's food – bits of meat, rice, things that the family ate – and they gave me a few beans and

hard tortillas, that hurt me very much. The dog had a good meal and I didn't deserve as good a meal as the dog. Anyway, I ate it, I was used to it.... But I felt rejected. I was lower than the animals in the house. (Menchú 1984, 92)

The mistress used to watch me all the time and was very nasty to me. She treated me like... I don't know what... not like a dog because she treated the dog well. She used to hug the dog. So I thought: 'She doesn't even compare me with the dog'. (Menchú 1984, 94)

Clearly the exploitation suffered by Rigoberta Menchú was in part motivated by economic reasons. It makes economic sense for the plantation owners not to distinguish between Indians and animals, so that they can save on the transportation costs of transferring their workforce from the highlands to the south coast. Similarly by treating her as less than their dog the rich *Ladino* family was saving money on the costs of giving Rigoberta Menchú a proper meal. Yet it would be wrong to think that the exploitation Rigoberta Menchú suffered is exclusively of an economic nature. Intertwined with the economic motivation, there is also a desire to humiliate and degrade her as an Indian woman.

The humiliation suffered by the Guatemalan Indians is a recurring theme in the literature on Guatemala.[18] Yet this humiliation cannot and should not be reduced to economic motives. The desire to humiliate, degrade and take away the dignity of the Guatemalan Indians points to a more complex analysis of exploitation than the EM model suggests.[19] In Guatemala the desire to humiliate and degrade Mayan Indians can be a sufficient reason per se for exploiting them, apart from any economic advantage that may arise from the exploitation. As Stallybrass and White explain, the social agent continuously defines and re-defines itself through the exclusion of what it marked out as 'low' – as dirty, repulsive, noisy, contaminating; the very act of exclusion is constitutive of its identity. The exploitation of Guatemalan Indians has a lot more to do with humiliation than it has with capital accumulation.

Part VII: Conclusion

I started this chapter by posing the following question: what is the correct way of accounting for the relationship between injustice, in the form of exploitation, and violence. The standard answer says that exploitation simply is a type of violence, *structural* violence to be precise. While not refuting this claim, this chapter suggests that this is not the full story. Exploitation occurs when one person uses another person for their own advantage, and if exploitation is redefined as structural violence, the injustice of exploitation is reduced to the unfair circumstances or structural conditions in which agents (both exploiters and exploited parties) are forced to operate. The problem with this analysis is that it gives only a partial account of why exploitation is wrong.

This chapter suggests that in order to appreciate why exploitation is wrong, the starting point for our inquiry should be a theory of violence in general, and an account of why violence is bad in particular. An act of violence is bad and wrong because it insults and humiliates the victims, who are made to feel powerless and degraded. The same can be said for exploitation. To exploit someone entails both the general idea of using someone for one's own advantage, for example in order to extract an economic benefit, and the more specific idea of degrading or humiliating them for the purpose of establishing one's superiority, by identifying with a position of power over those being exploited.

Through a close analysis of exploitation in Guatemala, I have argued that exploitation can arise from two distinct sets of reasons: to secure an economic gain by using another person for one's economic benefits (the Economic Motive or EM model), or alternatively to humiliate and degrade another person for the sake of identifying with power (the Humiliating Motive or HM model). Contrary to what is being suggested by most contemporary theories of exploitation, Marxist and non-Marxist, the desire to humiliate and degrade is part of the general phenomenon of exploitation, and it is ultimately why exploitation is wrong. It is only on account of a theory of violence that this aspect of exploitation becomes intelligible, reinforcing the idea promoted in the previous chapter that a theory of violence plays a determining role at the core of any theory of social justice.

Notes

1. See Goodin (1987).
2. Today most Marxists, or at least those who are not afraid to argue for a Marxist theory of justice, see exploitation as fundamentally unjust. This is the view of Elster (1986, 79), who claims that 'exploitation is a normative concept that is part of a wider theory of distributive justice'.
3. For more recent accounts of the classic Marxist analysis of exploitation, see Reiman (1987).
4. Roemer's theory of exploitation is much more complex, and much more sophisticated, than suggested by my brief overview. The *locus classicus* of Roemer's theory remains his *A General Theory of Exploitation and Class* (Roemer 1982). He has since slightly modified his position, therefore see also Roemer (1988 and 1994).
5. On left-libertarianism, see Steiner and Vallentyne (2001).
6. The same is often also said about slavery, for example Bales (2004) argues that slavery is exploitation, violence and injustice all rolled together in their most potent combination.
7. Following Galtung, Bourgois (2001) argues that the contemporary world (dis)order is infused with structural violence, to the extent that the political–economic organization of society imposes conditions of physical and emotional distress rooted, at the macro-level, in structures such as unequal and unfair international terms of trade, and at the local level in exploitative labour markets.
8. See Warren (1978); Melville and Melville (1971); McClintock (1985); Gómez and Ángel (1994).
9. *Caribbean and Central America Report*, 31 October 2000. The data reported in the 1979 official land census is not very different from the census of 1953. The 1979 census reveals that 2.9% of the farms cover 66% of arable land, while in 1953 3.2% of the farms covered 72.2% of arable land. See *Land in Guatemala: A Comprehensive Account of the Land Situation in Guatemala*, London: Guatemala Solidarity Network Report, 1998.
10. *Mesoamérica*, ICAS (Institute for Central American Studies), Vol.19, No.8, August 2000. Maquilas (or maquiladoras) are assembly plants where companies (usually foreign) import raw materials of product parts for assembly and export the finished product. See 'Plan to Entrench Inequality: Guatemala and the Free Trade Area of the Americas', in *Report on Guatemala*, Vol.22, No.2, Summer 2001.
11. I should add that 'motivational approach' is my terminology, not one used by Wood. I don't know whether Wood would agree with the use of this terminology.
12. Barry (1995) is absolutely right when he remind us that any theory of justice must address the question: 'What is the motive for behaving justly?'. Indeed, the issue of the motives of justice is central to many contemporary debates on social justice.

13. See Murphy (1985); Giddens (1995); Young (1990).
14. Gert (1998, 90) argues that 'there is a close relationship between the objects of irrational desires and evils. In fact, an evil or a harm can be initially defined as the object of an irrational desire'.
15. I am grateful to Jools Gilson-Ellis for making me aware of this book.
16. Tumin (1952, 114–115).
17. 'Those of the middle class of San Martin treat us as if we were irrational animals. They have us very oppressed, and they are very contemptuous of us', Sexton (1985, 70). This quote is taken from a detailed and faithful account of life as a Guatemalan Indian peasant.
18. Manz (1988, 140) refers to the 'constant humiliation' suffered by Indians in the military model villages built by the military in the early 1980s: 'The daily treatment Indians receive is discriminatory and contemptuous. Though this treatment is not new in Guatemala, it has particularly unpleasant overtones, given their dependence on the military today. Indians are shouted at, ignored, and summoned for errands and labor at whim. . . . A once independent and self-assured people, they now encounter constant humiliation'. Black (1984, 81; 38) refers to the 'humiliation' of the annual migration to work in coastal plantations: 'more than any other of Guatemala's 22 Maya-descended ethnic groups, the Ixiles know the humiliation of annual migration to the coastal plantations'. In the 1970s, for the 600,000 Indian peasant families who migrate to the coast each year for three months to earn a meagre wage, life in plantation is on the verge of being inhuman: 'the vast cotton plantations of Guatemala's south coast stink of toxic chemicals; small crop-duster planes wheel constantly over the hot flatlands, spraying even as the migrant Indian cotton-pickers are bent on their task. Set back from the fields are communal dormitory shacks, described by the International Labour Office as "totally unacceptable with regard to hygiene, health, education and morality". Malaria is rampant; babies are poisoned by the insecticide residues in the mother's milk'.
19. As Nelson (1999) rightly points out, economic reductivism downplays racism.

9
Violence for Justice

In the previous chapters I regularly postponed the question whether it is legitimate to promote justice through the use of violence. Instead Chapter Six explored the issue of what makes violence wrong, Chapter Seven asked whether an injustice is a type of violence, and Chapter Eight suggested how a theory of violence could facilitate our understanding of what makes an injustice both bad and wrong. But a book on violence and social justice would be incomplete without an analysis of the justifications of violence. Therefore the aim of this chapter is to address the question of whether the use of violence, notwithstanding its badness and prima facie wrongness, ought to be employed for the sake of promoting the goodness and rightness of justice.

Needless to say, this is a large, complex and multi-faceted topic, and any attempt to do justice to all its dimensions in one short chapter is almost inevitably going to result in failure. For all these reasons, the ambitions of this chapter will remain modest. The reader is warned not to expect any original insights in the pages that follow, but only an overview of the major issues and theoretical distinctions that inhabit this body of literature. Thus starting from an outline of the major stances on why violence is a legitimate means towards promoting justice (Part I), two dominant positions often invoked for the justification of violence will come under consideration, the Identity Argument (Part II) and the Consequentialist Argument (Part IV). Although both arguments make powerful claims, and deserve to be taken seriously, ultimately they are found wanting (Parts III and V, respectively). Yet the fact that the Identity and Consequentialist arguments per se fail to justify violence does not mean that violence cannot in principle be justified. There are times when violence ought to be used, but only in extreme circumstances, and if and only if certain conditions are firmly in place. These conditions require the adherence to a set of key principles, which will come under some scrutiny (Parts VI and VII).

Part I: Violence for justice

It is tempting to take a hard line on violence and defend the uncompromising position that violence can never be justified, under any circumstances, not even for the sake of justice. The view that there is always an alternative to violence, namely non-violence, is a powerful paradigm, which has been voiced by many distinguished thinkers over the centuries, including Tolstoy, Gandhi and Martin Luther King.[1] I will not engage directly with the theory of non-violence, instead in what follows the focus will be exclusively on the attempts to articulate ethically sound reasons for the use of violence.

Even though no one would deny that violence is bad and *prima facie* wrong, there are times when at least in principle violence can and ought to be justified. As Gert (1969) points out, although the overwhelming majority of acts of violence are prohibited by public reason and thus completely unjustified, it would be wrong to deny that violence is sometimes required by public reason. What we need to do is identify the public reasons that could, in principle, justify violence.

The place to start is by investigating our duties towards justice, in order to see whether these duties extend to the use of violence for the sake of justice. Generally speaking, our duties towards justice are of two different types: a duty to uphold justice and a duty to promote justice. As Rawls (1971, 334) explains in Chapter Six of *A Theory of Justice*, on 'Duty and Obligation', the most important natural duty is that to support and to further just institutions:

> This duty has two parts: first, we are to comply with and to do our share in just institutions when they exist and apply to us; and second, we are to assist in the establishment of just arrangements

when they do not exist, at least when this can be done with little cost to ourselves.

The duty to uphold justice speaks to our obligation to accept and live by the principles of justice. On the other hand, the duty to promote justice speaks to our obligation to facilitate the application and enforcement of the principles of justice. This includes an obligation not only to sustain the process of fair procedures, even if prolonged, at the expense of expediency, but of voicing one's concern for justice, even when this carries personal costs (within limits), for example in the case of peaceful demonstrations and other instances of civil disobedience.

The duties we have towards justice, to uphold and to promote justice, will have different implications depending on whether we live in a just or unjust society. Rawls's conception of natural duty assumes that the basic political, economic and social structure of society is, on the whole, organized according to the demands of publicly recognized principles of justice. Thus, in a state of 'near justice', as Rawls (1971, 350–351) calls it, we are under a duty to comply with unjust laws, provided that these laws do not exceed certain bounds of injustice:

> Now it is sometimes said that we are never required to comply in these cases. But this is a mistake. The injustice of a law is not, in general, a sufficient reason for not adhering to it.... When the basic structure of society is reasonably just, as estimated by what the current state of things allows, we are to recognize unjust laws as binding provided that they do not exceed certain limits of injustice.

Rawls is undoubtedly right, but what if there are serious restrictions to justice in society? What if one finds oneself living in a grossly unjust society? What obligations do we have towards justice when certain limits of injustice are being exceeded? Rawls does not discuss those cases, so we must look elsewhere for a guide. I believe that this is where questions of violence for justice arise. It is if, and only if, society is profoundly unjust, if laws exceed certain bounds of injustice, that violence becomes not only an option, but perhaps even a duty.

There are, generally speaking, two different types of argument for our duty to promote justice via the use of violence: the argument from necessity, and the strategic argument. The justifications for violence put forward by Audi (1971) and Geras (1990) are, respectively, representative of these two arguments.

Audi is uncomfortable with the idea that violence is always wrong. He considers the argument that violence should be used to stop a Hitler from carrying out his planned atrocities, as well as the counterargument that in fact it is never necessary to use violence, even to stop a man like Hitler, particularly if non-violent protests are used at the first sign of evil. Audi's (1971, 86) own assessment is that a thorough analysis of each actual case is mandatory, although

> it is certainly conceivable that a man like Hitler might be stopped only through violence; and insofar as there is good reason to think that only violence can stop him, the use of at least some violence, especially nonhomicidal violence aimed at bringing about a coup or forcing the needed change in social policy, might obviously be justified by the moral principles to which I am appealing.

Geras (1990, 23) would not disagree with the substance of Audi's argument, while at the same time emphasizing the fact that violence is at times strategically the only option open to the victims of injustice, and therefore ought to be available to them in their efforts to promote justice. Geras provides a compelling argument to refute the doctrine that the use of violence is never justified:

> where it is genuine, held scrupulously, consistently, on pacifist-type grounds, it [non-violence] is a doctrine that would deprive people of all weapons save passive resistance in the face of any oppression or threat, however terrible. If that is not a sufficient case against it, I am unsure what could be.

What Geras is telling us is that history is full of examples of violence being used as a means to impose injustice, and we must allow for the possibility that the only way to fight an injustice is through the same violent means.[2]

Of course this does not mean that with regards to political violence, including revolutionary violence, no question of justification arises. The fact that some type of violence can in principle be justified does not mean that any type of violence is automatically justified. A positive answer to the question 'Can violence in theory be justified?' must be followed by two further questions, of a less theoretical nature: First, 'What good can possibly come out of an evil?' and secondly, 'Assuming that violence can be justified, what type of violence, and how much violence, is justifiable?'.

The first question will be discussed in Parts II, III, IV and V below, where two arguments outlining for potential goods to be enjoyed via the evil of violence are put forward, the Identity argument and the Consequentialist argument. The second question will be dealt with in Parts VI and VII, where some of the main principles in the just war tradition will be introduced.

Part II: The Identity Argument

Definitions of violence vary, as we have seen, yet most definitions share an emphasis on the suffering and injury caused by the act of violence. It follows that to justify violence is to justify an evil.[3] After all, if violence were not an evil, the question of justifying it would not even arise. Therefore in order to justify violence, the evil produced by an act of violence must somehow be accounted for, and arguments suggesting how such evils are compensated by greater goods must be put forward.

One way of justifying violence is to argue that violence is not entirely bad, instead violence is both good and bad, and violence can be justified in terms of its goodness. The claim that violence can be good is counterintuitive, and needs to be explained. First of all, good for whom? Certainly not for the victims of violence, even though there are people who entertain this idea. Enduring violence is often seen as a rite of passage into manhood, therefore violence is held to be good for the victim to the extent that it defines their masculinity.[4] Thus Peteet (2002) suggests that the Israeli policy and practice of beating and imprisoning young Palestinian males in the occupied West Bank are framed as rites of passages now central in the construction of manhood and masculinity among Palestinian male youths, with critical consequences for political consciousness and agency.

Nietzsche (1977, 100–101) probably deserves much of the blame for giving credibility to this perilous argument, when he ponders whether violence does not belong to the *favouring* circumstances that make the increase in virtue possible:

> Examine the lives of the best and most fruitful men and people, and ask yourselves whether a tree, if it is to grow proudly into the sky, can do without bad weather and storms: whether unkindness and opposition from without, whether some sort of hatred, envy, obstinacy, mistrust, severity, greed and violence do not belong to the *favouring* circumstances without which a great increase even in virtue is hardly possible.

Pace Nietzsche, it could be argued that if not for the victim, at least violence is good for the perpetrator of violence, but in what sense can violence be good to the person doing the violence? The simple answer has less to do with benefits this action brings (this is the Consequentialist Argument discussed in Part III below), instead violence is good because of the way it makes the perpetrator of violence feel about himself or herself. This begs the question: how can doing violence, that is to say violating the integrity of another person, make someone feel good about themselves? The Identity Argument provides us with an answer.

The Identity Argument can be stated as follows: *Violence is good if, through an act of violence, the perpetrator is able to re-establish his or her own identity as a person of equal moral value, deserving the respect of others.* The most famous statement along these lines can be found in Frantz Fanon's powerful account of violence against colonial powers, and in Jean-Paul Sartre's endorsement of Fanon's argument. An analogous argument has also been put forward more recently by Julia Kristeva. The arguments of these three authors will be considered in turn.[5]

Fanon's (1970) *The Wretched of the Earth* was first published in French in 1961 at the height of the Algerian war. A psychiatrist by training, Fanon's argument is both normative and psychological. The essence of his argument, which could almost be described as therapeutic, is the belief that colonization constitutes a special type of violence, which can be overturned only if it is countered with violence. The violence of colonization is special in the sense that it has both a physical and a psychological component. The physical component is the overt aspect of any colonization, namely the act of taking away by force what rightfully belongs to those being colonized. From this point of view the colonization of Algeria by France until 1962 was not different from any other act of imperial violence, including the conquering wars of Alexander the Great, the Roman Empire, the British Empire and (some would argue) the American Empire since the end of the Second World War. But apart from the overt physical violence, colonization also entails a covert psychological violence. It is the latter that is the focus of Fanon's reflections on violence.

According to Fanon, colonization represents a power relation between the colonizers and the colonized, whereby the former are in a position of superiority, and the latter are made to feel inferior. It is this sense of inferiority that comes with being colonized that Fanon is most concerned with. Colonization is humiliating on a very personal level, undermining the sense of identity and self-respect of those being colonized. This is why the violence of colonization calls for the violence of decolonization, where decolonization stands for the process of reversing these power relationships. It is through this process that the colonized re-establish their moral identity and regain their self-respect.[6]

Fanon's thesis became very influential in France in the late 1960s, and more recently in many other countries with a colonial past, including Algeria, where Fanon is invoked today as an inspiration by Islamic fundamentalists in their armed struggle.[7] Crenshaw (2002, 103) even goes as far as to suggest that intellectuals such as Fanon 'have significantly influenced terrorist movements in the developed West by promoting the development of terrorism as routine behaviour'. Yet as Macey (2001) rightly points out, critics often trivialize Fanon's argument, making it sound as if Fanon glorifies violence for its own sake. Following Tronto (2004), it is more accurate to think of Fanon as a political realist who is suggesting that the violence he observes in decolonization is a response to the violence of colonization.

Perhaps one of the reasons why Fanon quickly became very popular, but perhaps also misunderstood, is due to Sartre's famous preface to the 1961 French edition of the book. Sartre's starting point is that violence in the colonies does not only have for its aim the protection of the interests of the colonizing powers, but it also seeks to dehumanize the colonized. Sartre's argument suggests that the reason behind using violence is to rediscover one's true identity. As Sartre (2004, 231) points out, in the act of violence a person recreates itself: 'we only become what we are by the radical and deep-seated refusal of that which others have made of us'. Within the context of colonization, Sartre (2004, 233) gives the impression that violence has the power to ennoble or liberate the perpetrator, since the colonized subjects can only regain their humanity through acts of revolutionary violence: 'the native cures himself of colonial neurosis by thrusting out the settler through force of arms. When his rage boils over, he rediscovers his lost innocence and he comes to know himself in that he himself creates his self'.

Considering that Julia Kristeva was also trained in psychoanalysis, and like Fanon she also wrote on the imperative to revolt, it is surprising that she never read Fanon.[8] At the same time, her arguments on revolt are not dissimilar to those of Fanon and Sartre, being founded on the idea of identity formation.[9] Kristeva (2002, 12) sustains that revolts, as in the case of the May '68 'contestation', are important because they express a fundamental version of freedom: 'liberty-as-revolt isn't just an available option, it's fundamental'. The difference between Fanon and Kristeva is that whereas Fanon was concerned specifically with the humiliation of being colonized, Kristeva (2002, 13) refers to the humiliation of the most disadvantaged citizens in general, thus the revolts of May '68 can be explained in terms of a desire by those classes to regain their dignity: 'it was the desire of the most disadvantaged citizens – the "humiliated" and the "offended" – to claim a dignity beyond and actually in spite of the political structures that had usually served them since the industrial revolution'.

The Identity Argument suggests that violence can (in part) be good, since through the act of violence those who have been humiliated by violence are able to reclaim their own identity. Fanon's original argument focused on the humiliation and search of identity of the victims of colonization, although Kristeva stretches the same argument to include the humiliation of the most disadvantaged citizens.

Part III: A critique of the Identity Argument

The appeal of the Identity Argument cannot be denied. Even Keane (1996), who is less than enthusiastic about the Identity Argument, agrees that there are times when acts of collective violence serve to lift the spirits of the unjustly treated, to give them hope and courage to stand up against their oppressors, as for example in the case of the American Revolution. Apart from the Algerian war (1954–1962), other examples from the twentieth century would include the Irish War of Independence (1919–1922), the armed struggle against apartheid in South Africa (1961–1994), or the velvet revolution in Eastern Europe in 1989.[10] There is also ample empirical evidence suggesting that violence plays an important role in the social construction of ethnic identities.[11] Yet the appeal of the Identity Argument can easily be romanticized, and violence glorified. Keane (1996, 75) points to the limits of Fanon's argument with some vigour:

> It is questionable whether the exercise of violence can always have a liberating cathartic impact upon the violent individual, as for instance Fanon's call for revolutionary violence of the colonized against the colonizers supposed. Fanon's account of how the depersonalized colonial subject can violently defeat the system of violence that dislocates and disempowers it.... romanticizes the gun and the bomb.

Keane goes on to say that the tactic of violence is invested with a hotchpotch faith in existentialist humanism and a crudely modernist belief in history as progress.

Apart from the risk of romanticizing violence, the Identity Argument falls foul of two other fallacies. First, there is a thin line between using the Identity Argument to justify violence and using the Identity Argument as an excuse for violence. The stakes are too high to risk confusing one for the other. It is important to stress that when Fanon was writing about violence, he was thinking exclusively within the context of colonization. But the reality today is that the Identity Argument can and has been used to justify the most brutal atrocities, even when colonization is not an issue. To put it bluntly, the Identity Argument per se makes it too easy to justify violence. One must be careful not to give unjustified violence the semblance of a valid justification.

Finally, with the Identity Argument the justification of violence takes the form of two negatives making a positive. There seems to be a dialectic of negation at work here, whereby violence is necessary as an act of negation of the original violence. Thus Sartre (2004, 231) talks about becoming what we are 'by the radical and deep-seated refusal of that which others have made of us', and Kristeva (2002, 114) sees revolt as a dialectical process, where negativity is assigned a central role: 'without negativity, there is no longer freedom or thinking... If this aspect of the negative were eliminated, it would lead straight into the robotization of humanity'. Unfortunately this logic does not apply to ethics, and violence in particular. In ethics the good cannot be constructed from two evils. With violence we are looking at a scenario where two evils make an even bigger evil, therefore the dialectic of negation is not a valid justification for the evils of violence.

Part IV: The Consequentialist Argument

Unlike for the Identity Argument, the Consequentialist Argument has no qualms on the evil of violence. Yet violence can still be justified, as long as the violence is a necessary evil. The Consequentialist Argument can be stated as follows: *Violence is justified when it is a necessary evil, an indispensable means towards preventing an even greater evil and/or promoting a greater good.*

The logic of this argument is strictly consequentialist, and it is arguably still the most common line of reasoning used to justify the use of violence, in fact the Consequentialist Argument is invoked by a variety of scholars across the ideological spectrum, including Robert Audi, Bernard Gert and Kai Nielsen. Audi (1971, 89) argues that violence, contemplated as a strategy for achieving social reform, particularly where the reform envisaged is regarded as the rectification of grave moral wrongs, can be justified only to maximize the proportion of happiness to suffering, giving priority to the reduction of suffering over the increase of happiness, and to the increase of happiness below the minimum acceptable level of well-being, over comparable increases above it.

What I propose is that in deciding whether violence would be justified in a given case in which it is being considered as a means of correcting certain grave moral wrongs, we would ascertain its probable consequences for justice, freedom and human welfare, and compare these with the probable consequences of the most promising non-violent alternative(s).

Gert (1969), who defines violence as the unwanted intentional violation of the moral rules (do not kill; do not cause pain; do not disable; do not deprive of freedom or opportunity; do not deprive of pleasure), argues that reason requires a certain public attitude towards these moral rules. Gert (1969, 621) goes on to say that everyone is to obey the moral rule with regard to everyone except when they would publicly advocate violating it, and that 'one kind of violation allowed by public reason is one in which significantly greater evil is prevented by breaking the [moral] rule than would be caused by the violation'. Gert (1969, 623) is adamant that the evil being prevented is *significantly greater* than the evil caused, 'it must be indisputable that the evil being prevented by the violence is significantly greater than the evil caused'. He gives the example of an innocent child plagued by some highly dangerous and infectious disease. In this case, it will be justifiable to use violence against the child in order to keep the plague from spreading. But this is not something to be done lightly, and one would demand an extremely high proportion of evil prevented to evil caused before publicly advocating violence.

Arguing along similar lines as Audi and Gert, but dealing specifically with the question of justifying a violent revolution, Nielsen (1981, 29) also argues that violence can be justified on consequentialist grounds:

Again the centrally relevant considerations would be for the most part, but not necessarily decisively or exclusively, utilitarian ones. We would need in the particular circumstances to weigh carefully what would be the probable consequences of resorting to such violence. If, on the one hand, only more suffering all around would result, then resort to such violence is wrong; if, on the other hand, such acts of violence are likely to lessen the sum total of human suffering and not put an unfair burden on some already cruelly exploited people, then the violence is justified.

Although Nielsen says that the centrally relevant considerations are 'utilitarian ones', what he really means to say here is that the relevant considerations are 'consequentialist ones'. As Geras (1990) rightly reminds us, the consequentialist judgement does not have to rest on some form of philosophical utilitarianism, since the judgement need not be unified by reliance on the single measure of utility (suffering/happiness). Instead, consequentialist considerations can use a number of indices, including freedom, equality and rights, which are not reducible to utility. On the issue of revolutionary violence, Nielsen (1976–1977, 527–528) suggests that consequentialism is once again the principle to follow: 'revolutionary violence is only justified when, of the alternatives available, it will, everything considered, make for less misery and human degradation all around'.

Following Moore (1962), the type of logic found in the arguments put forward by Audi, Gert and Nielsen can appropriately be called 'the calculus of suffering'. As Geras (1990, 27) explains, we evaluate 'the costs and benefits of projected or anticipated violence relative to those of a continuation of the status quo'. The consequentialist argument is essentially counterfactual, whereby roughly speaking violence is justified on the condition that it would deprive the world of X units of suffering that would have been present had violence not taken place, or in other words violence is justified because the welfare level at the nearest world where violence occurs is X units higher than at the nearest world where violence did not occur. The well-known difficulties with making counterfactual predictions can also be found in attempts to make consequentialist calculations regarding the outcome of violence.

Part V: A critique of the Consequentialist Argument

Some of the problems we encountered with the Identity Argument are replicated in the Consequentialist Argument. In particular there are two arguments that expose the dangers of justifying violence according to a calculus of suffering: the slippery-slope argument, and the cycle-of-violence argument.

The slippery-slope argument occurs when the occurrence of one event makes another event more likely to occur. Let's assume that A, B denote two distinct events. If A occurs, then the chances increase that

B will also occur. When applied to the context of violence, the (justi-fied) act of violence A triggers a process that increases the chances of (unjustified) act of violence B also occurring. The fact that A increases the chances of B does not mean that B will inevitably occur when A occurs, nevertheless the fact that A increases the chances of B occur-ring is sufficient to consider this a potentially serious problem for the Consequentialist Argument. An example will help to clarify the issues at stake here.

The calculus of suffering may justify the act of violence of killing one terrorist in order to prevent the killing of, say, 1,000 innocent people. But does the calculus of suffering also justify the torturing of one terrorist? In the well-known ticking-bomb scenario, the police apprehend three terrorists who are suspected of recently planting a bomb somewhere in the city, but the terrorists remain silent. As the bomb is ticking away, the police start by torturing one of the three terrorists, then proceed to shoot the terrorist in the head. Having witnessed the torture, the two other terrorists talk, the bomb is defused and countless lives are saved.[12] The Consequentialist Argu-ment here would appear to justify both the killing and the torture of a terrorist. In fact even Gert (1969, 623) is prepared to argue that while all killing and torturing for pleasure or profit is clearly immoral, 'killing and torturing to prevent greater killing and torturing may sometimes be allowed by public reason'.

Contrary to what Gert claims, torture of terrorists can never be justi-fied, for all the reasons recently suggested by Arrigo (2004).[13] First of all, there is a lot of empirical evidence suggesting that torture does not work as a method for obtaining information: bodily injury impairs a subject's mental ability to convey the truth; subjects die prema-turely; lengthy interrogation diminishes the value of the information obtained; subjects' true statements cannot be distinguished from the erroneous or deceitful. Secondly, empirical evidence suggests that torture motivates more terrorists than it incapacitates; Thirdly, if we allow the torturing of terrorists, there is a greater risk that inno-cent people will also be tortured. Fourthly, the establishment of a State sponsored torture interrogation unit, with training of torturers in sophisticated methods, including biomedical and psychological research into techniques, detection and concealment of torture, may lead to breakdowns in key State institutions – health care, biomedical research, police, judiciary and military. To these arguments I would add a fifth, of a more philosophical nature. A State that sets up torture interrogation units will lose its moral legitimacy, and therefore undermine the political obligation of its citizens. The moral difference between a legitimate State and its illegitimate enemies lies in part in the fact that unlike its enemies, the State does not employ methods like torture, which violate the fundamental rights of every citizen. In 1764 Cesare Beccaria (1995) argued that punishment is justified only to defend the social contract and to ensure that everyone will be motivated to abide by it. Beccaria also argued that there is no justification for severe punishments, famously rejecting the use of capital punishment. Part of his argument rested on rejecting the Lockean view that people forfeit their right to live when they initiate a state of war with other people. If the State does not have the moral authority to use capital punishment, as Beccaria argued, then the State certainly does not have the moral authority to use torture.

The second argument against justifying violence according to a calculus of suffering is that whenever violence is used, even justifiably, there is the risk of triggering a cycle-of-violence: when A uses legitimate violence to counter B's illegitimate violence, B may respond with more violence against A, which will in turn lead to A using even more violence against B, and so on *ad infinitum*. The cyclical nature of violence is well documented.[14] When an act of violence occurs, it is usually not an isolated event unconnected to others instances of violence, instead more times than not an act of violence is part of an on-going process linking many acts of violence. In justifying a certain act of violence, a theory of violence must not only justify the harm that will be inflicted on the recipient of such act, but also the foreseeable potential consequences of such act, which includes the spiral of retaliation that is being triggered. Martha Minow (2003) reminds us that victims of violence usually respond to such events not by lying down and accepting the violence, but by instigating revenge, which in turn inspires a cycle of retaliation. This is true of all victims of violence, be it sovereign States operating at the international level, citizens at the national level, or family-members at the domestic level. The empirical evidence on the cyclical nature of violence is overwhelming.[15] The cyclical nature of violence suggests that in

measuring the cost of violence, one must take into account something like a multiplier effect, the process by which an act of violence will prompt other acts of violence of a potentially greater
magnitude.

Part VI: How to justify violence

Pacifists refuse to accept that violence can ever be justified, in part
because they are afraid that once violence is warranted, even for a
just cause, there is no way of limiting the amount of violence being
unleashed. Their argument is not unfounded, and some of the worse
atrocities have been committed in the name of justice, by the same
people that were themselves the victims of violence. The war on
Nazism is one of the most blatant and most frequently used examples
of justified violence, yet many unjustified atrocities were committed
during this just war. Beevor (2002) recounts how in the two-week
battle for Berlin in 1945, rape ran at epidemic levels. During the battle,
130,000 women were raped, 10,000 of whom committed suicide. The
Red Army gang raped girls and women of all ages. This orgy of rape
could never be justified, even when your enemy is Hitler.

Given humanity's track record, the fear that to justify violence is to
open the floodgates to sickening acts of barbarism is understandable,
but this is not sufficient per se as an argument against the use of
violence *tout court*. This thing called 'violence' does not come in
a single, indivisible unit. Therefore the fact that violence could in
principle be justified does not say anything about the type or amount
of violence being justified. But the onus is on those who believe that
violence can be justified to explain with the utmost precision what
type of violence is justifiable. For example we may want to say that the
so-called war on terrorism unleashed after the events of September 11
2001 may justify some violence against terrorists, perhaps even the
killing of terrorists, but it certainly does not justify the bombing of
innocent people, the rape of war prisoners, or the institutionalization
of torture. What is required here is a set of principles that will help us
to navigate the hazardous waters of violence, by discerning between
the different types of violence.

As a starting point, we might want to say that to be justified,
violence must conform to a Fundamental Principle, which states that
ceteris paribus the life and dignity of all persons should be respected

at all times.[16] Another way of stating this principle is along the lines suggested by Geras (1990, 49), who argues that it is imperative, when justifying violence, to start from the assumption that individual rights against being killed or violated are all but absolute: 'That is to say that they may be overridden if and only if doing so is the sole means of averting imminent and certain disaster. I repeat: the sole means; and disaster which is otherwise imminent and certain. This is a proviso of impending moral catastrophe'.

This Fundamental Principle provides us with a useful starting point, but much more needs to be said. Apart from the Fundamental Principle, it may be possible to agree on a number of other principles, of a more precise nature, that must also be complied with in order for an act of violence to be justified. As we shall see, each of these principles is open to a myriad of interpretations, and each principle can be applied more or less stringently, more or less intransigently. In what follows four principles will be analysed in some detail, and in each case it will be suggested that each principle must be interpreted in the strictest possible sense, so that the bar is set at the highest possible level. In Part VII below a fifth principle will then be introduced, often neglected by the literature on violence or just war, which must also be adhered to in order for violence to be justified. This fifth principle is particularly useful in ascertaining whether and what type of terrorism is justifiable.

First, the Principle of Self-Defence. This states that violence is only permissible as a response to violence, in order to repel the attack of the aggressor. The Principle of Self-Defence finds confirmation in international law, where Article 51 of the United Nations Charter permits the use of force in self-defence against an armed attack. There is a dispute however on the issue whether the Principle of Self-Defence justifies using violence to pre-empt or prevent future attacks.[17] Much depends on the assessment of the situation, and in particular on the probability of future attacks, yet it is important to remember that pre-emptive self-defence is unlawful under international law, furthermore pre-emptive or preventive self-defence is to be distinguished from anticipatory self-defence, a narrower doctrine that authorizes armed responses to attacks that are on the brink of launch, or where an attack has already occurred and more attacks are anticipated. This suggests that the Principle of Self-Defence allows for some violence to repel violence, where the attack has either already occurred or is inevitable, but not when the attack is merely likely.

Second, the Principle of Reasonable Success. This states that one is justified to use violence only when there is a reasonable probability of success. Once again there is a debate on the issue of what constitutes 'reasonable success'. According to the Principle of Reasonable Success, the notion of 'success' does not refer to intermediate goals, such as securing positional advantages of a strategic nature, but to the final result of bringing violence to an end, or to extinguishing the original threat of violence. The thrust of the Principle of Reasonable Success emphasizes that human life should not be wasted, not even during war. To risk the lives of people when there is no reasonable chance of success (as defined above) is to contradict the Fundamental Principle that the integrity of all people should be respected at all times, including those who are prepared to die for a just cause. Furthermore, due to the cyclical nature of violence, the unsuccessful use of violence will only bring about more misery and destruction, hence on strictly consequentialist grounds violence can only be justified if and when there is a reasonable chance of success. As Nielsen (1981, 35) rightly points out: 'it is – concentration-camp-type circumstances apart – both immoral and irrational to engage in violence when all is in vain, for this merely compounds the dreadful burden of suffering'. The Principle of Reasonable Success is also crucial to Honderich's (2003; 2004) consequentialist argument for the justified use of violence.

Third, the Principle of Proportionality. This states that the use of violence must be proportional to the violence it counters. Referring to the war convention, Henry Sidgwick defines this principle as follows: it is not permissible to do any mischief of which the conduciveness to the end is slight in comparison with the amount of the mischief.[18] Walzer (1977, 129) explains that the notion of proportionality presumably means not only the immediate harm to individuals but also 'any injury to the permanent interest of mankind, against the contribution that mischief makes to the end of victory'. The Principle of Proportionality applies not only to war conventions. To punish jaywalking with immediate execution by firing squad may well be effective in stopping people from jaywalking, but this policy could never be justified on consequentialist or any other moral grounds. Once again, there is some dispute on the way the term 'proportionality' ought to be interpreted. One possible interpretation suggests 'reciprocity', whereby one is justified to use against the aggressor the same violence that the aggressor used. This cannot be right, since the principle would justify raping rapists or torturing torturers, acts that can never be justified under any circumstances. An alternative, stricter interpretation suggests 'sufficiency', that is to say the minimum necessary violence. This interpretation is consistent with the Fundamental Principle to the extent that the life and dignity of every person is more likely to be respected if an effort is made to minimize destruction and casualties.

Fourth, the Principle of Last Resort. This states that violence can be morally justified if and only if all peaceful alternatives have been exhausted. This criterion is essentially a prudential one. As Walzer (1977) points out in the case of wars, the unpredictable, unexpected, unintended and unavoidable horrors that war regularly brings makes it imperative to exhaust all other available channels before going to war. Needless to say, the concepts of 'last resort' or 'exhausting all alternatives' are notoriously difficult to define, and open to many interpretations. Following Walzer (1988, 239), the idea of 'last resort' should be interpreted in the strictest sense: 'it is not easy to reach the "last resort". To get there, one must indeed try everything (which is a lot of things) and not just once.... Politics is an art of repetition'. The Principle of Last Resort is important because it reinforces the point that even when it is justified, violence is always *prima facie* bad and wrong. In the words of Geras (1990, 49), to justify violence is to permit to do a moral wrong in order to escape some very terrible consequence, 'but it is, then, precisely a wrong that is done. Justifiable in one perspective, it remains unjustifiable in another. "It does not become *all right*" '.

Part VII: The Principle of Gradual Progression

In an effort to specify the principles that may allow for the use of violence, it has been suggested that the starting point should be the Fundamental Principle, which states that the life and integrity of all persons should be respected at all times. To make this principle more precise, four further principles were introduced: the Principles of Self-Defence, Reasonable Success, Proportionality and Last Resort. All four principles appear prominently in the literature on just war theory, and the concept of *jus in bello* (the rules of just or fair conduct in war) in particular. There is however a fifth principle that ought to be introduced, one that so far has not received the attention it deserves in the literature. For lack of a better term, I will refer to this as the Principle of Gradual Progression or Escalation.

The Principle of Gradual Progression states that when using violence, one has a duty to always start with the minimum amount of violence, and only gradually move up the scale of violence. This means not only that non-violent strategies must be tried before resolving to violent strategies, as implied by the Principle of Last Resort and as endorsed even by Marcuse (1966), but also that within the possible range of violent strategies, one should always adopt the least violent, and only progress to more violent strategies when those fail. To give a rough idea of how the Principle of Gradual Progression works, in a political confrontation the first strategy should always be to dialogue, and only when this fails it should be replaced by other strategies, starting from non-violent civil disobedience, followed by violent civil disobedience and only subsequently low intensity conflict, guerrilla warfare and revolutions.

Faced with the possible scenario of seeing non-violence strategies fail, the decision to use violence must always follow the Principle of Gradual Progression, in the first instance targeting inanimate objects before people. The Suffragette movement clearly adhered to this principle, which in part accounts for the moral success of this important but violent political movement. Thus, when non-violence fails, and only when it fails, sabotage can justifiably be contemplated as the next morally acceptable step. And when sabotage fails, one may then contemplate to use violence on human targets. When violence is aimed at a person, the Principle of Gradual Progression should again apply, whereby a minor injury should come before a more serious injury, and homicide should always be the last of all possible options. Something along the lines of the Principle of Gradual Progression appears to be endorsed by Nielsen. As Nielsen (1981, 35) says, violence is something that admits of degree, and of kind: 'it is, for example, extremely important to distinguish between violence against property and violence against persons'.

The strictest adherence to all the principles discussed so far is necessary before violence can be contemplated. But this only leads us to a further question. If the principles are in place, and political violence is justified, does it mean that terrorism is also justified? Before we attempt to answer this question, it is important to distinguish political violence from terrorism, and to emphasize the fact that to justify one does not automatically justify the other. As Nielsen (1981, 22) says: 'the thesis that sometimes the employment of violence is justified is not at all the same as defending terrorism'.[19] Regarding terrorism, much depends on exactly what we mean by this controversial and contested term. For example if, as Walzer (1988) suggests, terrorism is defined as the indiscriminate and arbitrary killing of innocent people, then terrorism cannot be justified, ever, under any circumstances. But as Fullinwider (1988) points out, terrorists do not always target innocent people, furthermore terrorism does not even have to involve killing anyone. The sabotage of a military base can be construed as an act of terrorism, even though it does not target people and it is not homicidal.[20] This is the sort of political violence that Nelson Mandela contemplated, and endorsed, before he was arrested in 1961.

The problem with terrorism is that too often terrorists embrace homicide as the only viable strategy. This is simply wrong, being contrary to all the principles that must be adhered to before violence can be justified. In particular, to start from the top, with homicide, as many terrorists do, is contrary to everything the Principle of Gradual Progression stands for. Terrorists that have no time or desire to exhaust all the other strategies prior to homicide cannot be justified in their acts. Honderich's (2003, 118) consequentialist approach seems to appeal to the Principle of Reasonable Success in condemning the terrorist attacks of September 11, 2001: 'What was done [on September 11] was wrong because there could be no certainty or significant probability, no reasonable hope, that it would work to secure a justifying end, but only a certainty that it would destroy lives'. Failure to comply with the Principle of Gradual Progression makes the attacks of September 11 even more deplorable.

Jaggar (2005) is absolutely right when she reminds us that terrorism is not a specific type of conflict, instead it is a tactic that may be employed in various types of conflict. Furthermore terrorism should not be equated with any particular method of intimidation, instead terrorists use a variety of methods. It follows that any sweeping statement about the moral status of terrorism is bound to be misguided. The question 'Can terrorism be justified?' cannot be answered in abstraction from knowledge of concrete, hence it ought to be replaced by the more specific question 'What type of terrorism can be justified?'. The terrorist attacks we witnessed on September 11 2001 represent the most extreme type of terrorist strategy, and can never be justified, but other less extreme forms of terrorism, of a non-homicidal nature, may be legitimate, depending on the context, and cannot be rejected *a priori* on moral grounds.

In order to know whether terrorism, in a certain context, and of a certain type, is justifiable, we need to think in terms of a principled approach. If the Fundamental Principle plus the other five principles discussed in this chapter are in place and strictly adhered to, then there is no reason why a certain type of terrorism could not be justified. In his celebrated autobiography *Long Walk to Freedom*, Mandela (1995, 336) explains that in planning the direction and form that the military wing of the ANC (Umkhonto we Sizwe – or MK for short – The Spear of the Nation) was to take, four types of violent activities were considered: sabotage, guerrilla warfare, terrorism and open revolution. He goes on to explain that 'since the ANC had been reluctant to embrace violence at all, it made sense to start with the form of violence that inflicted the least harm against individuals: sabotage'. This suggests that Mandela was thinking along the lines of the Principle of Gradual Progression. He goes on to state that he did not rule out other types of violence: 'If sabotage did not produce the results we wanted, we were prepared to move on to the next stage: Guerrilla warfare and terrorism'. Once again it is the Principle of Gradual Progression that makes it justifiable for Mandela to contemplate terrorist actions.

Part VIII: Conclusion

Can violence be justified? This chapter suggests that yes; violence can be justified, at least in theory. But it is extremely difficult to do so in practice, and it is even more difficult to justify terrorism, although not impossible. After assessing, but ultimately refuting, two dominant arguments often used to justify the use of violence, the Identity Argument and the Consequentialist Argument, this chapter argues for an alternative approach, which calls for the adherence to a set of principles, starting from the Fundamental Principle that demands that the life and integrity of all persons should be respected at all times, followed by five other key principles: Self-Defence; Reasonable Success, Proportionality, Last Resort and Gradual Progression. According to these principles, the overwhelming majority of acts of violence are groundless and inexcusable. In particular, homicide is virtually never justified, except in the most extreme circumstances. But this does not mean that in principle violence cannot be justified, and that includes terrorism.

Notes

1. There is a very extensive literature on the ethics of pacifism, see for example Steger and Lind (1999); Zinn (2002).
2. For a haunting account of how injustice has been imposed through the use of violence during the twentieth century, see Glover (2001). Geras is the author of a very influential political blog, where he takes the line that the British Left should support the war effort against Saddam Hussein's Iraq, since for any socialist there is no greater evil than a totalitarian dictatorship, which ought to be defeated using all available means. See *www.normblog.org*.
3. The relationship between violence and evil is extremely complex. For an enlightening analysis of this relationship, see Garrard (2006).
4. See Katz (1999) for some extremely interesting work on the culture of violence and masculinity. See also his educational video for schools and colleges *Tough Guise: Violence, Media and the Crisis of Masculinity* (2000).
5. Something along the lines of the Identity Argument is also invoked by those who defend the moral appropriacy of revenge, see for example Murphy (1995) and Solomon (1990). For a moral argument against revenge, see Govier (2002).
6. Fanon's argument should not be confused with Peteet's analysis of how being a victim of violence engenders masculinity and political agency. As Peteet (202, 258) points out 'Palestinian males need not necessarily do violence to become political agents as Fanon argued for the Algerian revolution. As its recipients, they acquire masculine and revolutionary credentials'.
7. Fanon's work has since been translated into seventeen languages. On the persisting appeal of Fanon, see Humphrey (2000), Presby (1996) and Fairchild (1994). Tronto (2004) argues that since decolonization is still one of the key problems that political thinkers will have to address in the twenty-first century, Fanon's work still remains extremely relevant to us today.
8. In a recent interview, when asked about the surprising absence of references to Fanon in her work, Kristeva (2002, 110) replies: 'I have often heard people speak of him [Fanon.], but I have never read anything by him. He isn't part of the mainstream of Psychoanalytic Studies.'

9. It is also important to stress that Kristeva (2002) distinguishes between revolt and violence, arguing that the term 'violence' can be misleading: 'In revolt there is violence, there is destruction, but there are also many other elements. I like the term revolt because of its etymological association with return, patience, distance, repetition, elaboration. Revolt is not simply about rejection and destruction; it is also about starting over. Unlike the word "violence", "revolt" foregrounds an element of renewal and regeneration'.

10. Vaclav Havel (1990) powerful essay *The Power of the Powerless*, written in 1978, encouraged people in Czechoslovakia to rebel against the dominant Soviet ideology and to 'live within the truth', something that he referred to as a basic existentialist starting point. According to Havel, ideology offers human beings the illusion of an identity, of dignity, and of morality while making it easier to part with them.

11. See Fearon and Laitin (2000).

12. This is a slightly different account of the one given by Bruce Hoffman, from Rand Corporation, in *The Atlantic Monthly*, January 2002, quoted in Arrigo (2004).

13. See also Bufacchi and Arrigo (2006).

14. On the view that violence breeds violence, and the dangers of violence starting an endless cycle of violence, see Hook (1976).

15. See for example May (2001) for a chilling account of how violence in Guatemala followed a cyclical pattern during the past four decades, escalating into genocide in the early 1980s.

16. This is the fundamental principle of international humanitarian law.

17. On the principle of self-defence in international law after the terrorist attacks on the US on 11 September 2001, see Cassese (2001).

18. Quoted in Walzer (1977, 129).

19. It is unfortunate that Honderich (2003) fails to distinguish between political violence and terrorism, giving the same definition for both terms.

20. There is some dispute regarding the targets of terrorist violence. Thus Held (2004) argues that the targets of terrorism can be both civilian and military, while Jaggar (2005) argues that apart from human targets terrorism can also include attacks on non-human targets, such as infrastructure, businesses, homes and buildings of religious, political or other symbolic significance, as long as those primarily affected are innocent civilians.

Conclusion

Violence and the essence of politics

When I started writing this book, I had a very simple aim in mind, namely, to explore the relationship between arguably the two most significant, powerful and widely debated concepts in politics and political philosophy: violence and social justice. Sometime between the end of the 1960s and the start of the 1970s the focus of attention in political philosophy switched from being concerned with the nature and ethics of violence, to a yearning for social justice. Yet, surprisingly, there has been virtually no overlap between these two bodies of literature. Instead, the literatures on violence and social justice have diverged to such an extent that the problems of political violence have disappeared from mainstream political philosophy radar-screens. This book is therefore nothing more than an initial effort to embark on the process of closing the gap between the existing literatures on violence and social justice. If, as a result of this book, political philosophers in general, and theorists of social justice in particular, begin to pay more attention to issues of political violence, my efforts will have been repaid.

In this concluding chapter I will not go over the grounds covered in the previous nine chapters. Instead the aim here will be to seek an answer to the following question: if political violence and social justice are essential to the concerns of political philosophy, what does that tell us about the subject matter of politics? More specifically could it be the case that political violence, including violence for social justice, is the essence of politics?

187

Part I: Violence and the essence of politics

The logical starting point for this inquiry on the essence of politics is a brief analysis of the concept of essence. In what follows 'essence' will be defined in terms of two distinct properties: First following G.W.F. Hegel (1969), we want to say that 'essence' refers to something *permanent*: the unchanging nature of a thing or class of things.[1] Secondly following Saul Kripke (1980), essence refers to a *necessity*: essential properties are necessary to something, whereas by contract accidental features are properties something merely happens to have, but are either not needed or secondary. Needless to say, there is a lot more than could be said about the concept of essence, but that would only distract us from our enquiry. I suggest therefore that we restrict our understanding of essence to only these two properties. On the basis of this minimalist account of 'essence', it is now possible to enquire on the nature of 'politics', and ask whether there is a feature of politics that is both permanent and necessary.

Regarding the essence of politics, the aim of this chapter is to test the validity of the following thesis: politics does have an essence, and it is to be found in the idea of violence. Needless to say, the validity of this thesis rests on the ability to show that violence is both a permanent and a necessary feature of what passes for politics. So our first task is to establish whether violence is both a permanent and a necessary feature of politics.

The first claim, that violence is a permanent feature of politics, is undoubtedly disturbing. Indeed it is very tempting to briskly reject this claim, and find solace in the reassuring view that modern politics is the antithesis of barbarism, and that the relentless progress of history towards an unprecedented echelon of civility stands in reverse correlation to violence, misery and destruction. While it is comforting to believe that democracies are a potent antidote against political violence, and that well-organized societies are characterized by a low intensity of political violence, these views are as widespread as they are false.[2]

Jonathan Glover's (2001) outstanding short history of the twentieth century, recounting the atrocities of the Holocaust, Hiroshima, the Gulags, Cambodia, Yugoslavia, Rwanda and many others, dissipates any lingering false illusions about the impact of modern politics. And Glover is not the only one voicing such concerns; John Keane

(1996) similarly defines the twentieth century as the long century of violence. The number of victims, the magnitude of devastation and the new technologies of destruction are without historical parallel.[3] This was the century of genocides and ethnic-cleansing, of concentration camps and gulags, of gas chambers and electric chairs, of labour camps and systematic rape as a weapon of war, of nuclear explosions and chemical warfare, of terrorism against the state and state terrorism. Estimates vary, but it has been calculated that war-related killings in the twentieth century exceeded 105 million people, including 62 million civilian victims.[4] And of course, the dead are not the only victims of violence. For every person killed by an act of violence there are many more who have survived torture, physical abuse, persecution, the loss of loved ones, or (if they are lucky) the loss of all their belongings and livelihood. One can safely speculate that every living person today at some stage in their lives will experience, directly or indirectly, some type of violence. There is also every reason to believe that the twenty-first century will be as blood-spattered as its predecessor. All empirical evidence seems to point to the fact that violence is, and always will be, a permanent feature of political affairs.

Perhaps violence is a permanent feature of politics, but is violence also a necessary part of politics? It may be possible to make this argument, on the grounds that no one is immune from violence, whether living in a wealthy Western democracy, or in a country undergoing late economic development. For example, there are convincing arguments emerging from the discipline of political economy suggesting that violence is a necessary condition for economic prosperity.[5]

Leaving aside issues of political economy it may also be possible to argue that all political regimes rely on either the use or the threat of violence, to maintain social order, and democracies are not an exception. Violence has always had a difficult relationship with democratic politics. In its ideal form democratic politics is a procedure aimed at resolving and averting violent conflict, yet violence can be used in the name and for the sake of the democratic political process. Modern democracies have not diminished the level of violence; they have merely learned how to conceal it under the moral fabric of legitimacy.[6] Laws stem violence yet laws also justify and legitimate violence. It has become orthodox to believe that when violence is legitimized, it is no longer violence. Violence applies specifically to the illegitimate act of imposing one's will upon another whereas the imposition is held to be legitimate in the case of force.[7] The celebrated cliché that the state uses authorized force, not violence, whereas enemies of the state use violence, is a convenient illusion. The force used by state institutions may be legal, even legitimate, but it is still violence. Furthermore and contrary to what many people think, many political scientists are converging on the view that the democratic experience has the unexpected corollary of acerbating violence, not reducing it.[8]

It is on the basis of the arguments presented so far that a long and distinguished tradition in the history of political thought has emerged, advocating the view that violence is, indeed, the essence of politics. This tradition will come under closer scrutiny in Part II below, before the thesis holding that violence is the essence of politics is challenged, and ultimately refuted, in Part III.

Part II: Violence and politics from Hobbes to the present

The thesis that violence is the essence of politics, far from being an original idea, has been around a long time. There is a long tradition in the history of political thought that identifies violence as the essence of politics. This tradition, which inevitably pays tribute to Thomas Hobbes, is embraced by political theorists on both the Left and the Right, and it includes influential twentieth-century thinkers of the calibre of Max Weber and Carl Schmitt.

Writing in the seventeenth century at a time when the modern state, and modern philosophy, acquired its present identity, Thomas Hobbes (1994) understood that in political affairs, violence constitutes both the problem and the solution. The problem of violence is famously depicted in the pre-political 'state of nature', a place of unbound licence, where everyone endeavours to destroy or subdue one another, making life solitary, nasty and short. We escape the pre-political state of promiscuous violence by forming a political society under the rule of a centralized authority that has the right to use violence on all those who fail to comply with the laws of nature, primarily to seek peace by way of a mutually constraining contract.

Fear plays a key role in the construction of Hobbes's theory, both in the pre-political state of nature and in the conduct of the sovereign within a political community. It is the fear of death in the state of nature that drives us to lay down our rights to all things and transfer such rights to the sovereign, the Leviathan, who in turn rules by instilling fear into us.[9] As Hobbes points out in Chapter 17 of his *Leviathan*, it is because we fear for our lives in the state of nature, 'that miserable condition of war', that we seek peace through a covenant, but we are tied to the performance of our covenants only by 'fear of punishment', or in other words by 'the terror of some power to cause them [the laws of nature] to be observed', since 'covenants without the sword are but words'. The fear Hobbes refers to in both the state of nature and in the commonwealth is not simply the fear of death, but premature death, that is to say death as an outcome of violence; in the last analysis, it is the fear of violence that Hobbes is primarily concerned about.[10]

It is important to emphasize that in the same chapter Hobbes goes on to say that in the unlimited powers of the sovereign we find the essence of the commonwealth, and since the sovereign is the embodiment of violence, in violence we find the essence of politics:

> The multitude so united in one person, is called a commonwealth, in Latin civitas. This is the generation of that great Leviathan, or rather (to speak more reverently) of that Mortal God to whom we owe, under the Immortal God, our peace and defence. For by this authority, given him by every particular man in the commonwealth, he hath the use of so much power and strength conferred on him that by terror thereof he is enabled to conform the wills of them all to peace at home and mutual aid against their enemies abroad. *And in him consisteth the essence of the commonwealth.* (Book II, Chapter 17, emphasis added).[11]

Hobbes' view on the nature of the commonwealth is one of the most disturbing truths ever articulated about the nature of politics. Given that the 'leviathan' in Hobbes' work represents the sole entity authorized with the exclusive use of violence, and the 'commonwealth' stands for the political arena, Hobbes tells us that violence is, quite simply, the essence of politics.

Hobbes' claim that violence, through the sovereign, constitutes the essence of politics, is echoed by two prominent German thinkers in the early part of the twentieth century, Max Weber and Carl Schmitt.

In *Politics as a Vocation*, a speech delivered at Munich University on 1918, Max Weber (1970, 77) starts by embracing a narrow conception of politics, based on the notion of the state:

> What do we understand by politics? The concept is extremely broad and comprises any kind of independent leadership in action.... Tonight, our reflections are, of course, not based upon such a broad concept. We wish to understand by politics only the leadership, or the influencing of the leadership, of a political association, hence today, of a state.

Weber (1970, 77–78) goes on to spell out the attribute which is most distinctive of the state, namely, the use of physical force: 'Ultimately, one can define the modern state sociologically only in terms of the specific means peculiar to it, as to every political association, namely, the use of physical force'.

It quickly became apparent that what Weber (1970, 78) means by physical force is nothing more than violence, indeed he quotes Trotsky with surprising approval on this issue: ' "Every state is founded on force", said Trotsky at Brest-Litovsk. That is indeed right. If no social institution existed which knew the use of violence, then the concept of "state" would be eliminated'. Weber (1970, 78) goes on to clarify the important point that force is not the normal or the only means of the state, instead 'force is a means specific to the state', before presenting us with arguably the most precise, succinct and influential definition of the modern state to date: 'Today the relation between the state and violence is an especially intimate one... Today, however, we have to say that a state is a human community that (successfully) claims the monopoly of the legitimate use of physical force within a territory'. Weber's powerful claim that the relation between the state and violence is 'an especially intimate one' adds support to the thesis that violence, principally but not exclusively through the state, is the essence of politics.

The intimate relationship between the state, violence and politics is given its most power (but sinister) theoretical argumentation in the work of one of Weber's students, Carl Schmitt. In *The Concept of the Political* first published in 1932, Schmitt famously identifies in the friend – enemy distinction the core of the political, and while the distinction between friend and enemy is the most celebrated aspect of Schmitt's political theory, it is worth emphasizing that there is something even more basic, and more substantial, lurking behind the notion of the enemy.

According to Schmitt and contrary to what may appear at first, the essence of politics is not captured by the friend – enemy distinction. As Julien Freund (1995, 15) reminds us,

> *The Concept of the Political* is not an attempt to define the essence of politics, only to find a criterion – a conceptual marker – to identify the phenomenon of politics. This criterion is the distinction between friend and enemy. It is not a question of elaborating a theory of ideal politics but of learning from experience that ever since men have practiced politics they have organized as friends within a particular community (tribe, polis, empire, state) and tried to preserve their identity against the threats of those who might want to destroy it.

Freund is right, the distinction between friend and enemy is not the essence of politics, indeed Schmitt (1996, 26) is very clear on this point: 'The specific political distinction to which political actions and motives can be reduced is that between friend and enemy. This provides a definition in the sense of a criterion and not as an exhaustive definition or one indicative of substantial content'. But even if we accept that the distinction between friend and enemy is not an attempt to define the essence of politics, it does not mean that we cannot try to infer from Schmitt's political writings what the essence of politics might be.

It may be worth distinguishing between the essence of politics, and what Schmitt (1996, 67) calls 'the high points of politics'. The high points of politics are the moments in which the enemy is recognized as the enemy, whereas the 'essence' of politics (although Schmitt does not use this term) is about combat, war, physical killing or in other words 'the negation of the enemy' (33). We can infer this distinction by the fact that Schmitt is keen to point out that the friend and enemy concepts are to be understood in their concrete and existential sense, not as a metaphor or symbol, and least of all as a psychological expression of private emotions and tendencies. The existential sense to which Schmitt refers to is captured by an act of violence, to be precise the act of physical killing as the existential negation of the enemy. As Schmitt (1996, 32–33) says:

> For the enemy concept belongs the ever present possibility of combat.... Just as the term enemy, the word combat, too, is to be understood in its original existential sense. It does not mean competition, nor does it mean pure intellectual controversy nor symbolic wrestling... The friend, enemy, and combat concepts receive their real meaning precisely because they refer to the real possibility of physical killing.

In his emphasis on causing death through violence Schmitt is clearly influenced by both Hobbes and Weber,[12] indeed the concept of the modern state as an omnipotent leviathan is present throughout Schmitt's (1996, 45) work: 'To the state as an essentially political entity belongs the *jus belli*, i.e., the real possibility of deciding in a concrete situation upon the enemy and the ability to fight him with the power emanating from the entity'. What is important to emphasize here is that according to Schmitt it is not sufficient to simply identify or recognize the enemy, but we must also be prepared to act upon it, through acts of violence, primarily war and combat. Schmitt (1996, 46) leaves no room for ambiguity here:

> The state as the decisive political entity possesses an enormous power: the possibility of waging war and thereby publicly disposing of the lives of men. The *jus belli* contains such a disposition. It implies a double possibility: the right to demand from its own members the readiness to die and unhesitatingly to kill enemies.

In the work of Schmitt, just as in the case of Hobbes and Weber before him, all evidence seems to point to violence as the essence of politics.

The political theories of Hobbes, Weber and Schmitt are evidence that there is an important tradition in the history of political thought that sees violence as the essence of violence. While there are obvious similarities in the political theories of Hobbes, Weber and Schmitt, one should not make the mistake of ironing out the differences between these thinkers. For example, there are significant discrepancies between Weber and Schmitt, in fact Schmitt faults Weber for limiting his understanding of violence to the state, and more generally for equating politics with the state. As Schmitt (1996, 20) points out: 'One seldom finds a clear definition of the political.... In one way or another "political" is generally juxtaposed to "state" or at least is brought into relation with it. The state thus appears as something political, the political as something pertaining to the state – obviously an unsatisfactory circle'. There are also important differences between Schmitt and Hobbes. Giovanni Sartori (1989, 73) points out that the major difference is that in Hobbes the state of nature, *status naturalis*, is repudiated and superseded by the *status civilis*, whereas 'Schmitt turns this argument around: he reinstates the *status naturalis* as the condition in which politics manifests its genuine essence'.[13] While the differences between these three authors cannot be denied, we can let scholars worry about these issues, while retaining the general sense of the common thesis defended by Hobbes, Weber and Schmitt, namely that violence is the essence of politics.

Part III: A refutation of the thesis

It is important to recall that the concept of essence has two fundamental requirements: permanence and necessity. In Part I above it was suggested how it may be possible to see violence as the essence of politics, to the extent that violence may be interpreted to be both a permanent feature of politics, and a necessary requirement of politics. In Part II the political theories of Hobbes, Weber and Schmitt were introduced as representative of this thesis about the nature of politics.

But is violence really the essence of politics? Is the thesis advocated by Hobbes, Weber and Schmitt to be embraced, albeit reluctantly, or can it be refuted? In what follows I will argue that in fact this thesis ought to be refuted, even though it will be treated with greater respect than it usually receives, and it will be taken more seriously than many may feel it deserves. Of the two requirements that define the idea of essence, permanence and necessity, it will be argued that only the first applies, giving some credence to the thesis, but not the second. In order to show why this is the case, hence why the thesis ought to be refuted, the attention will fall exclusively on Schmitt's political theory.[14]

As we said before, it is necessary to distinguish between the point or purpose of politics, and its essence. That violence in the form of war is not the point of violence, is something that even Carl Schmitt would admit to. In *The Concept of the Political*, Schmitt (1996, 34) has this to say about war and politics:

> War is neither the aim nor the purpose nor even the very content of politics. But as an ever present possibility it is the leading presupposition which determines in a characteristic way human action and thinking and thereby creates a specifically political behaviour.

Schmitt's distinction between the point of politics (what he refers to as the aim or purpose or very content of politics), and the essence of politics, is crucial. Clearly violence is not the point or purpose of politics, but it may be its essence. War is the essence of politics because it is permanent, or what Schmitt calls 'an ever present possibility'. Furthermore war plays a determining role in identifying what constitutes political behaviour.[15] Given that 'essence' refers, in part, to the permanent element of being, it would appear that violence has met the first requirement towards being identified with the essence or politics.

It is on the second requirement, the issue of necessity, that the thesis comes undone. It is simply false to claim that everything that goes on in politics requires the use of violence, or that there cannot be politics without violence. This in part explains why Schmitt's thesis has met with much disapproval and condemnation. In his critical analysis of Schmitt's famous thesis, Sartori (1989, 74) contrasts Schmitt's 'politics of hostility' or 'politics as conflict', with what he calls 'politics-as-peace':

> The fact nevertheless remains that we *are* confronted with two 'models', with two 'paradigms', of the political. The mode of politics theorized by Schmitt – politics-as-war – certainly exists. But Schmitt cannot belittle and indeed cancel out of existence the alternative mode of politics – peace-like politics – by simply

calling it non-politics. Politics need not be, in order to be, life-threatening (a life-threatening intensity of dissociation). *Pace* Schmitt, unthreatening, peace-like politics still is politics.

Sartori is right to remind us that politics is as much about peace as it is about war. In fact, politics is often the negation of violence, especially in liberal democracies. Democratic politics is, in the last analysis, a way of managing conflict without resorting to violence, or as Norberto Bobbio explains (1987, 212): 'By a democratic state I mean a state founded on a pact of non-aggression between different political groups, and on the acceptance by these same political groups of a set of rules that makes it possible for conflicts to be resolved by peaceful means'. In other words politics is a substitute for violence, and we engage in democratic politics exactly in order to avoid violence as a way of resolving conflicts.

It may not be the essence of politics in general, but the essence of democratic politics would appear to be peace,[16] not violence, which explains why Joseph Schumpeter (1954, 283, emphasis added) sees in political parties' competitive struggle for power, and in particular their efforts at manufacturing consent through peaceful means, the essence of politics: 'The psycho-technics of party management and party advertising, slogans and marching tunes, are not accessories. They are of *the essence of politics*. So is the political boss'.

Part IV: Conclusion

Violence may not be the essence of violence, but it comes close to it. The concept of essence in philosophy has a very precise meaning, being defined in terms of the requirements of permanence and necessity. Based on this definition of essence the thesis that violence is the essence of politics cannot be defended, even though it is not obvious what, if not violence, captures the essence of politics, or indeed if politics in general has an essence at all.

The fact that violence is not the essence of politics does not take away from the fact that violence, like social justice, is a cardinal concept in the realm of politics, and the more we study these two concepts, and how they interact, the better understanding of politics we gain.

Notes

1. See in particular Volume 1 (The Objective Logic), Book 2 (The Doctrine of Essence).
2. The extent of such mass-scale misconception should not come as a surprise. After all, the vast majority of readers of this book probably belong to that first generation of citizens lucky enough not to have fought or lived through a major war, and as the theory of democratic peace in international relations likes to remind us, the chances of democracies going to war against each other are almost non-existent.
3. Wolin (1963).
4. Steger (2003, xiii). Glover (2001, 47) gives an estimate of 86 million people killed by war for the period from 1900 and 1989: 'If these deaths had been spread evenly over the period, war would have killed around 2,500 people per day. That is over 100 people an hour, round the clock, for ninety years'.
5. On the role of violence in economic development, see Bates (2001).
6. Wolin (1963).
7. See for example Macfarlane (1974). On the relationship between violence and law, see Brady and Garver (1991).
8. On the use of violence in the context of democratic politics, see Weinberg and Rapoport (2001). On violence and politics in general, see Worcester, Bermanzohn, and Ungar (2002).
9. Especially on the 'fools' amongst us, those who may be thinking of breaking an agreement by taking advantage of other people's coopera-tion. Hobbes (Part 1, Ch. XV, Par. 4) has the 'fool' speak the following words: 'The kingdom of God is gotten by violence; but what if it could be gotten by unjust violence?'. In this passage the fool alludes to a contro-versial verse in Matthew: 'And from the days of John the Baptist until now, the kingdom of heaven suffereth violence, and the violent take it by force'. This is further evidence that violence is central to Hobbes's concerns. On the problem of 'the fool', see Hobbes Chapter XV.
10. As Strauss (1953) points out, what is doing much of the work in Hobbes's political theory is not simply the fear of death, but the fear of violent death.
11. 'Essence' for Hobbes is the same as 'formal cause', which in Aristotelian philosophy is the expression of what something is, or its defining feature. Needless to say, Hobbes rejected the idea that 'formal causes' are causes, since a cause must precede its effect. Nevertheless, he retained the idea of essence as a formal cause, thus for example in *De Corpore* (1655) he maintains that 'knowledge of the essence of anything, is the cause of the knowledge of the thing itself; for, if I know that a thing is rational, I know from thence, that the same is man' (Part II, Ch. X).
12. Schmitt (1996b) is the author of an important study on the idea of the leviathan in Hobbes: *The Leviathan in the State Theory of Thomas Hobbes*.
13. This point is also made by Strauss (1996).

14. Schmitt is often singled out as the 'bête noir' of twentieth-century political theory, a *persona non grata* amongst political theorists. See for example Huysmans (1997) and Holmes (1993). For a general overview of the recent revival of interest in Schmitt, on both the Right and Left, see Strong (1996).

15. Schmitt (1996, 37) reiterates this point again a few pages later: 'The political does not reside in the battle itself, which possesses its own technical, psychological, and military laws, but in the mode of behaviour which is determined by this possibility'.

16. Another possible contender for the essence of politics is captured by the notion of 'strategy'. This argument is put forward by Kjell Hausken and Thomas Plümper (1997, 47) in their attempt to defend the intrinsic validity and essential contribution of game theory to the study of politics: 'Game theory, or more specifically non-cooperative game theory, provides a powerful tool for the analysis of international affairs since strategy is the essence of politics'. This is an intriguing argument but ultimately unpersuasive. It is true that strategy plays an important role in much of what goes on in politics, but per se it is not sufficient to make strategy the *essence* of politics. Strategy is not a necessary condition of politics, but a secondary one. There is a crucial problem with the claim that strategy is the essence of politics, namely, it runs the risk of making every human action (and interaction) by definition political. The fundamental assumption of the rational choice theory paradigm is that social actors are rational beings, where rationality implies the ability to think about the consequences of one's actions and act in such a way as to bring about a desired future state of affairs. In other words rational agents think and act strategically, especially when the outcomes of one's actions are dependent on the actions of others. Since everything we do, as rational agents, involves strategy, it follows that just about everything a person does, being strategic, is also political. This divests the concept of political from any useful meaning. Strategy is at best a secondary rather than necessary property of politics.

Bibliography

Allen, B. (1996). *Rape Warfare: Hidden Genocide in Bosnia-Herzegovina and Croatia*, Minnesota: University of Minnesota Press.

Ambrose, S. (2002). *Nothing Like it in the World: The Men that Built the Transcontinental Railroad, 1863–69*, New York: Simon & Schuster.

Anderson, E. (1999). 'What is the Point of Equality?'. *Ethics*, Vol. 109, No. 2.

Anscombe, G.E.M. (1961). 'War and Murder' in W. Stein (ed.) *Nuclear Weapons: A Catholic Response*, New York: Merlin Press; reprinted in J. Rachels (ed.) *Moral Problems*, 3rd edition, New York: Harper & Row, 1979.

Apter, D.E. (ed.) (1997). *The Legitimization of Violence*, Basingstoke: Macmillan.

Archard, David (1998). *Sexual Consent*, Boulder, Colorado: Westview Press.

Arendt, H. (1969). *On Violence*, New York: Harcourt.

Arrigo, J.M. (2004). 'A Utilitarian Argument Against Torture Interrogation of Terrorists', *Science and Engineering Ethics*, Vol. 10, No. 3.

Audi, R. (1971). 'On the Meaning and Justification of Violence', in Jerome A. Shaffer (ed.) *Violence*, New York: David McKay Company.

Audi, R. (1974). 'Violence, Legal Sanctions, and Law Enforcement', in S.M. Stanage (ed.) *Reason and Violence: Philosophical Investigations*, Oxford: Blackwell.

Ayer, A.J. (1936). *Language, Truth and Logic*. London: Gollancz.

Bäck, A. (2004). 'Thinking Clearly about Violence', *Philosophical Studies*, Vol. 117, No. 1.

Bales, K. (2004). *Disposable People: New Slavery in the Global Economy*, California: University of California Press.

Bar On, B. (ed.) (1998). *Women and Violence*, Indiana: Indiana University Press.

Bar On, B. (2002). *The Subject of Violence: Arendtean Exercises in Understanding*, Lanham, MD: Rowman & Littlefield.

Barkan, S. and L. Snowden (2000). *Collective Violence*, Needham Heights, MA: Allyn and Bacon.

Barry, B. (1965). *Political Argument*. London: Routledge and Kegan Paul.

Barry, B. (1989). 'Is It Better to be Powerful or Lucky?', in B. Barry (ed.) *Democracy, Power and Justice: Essays in Political Theory*, Oxford: Clarendon.

Barry, B. (1990). *Political Argument: A Reissue with a New Introduction*, London: Harvester-Wheatsheaf.

Barry, B. (1995). *Justice as Impartiality*, Oxford: Oxford University Press.

Barry, B. (2001). *Culture and Equality: An Egalitarian Critique of Multiculturalism*. Cambridge: Polity.

Barry, B. (2005). *Why Social Justice Matters*. Cambridge: Polity.

Bates, R.H. (2001). *Prosperity and Violence: The Political Economy of Development*, New York: WW Norton.

Beccaria, C. (1995). *On Crimes and Punishments and Other Writings*, R. Bellamy (ed.), Cambridge: Cambridge University Press.

Bedau, H.A. (1961). 'On Civil Disobedience', *Journal of Philosophy*, Vol. 58.

Beevor, A. (2002). *Berlin: The Downfall*, 1945, London: Viking.

Besteman, C. (ed.) (2002). *Violence: A Reader*, Basingstoke: Palgrave-Macmillan.

Betz, Joseph (1977). 'Violence: Garver's Definition and a Deweyan Correction', *Ethics*, Vol. 87, No. 4, July 1977.

Black, G. (1984). *Garrison Guatemala*, London: Zed Books.

Bobbio, N. (1987). *The Future of Democracy*, Cambridge: Polity Press.

Bourgois, P. (2001). 'The Power of Violence in War and Peace: Post-Cold War Lessons from El Salvador', *Ethnography*, Vol. 2, No. 1.

Brady, J. and Garver, N. (eds) (1991). *Justice, Law and Violence*, Philadelphia: Temple University Press.

Bratman, M.E. (1987). *Intention, Plans, and Practical Reason*, Cambridge, Mass.: Harvard University Press.

Breines, W. and Gordon, L. (1983). 'The New Scholarship on Family Violence', *Signs: Journal of Women in Culture and Society*, Vol. 8, No. 3.

Brison, S. (2002). *Aftermath: Violence and the Remaking of the Self*, Princeton, NJ: Princeton University Press.

Bufacchi, V. (2004). 'Why is Violence Bad?', *American Philosophical Quarterly*, Vol. 41, No. 2.

Bufacchi, V. and Arrigo, J.M. (2006). 'Torture, Terrorism and the State: A Refutation of the Ticking-Bomb Argument', *Journal of Applied Philosophy*, Vol. 23, No. 3.

Bufacchi, V. and Fairrie, L. (2001). 'Execution as Torture', *Peace Review*, Vol. 13, No. 4.

Carroll, S.J. and Zerilli, M.G. (1999). 'Feminist Challenges to Political Science', in S.Z. Theodoulpu and R. O'Brien (eds) *Methods for Political Inquiry: The Discipline, Philosophy, and Analysis of Politics*, Upper Saddle River, NJ: Prentice Hall.

Cassese, A. (2001). 'Terrorism is Also Disrupting Some Crucial Legal Categories of International Law', *European Journal of International Law*, Vol. 12, No. 5.

Chang, I. (2003). *The Chinese in America*, New York: Viking.

Coady, C.A.J. (1986). 'The Idea of Violence', *Journal of Applied Philosophy*, Vol. 3, No. 1.

Coleman, J.L. and Buchanan, A.E. (1994). *In Harm's Way: Essays in Honor of Joel Feinberg*, Cambridge: Cambridge University Press.

Conteh-Morgan, E. (ed.) (2004). *Collective Political Violence: An Introduction to the Theories and Cases of Violent Conflict*, London: Routledge.

Crenshaw, M. (2002). 'The Causes of Terrorism', in C. Besteman (ed.) *Violence: A Reader*, Basingstoke: Palgrave Macmillan.

Curtin, D. and Litke, R. (eds) (1999). *Institutional Violence*, Amsterdam: Rodopi.

Dahl, R. (1999). 'What is Politics?', in S.Z. Theodoulpu and R. O'Brien (eds) *Methods for Political Inquiry: The Discipline, Philosophy, and Analysis of Politics*, Upper Saddle River, NJ: Prentice Hall.

Daniels, C. (1997). *Feminists Negotiate the State: The Politics of Domestic Violence*, Lanham, MD: University Press of America.

Davidson, D. (1980). *Essays on Actions and Events*, Oxford: Oxford University Press.

Dewey, J. (1980). 'Force, Violence and Law' and 'Force and Coercion', in Jo Ann Boydston (ed.) *John Dewey, The Middle Works, 1899–1924, Vol.10: 1916–1917*, Carbondale: Southern Illinois University Press.

Dowding, K. (1991). *Rational Choice and Political Power*. Aldershot: Edward Elgar.

Dowding, K. (1996). *Power*, Milton Keynes: Open University Press.

Dworkin, A. (1974). 'Gynocide: Chinese Footbinding' *Woman Hating*, New York: Dutton.

Elster, J. (1984). *Ulysses and the Sirens*, Cambridge: Cambridge University Press.

Elster, J. (1986). *An Introduction to Karl Marx*, Cambridge: Cambridge University Press.

Fairchild, H. (1994). 'Franz Fanon's *The Wretched of the Earth* in Contemporary Perspective', *Journal of Black Studies*, Vol. 25, No. 2.

Fearon, J. and Laitin, D. (1996). 'Explaining Interethnic Cooperation', *American Political Science Review*, Vol. 90, No. 4.

Fearon, J. and Laitin, D. (2000). 'Violence and the Social Construction of Ethnic Identities', *International Organization*, Vol. 54, No. 4.

Feinberg, J. (1984). *Harm to Others*, New York: Oxford University Press.

Feinberg, J. (1985). *Offense to Others*, New York: Oxford University Press.

Feinberg, J. (1986). *Harm to Self*, New York: Oxford University Press.

Feinberg, J. (1988). *Harmless Wrongdoing*, New York: Oxford University Press.

Feldman, F. (1991). 'Some Puzzles About the Evil of Death', *The Philosophical Review*, Vol. C, No. 2.

Fischer, J. and Ravizza, M. (eds) (1993). *Perspectives on Moral Responsibility*, Ithaca, NY: Cornell University Press.

Fluehr-Lobban, C. (1995). 'Cultural Relativism and Universal Rights', *The Chronicle of Higher Education*, 9 June 1995.

Foot, P. (1978). 'The Problem of Abortion and the Doctrine of the Double Effect', in P. Foot (ed.) *Virtues and Vices*, Oxford: Blackwell. (Originally published in *The Oxford Review*, No. 5, 1967).

Foucault, M. (1977). *Discipline and Punishment*, New York: Pantheon Books.

Frappat, H. (ed.) (2000). *La Violence*, Paris: Flammarion.

Frankfurt, H. (1987). 'Identification and Wholeheartedness' in F. Schoeman (ed) *Responsibility, Character, and the Emotions: New Essays in Moral Psychology*, New York: Cambridge University Press.

French, S.G., Teays, W. and Purdy, L.M. (eds) (1996). *Violence Against Women: Philosophical Perspectives*, Ithaca, NY: Cornell University Press.

Freund, J. (1995). 'Schmitt's Political Thought', *Telos*, Winter 1995, No. 102.

Fullinwider, R. (1988). 'Understanding Terrorism', in S. Luper-Foy (ed.) *Problems of International Justice*, Boulder, CO.: Westview Press.

Galtung, J. (1969). 'Violence, Peace and Peace Research', *Journal of Peace Research*, Vol. 3.

Galtung, J. (1996). *Peace by Peaceful Means*, London: Sage.

Gambetta, D. (1993). *The Sicilian Mafia*, Cambridge, Mass.: Harvard University Press.

Gambetta, D. (1999). 'Primo Levi's Last Moments', *Boston Review*, Summer 1999.

Gandhi, M. (1997). *Hind Swaraj and other Writings*, (ed.) A.J. Parel. Cambridge: Cambridge University Press.

Garrard, E. (2006). 'Violence, Cruelty and Evil' in F. Omurchadha (ed.) *Violence, Victims, Justifications*, Bern: Peter Lang.

Garver, N. (1968). 'What Violence Is', *Nation*, 24 June 1968.

Garver, N. (1973). 'What Violence Is', in A.K. Bierman and J.A. Gould (eds) *Philosophy for a New Generation*, 2nd edition, New York: Macmillan.

Garver, N. (2003). 'Shadows of the 60s', *Buffalo Report*, 10 May 2003.

Geras, N. (1990). 'Our Morals', in N. Geras *Discourses of Extremity*, London: Verso.

Geras, N. (1998). *The Contract of Moral Indifference*, London: Verso.

Gert, B. (1969). 'Justifying Violence', *The Journal of Philosophy*, Vol. 66, No. 19.

Gert, B. (1998). *Morality: Its Nature and Justification*, New York: Oxford University Press.

Gibbard, A. (1990). *Wise Choices, Apt Feelings*, Cambridge, Mass: Harvard University Press.

Giddens, A. (1995). *A Contemporary Critique of Historical Materialism*, Basingstoke: Macmillan.

Glover, J. (1977). *Causing Death and Saving Lives*, Harmondsworth: Penguin.

Glover, J. (1995). 'The Implications for Responsibility of Possible Genetic Factors in the Explanation of Violence', in G. Bock and J. Goode (eds) *Genetics of Criminal and Anti-Social Behaviour*, London: John Wiley and Sons.

Glover, J. (2001). *Humanity: A Moral History of the Twentieth Century*, New Haven, CT: Yale University Press.

Gómez, C. and Ángel, M. (1994). *Discriminación del Pueblo Maya en el Ordenamiento Jurídico de Guatemala*, Guatemala: Cholsamaj.

Goodin, R. (1987). 'Exploiting a Situation and Exploiting a Person', in A. Reeve (ed.) *Modern Theories of Exploitation*, London: Sage.

Gordon, J. (2002). 'When Intent makes All the Difference in the World: Economic Sanctions on Iraq and the Accusation of Genocide', *Yale Human Rights and Development Journal*, Vol.5.

Gotesky, R. (1974). 'Social Force, Social Power, and Social Violence', in S.M. Stanage (ed.) *Reason and Violence: Philosophical Investigations*, Oxford: Blackwell.

Govier, T. (2002). *Forgiveness and Revenge*, London: Routledge.

Graham, H.D. and Gurr, T.R. (eds) (1969). *The History of Violence in America: Historical and Comparative Perspectives*, New York: Bantam Books.

Green, L. (1999). *Fear as a Way of Life: Mayan Widows in Rural Guatemala*, New York: Columbia University Press.

Gross, M.L. (1997). *Ethics and Activism*, Cambridge: Cambridge University Press.

Gross, M.L. (2005–2006). 'Killing Civilians Intentionally: Double Effect, Reprisal, and Necessity in the Middle East', *Political Science Quarterly*, Vol. 120, No. 4.

Grundy, K.W. and Weinstein, M.A. (1974). *The Ideologies of Violence*, Columbus, Ohio: Merrill.

Gurr, T. (ed.) (1989). *Violence in America*, 2 Vols, Newbury Park: Sage.

Gurr, T. (1993). *Minorities at Risk: A Global View of Ethnopolitical Conflicts*, Washington: United States Institute of Peace Press.

Hall, H. and Whitaker, L. (eds) (1999). *Collective Violence*, Boca Raton: CRC Press.

Hampshire, S. (1999). *Justice is Conflict*, Princeton: Princeton University Press.

Hardin, R. (1995). *One for All: The Logic of Group Conflict*, Princeton: Princeton University Press.

Harman, G. (1986). *Change in View*, Cambridge, Mass.: MIT Press.

Harris, J. (1980). *Violence and Responsibility*, London: Routledge & Kegan Paul.

Hart, H.L.A. (1961). *The Concept of Law*. Oxford: Oxford University Press.

Hart, HLA (1968). *Punishment and Responsibility*, Oxford: Oxford University Press.

Hausken, K. and Plümper, T. (1997). 'Hegemons, Leaders and Followers: A Game-theoretic Approach to the Post-war Dynamics of the International Political Economy', *Journal of World-Systems Research*, Vol. 3, No. 1, pp. 35–93.

Havel, V. (1990). *The Power of the Powerless*, (ed.) J. Keane, New York: M.E. Sharpe.

Hegel, G.W.F. (1969). *Science of Logic*. Translated by A.V. Miller. London: George Allen & Unwin, Ltd.

Held, V. (2004). 'Terrorism and War', *The Journal of Ethics*, Vol. 8, pp. 59–75.

Hester, M., Kelly, L. and Radford, J. (eds) (1996). *Women, Violence and Male Power*, Buckingham: Open University Press.

Hobbes, T. (1994). *Leviathan*, (ed.) Edwin Curley, Indianapolis: Hackett.

Holmes, R.L. (1971). 'Violence and Nonviolence', in J.A. Shaffer (ed.) *Violence*, New York: David McKay Company.

Holmes, R.L. (1973). 'The Concept of Physical Violence in Moral and Political Affairs', *Social Theory and Practice*, Vol. 2, No. 4, Fall 1973.

Holmes, R.L. (1989). *On War and Morality*, Princeton: Princeton University Press.

Holmes, S. (1993). *The Anatomy of Antiliberalism*, Cambridge, MA: Harvard University Press.

Honderich, T. (1989). *Violence for Equality*, London: Routledge.

Honderich, T. (2002). *After the Terror*, Edinburgh: Edinburgh University Press.

Honderich, T. (2003). *Terrorism for Humanity: Inquiries in Political Philosophy*, London: Pluto.

Hook, S. (1976). *Revolution, Reform and Social Justice*, Oxford: Blackwell.

Humphrey, M. (2000). 'Violence, Voice and Identity in Algeria', *Arab Studies Quarterly*, Vol. 22, No. 1.

Huysmans, J. (1997). 'Know your Schmitt. A Godfather of Truth and the Spectre of Nazism', *Review of International Studies*, Vol. 25, No. 2.

Huysmans, J. (1999). 'Know your Schmitt: A Godfather of Truth and the Spectre of Nazism', *Review of International Studies*, Vol. 25, No. 2, pp. 323–328.

Jaggar, A. (2005). 'What is Terrorism, Why is it Wrong, and Could it Ever be Morally Permissible?', *Journal of Social Philosophy*, Vol. 36, No. 2.

Jennings, J. (1985). *Georges Sorel*, Basingstoke: Macmillan.

Jonas, S. (2000). *Of Centaurs and Doves: Guatemala's Peace Process*, Boulder, Co.: Westview.

Kallen, E. (2004). *Social Inequality and Social Injustice: A Human Rights Perspective*, Basingstoke: Palgrave Macmillan.

Kamm, F.M. (1993). *Morality, Mortality*, Vol.I. Oxford: Oxford University Press.

Kant, I. (1991). *Kant: Political Writings*, (ed.) H. Reiss, Cambridge: Cambridge University Press.

Katz, J. (1999). 'Men, Masculinities, and Media: Some Introductory Notes', *Research Report, Wellesley Centers for Women*, Vol. 2, No. 2.

Keane, J. (1996). *Reflections on Violence*. London: Verso.

Kelman, H. (1973). 'Violence without Hostility: Reflections on the Dehumanization of Victims and Victimizers', *The Journal of Social Issues*, Vol. 29, No. 4.

King, P. (2003). *Fear of Power: An Analysis of Anti-Statism in Three French Writers*, London: Frank Cass.

Knobe, J. (2003). 'Intentional Action and Side Effects in Ordinary Language', *Analysis*, Vol. 63, No. 3, July 2003.

Kripke, S. (1980). *Naming and Necessity*, Oxford: Blackwell.

Kristeva, J. (2002). *Revolt, She Said*, Cambridge, MA: Semiotext(e)/MIT Press.

Ladd, J. (1991). 'The Idea of Collective Violence', in J. Brady and N. Garver (eds) *Justice, Law and Violence*, Philadelphia: Temple University Press.

Laing, R.D. (1990). *The Divided Self: an Existential Study in Sanity and Madness*. London: Penguin.

Laslett, P. (ed.) (1956). *Philosophy, Politics and Society*, Series I. Oxford: Blackwell.

Lawler, P. (1995). *A Question of Values: Johan Galtung's Peace Research*, Boulder, CO: Lynne Rienner.

Lee, S. (1996). 'Poverty and Violence', *Social Theory and Practice*, Vol. 22, No. 1.

Lee, S. (1999). 'Is Poverty Violence?', in D. Curtin and R. Litke (eds) *Institutional Violence*, Amsterdam: Rodopi.

Levi, P. (1988). *The Drowned and the Saved*, New York: Vintage.

Levy, B.S. and Sidel, V.W. (2005). 'The Nature of Social Injustice and its Impact on Public Health', in B.S.Levy and V.W.Sidel (eds) *Social Injustice and Public Health*, New York, NY: Oxford University Press.

Litke, R. (1992). 'Violence and Power', *International Social Science Journal*, Vol. 44, No. 132.

Lukes, S. (1997). 'Humiliation and the Politics of Identity', *Social Research*, Vol. 64, No. 1.

Macey, D. (2001). *Frantz Fanon: A Life*, London: Granta Books.

Macfarlane, L. (1974). *Violence and the State*, London: Nelson.

MacCallum, G. (1993). 'What is Wrong with Violence', in M. Singer and R. Martin (eds) *Legislative Intent and Other Essays in Law, Politics and Morality*, Madison, WI: Winsconsin University Press.

Mackie, G. (1996). 'Ending Footbinding and Infibulation: A Convention Account', *American Sociological Review*, Vol. 61, pp. 999–1017.

MacKinnon, Catharine (2001). *Sex Equality*, New York: Foundation Press.

Magnarella, P. (1993). 'Anthropology, Human Rights and Justice', *International Journal of Anthropology*, Vol.9, No.1.

Mandel, E. (1970). *An Introduction to Marxist Economic Theory*, New York: Pathfinder Press.

Mandela, N. (1995). *Long Walk to Freedom*, London: Abacus.

Mangan, J. (1949). 'An Historical Analysis of the Principle of Double Effect', *Theological Studies*, Vol. 10.

Manz, B. (1988). *Refugees of a Hidden War: The Aftermath of Counterinsurgency in Guatemala*, Albany, NY: State University of New York Press.

Marcuse, H. (1966). 'Ethics and Revolution', in R.T. DeGeorge (ed.) *Ethics and Society*, New York: Doubleday & Co.

Margalit, A. (1996). *The Decent Society*, Cambridge, MA: Harvard University Press.

Marquis, D. (1991). 'Four Versions of Double Effect', *The Journal of Medicine and Philosophy*, Vol. 16.

Marquis, D. (1997). 'An Argument that Abortion is Wrong', in H. LaFollette (ed.) *Ethics in Practice*, Oxford: Blackwell.

May, R. (2001). *Terror in the Countryside: Campesino Responses to Political Violence in Guatemala, 1954–1985*, Athens, OH: Ohio University Press.

McClintock, M. (1985). *The American Connection, Vol.II: State Terror and Popular Resistance in Guatemala*, London: Zed Books.

McCluskey, U. and Hooper, C. (eds.) (2000). *Psychodynamic Perspectives on Abuse: The Cost of Fear*. London: Jessica Kingsley Publishers.

McIntyre, A. (2004). 'Doing Away with Double Effect'. *Ethics* Vol. 111, No. 2.

Meili, T. (2004). *I Am the Central Park Jogger: A Story of Hope and Possibility*, New York: Simon and Schuster.

Melville, T. and Melville, M. (1971). *Guatemala: Another Vietnam?* Harmondsworth: Penguin.

Menchú, R. (1984). *I, Rigoberta Menchú, An Indian Woman in Guatemala*, London: Verso.

Mill, J.S. (1991). *On Liberty and Other Essays*, edited by John Gray, Oxford: Oxford University Press.

Miller, R. (1971). 'Violence, Force and Coercion' in Jerome A. Shaffer (ed.) *Violence*, New York: David McKay Company.

Minow, M. (2003). *Breaking the Cycle of Hatred: Memory, Law, and Repair*, Nancy L.Rosenblum (ed.), Princeton: Princeton University Press.

Moore, B. (1962). *Political Power and Social Theory: Seven Studies*, New York: Harper & Row.

Morriss, P. (1987). *Power: A Philosophical Analysis*. Manchester: Manchester University Press.

Mueller, J. and Mueller, K. (1999). 'Sanctions of Mass Destruction', *Foreign Affairs*, Vol. 78, No. 3, May/June.

Mullen, P.E., *et al.* (1996). 'The Long-term Impact of the Physical, Emotional, and Sexual Abuse of Children: A Community Study', *Child Abuse & Neglect*, Vol. 20, No. 1.

Murphy, J. (ed) (1971). *Civil Disobedience and Violence*, Belmont, CA: Wadsworth.

Murphy, J. (1995). 'Getting Even: The Role of the Victim', in J. Murphy (ed.) *Punishment and Rehabilitation*, Belmont, CA: Wadsworth.

Murphy, R. (1985). 'Exploitation or Exclusion?', *Sociology*, Vol. 19, No. 2.

Nagel, T. (1979). *Mortal Questions*, Cambridge: Cambridge University Press.

Nagel, T. (1986). *The View from Nowhere*, Oxford: Oxford University Press.

Nagel, T. (1997). *The Last Word*, Oxford: Oxford University Press.

Nelson, D.M. (1999). *A Finger in the Wound: Body Politics in Quincentennial Guatemala*, Berkeley, CA: University of California Press.

Nickel, J. (2007). *Making Sense of Human Rights*, Oxford: Blackwell.

Nieburg, N.L. (1969). *Political Violence: The Behavioral Process*. New York: St. Martin Press.

Nielsen, K. (1976–1997). 'On Justifying Revolution', *Philosophy and Phenomenological Research*, Vol. 37.

Nielsen, K. (1981). 'On Justifying Violence', *Inquiry*, Vol. 24.

Nietzsche, F. (1977). *A Nietzsche Reader*, Harmondsworth: Penguin.

North, L. and Simmons, A. (eds) (1999). *Journeys of Fear: Refugee Return and National Transformation in Guatemala*. Montreal and Ithaca: McGill-Queen's University Press.

Nozick, R. (1969). 'Coercion', in S. Morgenbesser, P. Suppes, and M. White (eds) *Philosophy, Science and Method*, New York: St. Martin's Press. Reprinted in R. Nozick, (1997), *Socratic Puzzles*, Cambridge, Mass.: Harvard University Press.

Nozick, R. (1974). *Anarchy, State, and Utopia*, Oxford: Blackwell.

Oliner, S.P. and Oliner, P.M. (1988). *The Altruistic Personality*, New York: The Free Press.

O'Leary, F.A. (2002). 'The Kurds of Iraq: Recent History, Future Prospects', *Middle East Review of International Affairs*, Vol. 6, No. 4.

Perry, C. (1970). 'Violence – Visible and Invisible', *Ethics*, Vol. 81, No. 1.

Peteet, J. (2002). 'Male Gender and Rituals of Resistance in the Palestinian *Intifada*: A Cultural Politics of Violence', in C. Besteman (ed.), *Violence: A Reader,* Basingstoke: Palgrave Macmillan.

Platt, T. (1992). 'The Concept of Violence as Descriptive and Polemical', *International Social Science Journal*, Vol. 44, No. 2.

Pogge, T. (1991). 'Coercion and Violence', in J. Brady and N. Garver (eds) *Justice, Law and Violence*, Philadelphia: Temple University Press.

Pogge, T. (2002). *World Poverty and Human Rights*. Cambridge: Polity.

Presby, G. (1996). 'Fanon on the Role of Violence in Liberation: A Comparison to Gandhi and Mandela', in L.R. Gordon, T.D. Sharpley-Whiting, and R.T.White (eds), *Fanon: A Critical Reader*, Oxford: Blackwell.

Quinn, W.S. (1989). 'Actions, Intentions and Consequences: The Doctrine of Doing and Allowing', *The Philosophical Review*, Vol. 98, No. 3.

Quinton, A. (1997). 'Humiliation', *Social Research*, Vol. 64, No. 1.

Rawls, J. (1969). 'The Justification of Civil Disobedience', in H.A.Bedau (ed.) *Civil Disobedience: Theory and Practice*, New York, NY: Macmillan.

Rawls, J. (1971). *A Theory of Justice*, Cambridge, MA: Harvard University Press.

Rawls, J. (1995). 'Reflections on Hiroshima: Fifty Years After Hiroshima', *Dissent*, Summer 1995.

Reeve, A. (ed.) (1987). *Modern Theories of Exploitation*, London: Sage.

REHMI (1999), *Guatemala: Never Again!*, Recovery of Historical Memory Project, Maryknoll, NY: Orbis Books.

Reiman, J. (1987). 'Exploitation, Force, and the Moral Assessment of Capitalism: Thoughts on Roemer and Cohen', *Philosophy and Public Affairs*, Vol. 16.

Reiman, J. (2004). *The Rich Get Richer and the Poor Get Prison*, Boston: Pearson.

Riga, P.D. (1969). 'Violence: A Christian Perspective', *Philosophy East and West*, Vol. 19.

Roemer, J. (1982). *A General Theory of Exploitation and Class*, Cambridge, Mass.: Harvard University Press.

Roemer, J. (1988). *Free to Lose: An Introduction to Marxist Economic Philosophy*, London: Radius.

Roemer, J. (1994). *Egalitarian Perspectives: Essays in Philosophical Economics*. Cambridge: Cambridge University Press.

Roth, J.J. (1980). *The Cult of Violence: Sorel and the Sorelians*, Berkeley, CA: University of California Press.

Roth, P. (2001). *The Human Stain*, New York: Vintage.

Runkle, G. (1976). 'Is Violence Always Wrong?', *The Journal of Politics*, Vol. 38, No. 2.

Salmi, J. (1993). *Violence and Democratic Society*, London: Zed Books.

Sanford, V. (2003). *Buried Secrets: Truth and Human Rights in Guatemala*, Basingstoke: Palgrave Macmillan.

Sartori, G. (1973). 'What is "Politics" ', *Political Theory*, Vol. 1, No. 1.

Sartori, G. (1989). 'The Essence of the Political in Carl Schmitt', *Journal of Theoretical Politics*, Vol. 1, No. 1, pp. 53–75.

Sartre, J.P. (2004). 'Preface to Frantz Fanon's Wretched of the Earth', in N. Scheper-Hughes and S.P. Bourgois, S.P. (eds) *Violence in War and Peace: An Anthology*, Oxford: Blackwell.

Scanlon, T. (1998). *What We Owe to Each Other*. Cambridge, Mass.: Harvard University Press.

Scheper-Hughes, N. and Bourgois, S.P. (eds) (2004a). *Violence in War and Peace: An Anthology*, Oxford: Blackwell.

Scheper-Hughes, N. and Bourgois, S.P. (2004b). 'Introduction: Making Sense of Violence', in N. Scheper-Hughes and S.P. Bourgois, S.P. (eds) *Violence in War and Peace: An Anthology*, Oxford: Blackwell.

Schick, F. (1997). 'On Humiliation', *Social Research*, Vol. 64, No. 1.

Schirmer, J. (2003). 'Whose Testimony? Whose Truth?', *Human Rights Quarterly*, Vol. 25.

Schmitt, C. (1996a). *The Concept of the Political*, Chicago: Chicago University Press.

Schmitt, C. (1996b). *The Leviathan in the State Theory of Thomas Hobbes*, London: Greenwood Press..

Schulhofer, S.J. (1998). *Unwanted Sex: The Culture of Intimidation and the Failure of Law*, Cambridge, Mass.: Harvard University Press.

Schumpeter, J.A. (1954). *Capitalism, Socialism and Democracy*, London: George Allen & Unwin.

Sen, A. (1982). *Choice, Welfare and Measurement*, Oxford: Blackwell.

Sexton, J.D. (1985). *Campesino: The Diary of a Guatemalan Indian*, Tucson, Arizona: University of Arizona Press.

Shapiro, I. (1999). *Democratic Justice*, New Haven, CT.: Yale University Press.

Shklar, H. (1990). *The Faces of Injustice*, New Haven, CT: Yale University Press.

Silverstein, H. (1980). 'The Evil of Death', *The Journal of Philosophy*, Vol. 77.

Simon, T. (1995). *Democracy and Social Injustice: Law, Politics, and Philosophy.* Lanham, MD: Rowman & Littlefield.

Simpson, E. (1970). 'Social Norms and Aberrations: Violence and Some Related Social Facts', *Ethics*, Vol. 81, No. 1.

Singer, P. (1972). 'Famine, Affluence and Morality', *Philosophy & Public Affairs*, Vol. 1, No. 3. Reprinted in P. Singer *Writings on an Ethical Life*, London: Fourth Estate, 2000.

Sinnott-Armstrong, W. (1987). 'Moral Realisms and Moral Dilemmas', *The Journal of Philosophy*, Vol.84, No.5.

Skillan, A. (1977). *Ruling Illusions: Philosophy and the Social Order*, Hassocks: Harvester.

Smith, A. (2002). *The Theory of Moral Sentiments.* (ed.) Knud Haakonssen, Cambridge: Cambridge University Press.

Solomon, R. (1990). *A Passion for Justice: Emotions and the Origins of the Social Contract.* New York: Addison-Wesley.

Sorel, G. (1961). *Reflections on Violence*, New York: Huebsch.

Spence, J. and Ching, A. (1996). *The Chinese Century: A Photographic History of the Last Hundred Years*, New York: Random House.

Stallybrass, P. and White, A. (1987). *The Politics and Poetics of Transgression.* Ithaca, NY: Cornell University Press.

Stanko, E. (2003). *The Meanings of Violence*, London: Routledge.

Starr, B. (2006). 'Can There e Moral Justification for State Violence? The Case of America', in F. O'Marchadha (ed.) *Violence, Victims, Justifications*, Bern: Peter Lang.

Steger, M. (2003). *Judging Nonviolence: The Dispute Between Realists and Idealists*, London: Routledge.

Steger, M. and Lind, N. (eds) (1999). *Violence and Its Alternatives: An Interdisciplinary Reader*, New York: St. Martin's Press.

Steiner, H. (1984). 'A Liberal Theory of Exploitation', *Ethics*, Vol. 94, No. 2.

Steiner, H. (1987). 'Exploitation. A Liberal Theory Amended, Defended and Extended', in A. Reeve (ed.) *Modern Theories of Exploitation*, London: Sage.

Steiner, H. (1994). *An Essay on Rights*, Oxford: Blackwell.

Steiner, H. and Vallentyne, P. (eds) (2001). *Left-Libertarianism and Its Critics*, Basingstoke: Palgrave Macmillan.

Stevenson, C. (1944). *Ethics and Language.* New Haven, CT.: Yale University Press.

Stewart, P.J. and Strathern, A. (2002). *Violence: Theory and Ethnography*, London: Continuum.

Strauss, L. (1952). *The Political Philosophy of Hobbes*, Chicago: University of Chicago Press.

Strauss, L. (1953). *Natural Rights and History*, Chicago, IL: Chicago University Press.

Strauss, L. (1996). 'Notes on Carl Schmitt, The Concept of the Political', reprinted in C. Schmitt, *The Concept of the Political*, Chicago: University of Chicago Press.

Strong, T. (1996). 'Foreword: Dimensions of the New Debate Around Carl Schmitt', in C. Schmitt, *The Concept of the Political*, Chicago: University of Chicago Press.

Summers, C. and Markusen, E. (eds) (1999). *Collective Violence*. Lanham, MD.: Rowan and Littlefield.

Taylor, L. (1984). *Born to Crime: The Genetic Causes of Criminal Behaviour*. Greenwood Press.

Tilly, C. (2003). *The Politics of Collective Violence*, Cambridge: Cambridge University Press.

Tronto, J. (2004). 'Frantz Fanon', *Contemporary Political Theory*, Vol. 3, No. 3.

Tumin, M. (1952). *Caste in a Peasant Society*, Princeton: Princeton University Press.

Turpin, J. and Kurtz, L. (eds) (1997). *The Web of Violence: From Interpersonal to Global*, Urbana, Ill.: University of Illinois Press.

Van den Anker, C. (ed.) (2004). *The Political Economy of New Slavery*. Basingstoke: Palgrave Macmillan.

Van den Haag, E. (1972). *Political Violence and Civil Disobedience*, New York: Harper & Row.

Varese, F. (2001). *The Russian Mafia: Private Protection in a New Market Economy*, Oxford: Oxford University Press.

Varese, F. and Yaish, M. (2000). 'The Importance of Being Asked: The Rescue of Jews in Nazi Europe', *Rationality and Society*, Vol. 12 No. 3.

Varese, F. and Yaish, M. (2005). 'Resolute Heroes: The Rescue of Jews During the Nazi Occupation of France', *Archives Européennes de Sociologie*, Vol.XLVI, No.1.

Veatch, R. (1978). 'Defining Death Anew: Technical and Ethical Problems' in T.L. Beauchamp and S. Perlin (eds) *Ethical Issues in Death and Dying*, Englewood Cliffs, NJ: Prentice-Hall.

Vincent, J. and Jouriles, E. (eds) (2000). *Domestic Violence: Guidelines for Research-Informed Practice*, London: Jessica Kingsley Publishers.

Wade, F.C. (1971). 'Comments and Criticism on "On Violence" '. *Journal of Philosophy*, Vol. 68

Waldenfels, B. (2006). 'Violence as Violation' in F. O'Murchadha (ed.) *Violence, Victims, Justifications*, Bern: Peter Lang.

Walzer, M. (1970). *Obligations: Essays on Disobedience, War, and Citizenship*, Cambridge, MA.: Harvard University Press.

Walzer, M. (1977). *Just and Unjust Wars*. New York: Basic Books.

Walzer, M. (1988). 'Terrorism; A Critique of Excuses', in S. Luper-Foy (ed.), *Problems of International Justice*, Boulder, CO.: Westview Press.

Walzer, M. (2002). 'Five Questions About Terrorism'. *Dissent*, Vol. 49, No. 1.

Warren, K.B. (1978). *The Symbolism of Subordination: Indian Identity in a Guatemalan Town*. Austin, TX: University of Texas Press.

Wasserman, D. and Wachbroit, R. (eds) (2001). *Genetics and Criminal Behaviour*, Cambridge: Cambridge University Press.

Weber, M. (1978). *Economy and Society*, Vol. 1 and 2, (ed.) G. Roth and C. ittich, Berkeley: University of California Press.

Weber, M. (1970). 'Politics as a Vocation', in H.H. Gerth and C.W. Mills (eds), *From Max Weber*, London: Routledge.

Weinberg, L. and Rapoport, D. (eds) (2001). *The Democratic Experience and Political Violence*, London: Frank Cass.

Wells, D.A. (1970). 'Is "Just Violence" Like "Just War"?', *Social Theory and Practice*, Vol. 1, No. 1, Spring 1970.

Welsh, B. (2002). 'Globalization, Weak States, and the Death Toll in East Asia', in K. Worcester, S.A. Bermanzohn, M. Ungar (eds) *Violence and Politics: Globalization's Paradox*, London: Routledge.

Wertheimer, A. (1987). *Coercion*, Princeton, New Jersey: Princeton University Press.

Williams, S. (1981). *Moral Luck*. Cambridge: Cambridge University Press.

Wolff, R.P. (1969). 'On Violence', *The Journal of Philosophy*, Vol. 66, No. 19, 1969.

Wolin, S. (1963). 'Violence and the Western Political Tradition', *American Journal of Orthopsychiatry*, Vol. 33.

Wood, A.W. (1995). 'Exploitation', *Social Philosophy and Policy*, Vol. 12.

Worcester, K., Bermanzohn, S.A., and Ungar, M. (eds) (2002). *Violence and Politics: Globalization's Paradox*, London: Routledge.

Young, I.M. (1990). *Justice and the Politics of Difference*. Princeton, NJ: Princeton University Press.

Zinn, H. (1968). *Disobedience and Democracy: Nine Fallacies on Law and Order*, New York: Random House.

Zinn, H. (ed.) (2002). *The Power of Nonviolence: Writings by Advocates of Peace*, Boston, MA.: Beacon Press.

Zur, J. (1998). *Violent Memories: Mayan War Widows in Guatemala*, Boulder, CO: Westview Press.

Index

accident, 66–7, 70, 73, 76, 79–81
act and omission doctrine, 54, 55
  see also, Foot, P.
Afghanistan, 78
aggression, 16
aid to poor countries, 105–7
Allen, B., 108
allowing, 51, 53, 73
alternativity, 55–9
Ambrose, S., 86
Anderson, E., 143
Ángel, M., 162
Anscombe, G.E.M., 68
Apter, D., 26
Aquinas, Thomas St., 68
Archard, D., 27, 127
Arendt, Hannah, 4, 15, 21, 26
arms trade, 98, 101–2
Arrigo, J.M., 108, 176, 186
Audi, Robert, 21, 22, 24–5, 27, 39,
    46, 71, 87, 137, 144, 167, 173–5
autonomy, 133
Ayer, A.J., 32

Bäck, A., 16, 86
Bales, K., 162
Bar On, B., 26, 28
Barry, Brian, 9, 10, 15–16, 32, 46, 47,
    128, 162
Bates, R., 198
BDSM, 20, 27, 127
Beccaria, C., 177
Bedau, Hugo Adam, 4
Beevor, A., 178
Bermanzohn, S.A., 26, 198
Besteman, C., 10, 26
Betz, Joseph, 23, 47
bilateral omissions, 51, 52, 53
Black, G., 163
Bobbio, N., 197

bomber
  strategic, 77, 80
  terror, 77, 80
Bourgois, S.P., 26, 124, 162
Brady, J., 198
Bratman, M., 72, 74, 86
Breines, W., 28, 108
Brison, S., 34, 35, 42–3, 47, 108, 127
Buchanan, A.E., 47
Bufacchi, V., 46, 108, 186
bystanders, 61–3, 95, 98

Cage, J., 64
Carroll, S.J., 108
Cassese, A., 186
Catholic Church
  ethics, 68
  sex scandals, 104–5
  Vatican, 105
Chang, I., 86
China, 35–6
Ching, A., 47
choice, 61
civil disobedience, 4, 99, 108, 128,
    166, 182
Climbie, Anna, 92–3
Coady, C.A.J., 18, 27, 28, 86
coercion, 17–18
Coleman, J.L., 47
colonization, 169–72
Comprehensive Conception of
    Violence (CCV), 6, 24–6, 28,
    38–9, 44, 45, 74
consent, 36–7
Consequentialist Argument, 9,
    173–8, 180
  critique, 175–8
  defined, 173
Crenshaw, M., 179
criminal behaviour, 137

culture, 30, 31, 36, 37, 38
Curtin, D., 28
cycle of violence, 177, 180, 186

Dahl, Robert, 96, 108
Daniels, C., 28
Davidson, D., 69, 86
death, 8
    asymmetry problem, 114, 116
    badness of, 110, 113–14, 123–4,
        125, 126
    equivocation problem, 116
    as extrinsic evil, 114–15
    as intrinsic evil, 114–15
    wrongness, 124
death penalty, 32
dehumanization, 120–1, 171
Deprivation Factor, 113–16, 126
Dewey, John, 19
dialectic of negation, 173
Doctrine of Double Effect (DDE), 68,
    77, 80, 86
domestic violence, 24, 27
Dowding, K., 26
drink-driving, 94, 108
duties
    negative and positive, 53–4, 65
    towards justice, 165–7
Dworkin, A., 36
dying, 126

economic justice, 141–2
economic sanctions, 98, 100, 108,
    109
Elster, J., 156, 162
Equivalence Thesis, 53, 55–9, 65
essence
    and the commonwealth, 191
    defined, 188
    of politics, 188–97
ethical relativism, 29–33
euthanasia, 126, 127
evil, 155, 185
exploitation, 8–9, 80, 81, 135, 144,
    145–61
    circumstances, 148, 153–4

compared to 'use', 147
defined, 146–7
economic motives, 155–61
humiliating motives, 155–61
Marxist analysis, 148–50
motivations, 153–8
as structural violence, 150–2
wrongness, 148, 153, 154, 161
see also transcontinental railroad
Extinction Factor, 114, 117, 124

Fairchild, H., 185
Fairrie, L., 46
Fanon, F., 169–72, 185
Fearon, J., 26, 186
Feinberg, J., 47
Feldman, F., 113
Fischer, J., 64
Fluehr-Lobban, C., 31
Foot, P., 52, 53–4, 55, 59, 64
footbinding, 18, 35–6, 38
foreseeability, 55–9, 67, 71–86,
    93–6
Foucault, M., 47
Frankfurt, H., 41
Frappat, H., 28
free-will, 69
French, S.G., 28
Freund, J., 193
friendly fire, 78, 80, 81, 82, 87, 98
Fullinwider, R., 108, 109, 183

Galtung, Johan, 22, 24–5, 28, 45, 73,
    83–5, 133–5, 144, 150–1, 152,
    162
Gambetta, D., 10, 127
Gandhi, M., 126, 165
Garrard, E., 185
Garver, Newton, 21–2, 27, 28, 41,
    47, 133–5, 144, 198
genetics, 137
Genocide Convention, 68, 86
Genovese, Kitty, 94–5, 108
Geras, Norman, 10, 23, 27, 49, 65,
    138, 167, 175, 179, 181, 185
Gert, Bernard, 19, 58, 65, 163, 165,
    173–5, 176

Gibbard, A., 86
Giddens, A., 163
global health fund, 98
Glover, J., 48, 54, 56, 59, 65, 86, 112, 126, 144, 185, 188, 198
Gómez, C., 162
Goodin, R., 162
Gordon, J., 86, 108, 109
Gordon, L., 28, 108
Gotesky, R., 27
Govier, 185
Graham, H.D., 27, 69
Green, L., 28
Gross, M., 65, 77
Grundy, K.W., 27, 28
Guatemala, 31, 35, 102–3, 119–21, 126, 146, 151–2, 158–61, 162, 163, 186
Gurr, T., 26, 27, 69

Halliday, Denis, 101
Hampshire, Stuart, 10
Harman, G., 74, 77
Harris, John, 13, 51, 55, 56, 59, 73, 138
Hart, H.L.A., 46, 75, 77, 86
Hausken, K., 199
Havel, V., 186
Hegel, G.W.F., 156, 188, 198
Held, V., 186
Herman, J., 47
Hester, M., 127
Hitler, A., 167, 178
Hobbes, Thomas, 190–1, 194–5, 198
Hoffman, B., 186
Holmes, Robert, 6, 27, 46
Holmes, S., 199
Honderich, Ted, 14, 49, 50, 55, 56, 59, 84–5, 87, 97–8, 108, 180, 183, 186
Hook, S., 186
Hooper, C., 127
humiliation, 153, 155–6, 160, 163, 170, 171
    ascriptive humiliation, 132
    see also exploitation, humiliating motives; Humiliation Factor

Humiliation Factor, 8, 118–26, 131–2, 139–41, 144, 145–6, 148
Humphrey, M., 185
hunger, 134
Huysmans, J., 199

identity, 156–8, 161, 170, 171, 193
Identity Argument, 9, 168–73, 185
    critique of, 172–3
    defined, 169
impartial standpoint, 38, 58
income inequality, 5
inequality, 84, 119, 140, 148–9, 151–2
injustice, 2–5, 8, 128–44, 136, 145–6, 165–7, 185
    as violence, 133–8, 145
    wrongness, 139–44, 145
institutional violence, 133–5
Insult Factors, 114, 117, 123, 125
integrity, 6, 29–30, 40–7, 89, 90–1, 118, 123, 124–5, 153, 158
    amoral concept, 41, 42, 46
    moral concept, 40–1, 46
    violence as violation of integrity, defined, 43–4, 131, 132, 140
intention-oriented (I-O) approach, 66–71, 79–81, 82, 84, 85
Iraq, 78, 87, 100–1, 102, 108, 109
Irish Nationalists, 75, 77, 86
Islamic fundamentalism, 170
Israel, 168

Jaggar, A., 183, 186
Jennings, J., 28
Jonas, S., 103
Jouriles, E., 127
Just War Doctrine, 68, 181–2

Kallen, E., 144
Kamm, F.M., 111, 112, 114, 117–18, 122–3, 125
Kantian ethics, 67
Katz, J., 185
Keane, John, 19, 25, 27, 49, 83, 172, 188–9

Kelly, L., 127
King, Martin Luther, 165
King, P., 28
Knobe, J., 87
Kosovo, 78
Kripke, S., 188
Kristeva, J., 169, 171, 173, 185, 186
kurds, 102
Kurtz, L., 26

Ladd, J., 27
Laing, R.D., 46
Laitin, D., 26, 186
Laslett, P., 32
Lawler, P., 28
Lee, S., 28, 135, 136
Levi, P., 34, 47, 125, 127
Levy, B.S., 130
Lind, N., 185
Litke, R., 28, 141
logical positivism, 32
Lukes, S., 132, 144

MacCallum, G., 42, 140, 144
McClintock, M., 162
McCluskey, U., 127
Macey, D., 170
MacFarlane, L., 198
MacIntyre, A., 86
Mackie, G., 47
MacKinnon, C., 45
mafia, 5
Magnarella, P., 31
Mandel, E., 148, 151, 153, 154
Mandela, N., 183, 184
Mangan, J., 68
Manz, B., 163
Marcuse, H., 182
Margalit, A., 119, 131–2, 140, 144
Marquis, D., 86, 126
Marx, Karl, 17
masculinity, 168, 185
master–slave dialectic, 156–7
May, R., 186
Meili, T., 92
Melville, M., 162

Melville, T., 162
Menchú, R., 159–60
Mengele, Josef, 66
Mill, John Stuart, 50, 130
Miller, R., 17, 27, 70
Minimalist Conception of Violence
    (MCV), 6, 23–6, 27, 38–9, 44,
    45, 74
Minow, M., 177
Moore, B., 175
moral absolutism, 59–61
moral analysis, 5–6
moral dilemma, 60
moral gradualism, 61
Morriss, P., 27
Mueller, J., 100
Mueller, K., 100
Mullen, P.E., 127
Murphy, J., 108, 185
Murphy, R., 163

Nagel, T., 38, 46, 111, 113–14, 126
negative action, 51, 52
negative causation, 51, 52
neglect, 49
Nelson, D.M., 163
Nickel, J., 144
Nieburg, N.L., 27
Nielsen, K., 10, 173–5, 180, 182, 183
Nietzsche, F., 110, 126, 169
non-violence, 165, 167
North, L., 28
Nozick, Robert, 22, 27, 136

O'Leary, F.A., 109
Oliner, M., 65
Oliner, S.P., 65
omitted action, 50, 52
omitting action, 50, 52
Oxfam, 56–9, 105

pain, 38
Palestine, 168, 185
Perry, C., 135
Peteet, J., 168, 185
Platt, T., 27, 28, 137
Plümper, T., 199

Pogge, T., 65, 69
political violence, 96–108, 183
politics, 96
  violence as essence of, 187–9
poverty, 134–5, 150, 152
power, 15–16, 96–7, 123, 124,
    125–6, 130, 132, 134, 139–41,
    146, 156, 157, 170
powerlessness, 2–3, 8, 117–18, 123,
    125, 139–41, 142, 143, 146, 153
Presby, G., 185
Principle of Gradual Progression,
    182–5
Principle of Last Resort, 181
Principle of Proportionality, 180–1
Principle of Reasonable Success, 180,
    183
Principle of Self-Defence, 179–80
Psychological Damage Factor, 116,
    117, 118, 125
public reason, 165
Purdy, L.M., 28

Quinn, W., 64
Quinton, A., 144

race riots, 133
Radford, J., 127
rape, 20, 32, 45, 91–2, 98, 104–5,
    108, 112, 116, 119–21, 122, 125
  during wartime, 92, 108, 119
Rapoport, D., 198
Ravizza, M., 64
Rawls, John, 2, 4, 46, 121, 126,
    128–9, 130, 136, 140, 142–3,
    144, 165–6
Reiman, J., 81, 162
rescue of Jews, 61–3, 65
Restriction of Freedom Factor,
    115–16, 118, 125
revolt, 167, 171, 172, 173, 174–5,
    182, 186
revolutions, *see* revolt
Riches, D., 47
Riga, P.D., 26
rights, 31, 130–1, 133–5, 136, 143,
    149, 153, 177, 179

Roemer, J., 148–50, 151, 153, 154–5,
    162
Roth, J.J., 28
Roth, P., 141
Runkle, G., 107
Rwanda, 48, 49, 188

Salmi, Jamil, 22, 45, 47, 84–5, 134
Sanford, V., 31
Sartori, G., 195, 196–7
Sartre, J.P., 156, 169–73
Scanlon, T., 61, 86
Scheper-Hughes, N., 26, 124
Schick, F., 144
Schirmer, J., 35
Schmitt, C., 190–7, 198, 199
school shootings, 27
Schulhofer, S.J., 20
Schumpeter, J., 197
self-esteem, 121–2, 125, 131–2, 140,
    153, 170
self-respect, *see* self-esteem
self-violence, 46
Sen, A., 27
Sexton, J.D., 163
sexual violence, *see* rape
Shapiro, I., 130
Shklar, Judith, 2, 139, 144
Sidel, V.W., 130
Sidgwick, H., 180
Silverstein, H., 126
Simmons, A., 28
Simon, T., 138
Simpson, E., 36
Singer, P., 89, 90
Sinnott-Armstrong, W., 60–1
smart bombs, 78, 80, 81, 82, 87, 98
Smith, A., 37
Solomon, R., 185
Sorel, Georges, 25–6, 28, 97–8
South Africa, 97
Spence, J., 47
Stallybrass, P., 156–7, 160
Stanko, E., 26, 32
Starr, Bill, 23
state, 192, 194, 195, 197

Steger, M., 14, 27, 69, 185, 198
Steiner, H., 127, 130, 149–50, 151,
    153, 154–5, 162
Stern report, 9–10
Stevenson, C., 32
Stewart, P.J., 30, 47
Strathern, A., 30, 47
Strauss, L., 198
Strong, T., 199
structural violence, 2, 20, 24–5, 35,
    73, 83–4, 134–5, 136, 147,
    150–2, 161, 162
subjectivism, *see* ethical relativism
suffragettes, 4, 10, 182

Taylor, L., 144
Teays, W., 28
terrorism, 98–9, 107, 109, 182–4
Tolstoy, L., 165
torture, 32, 98, 99–100, 108, 112,
    176, 178
    Convention Against Torture, 100
    ticking-bomb scenario, 100, 108,
        176
transcontinental railroad, 76, 79, 82,
    87, 151
trilateral omissions, 51, 52, 53
Tronto, J., 170, 185
Trotsky, L., 192
Tumin, M., 158–9, 163
Turpin, J., 26

Ungar, M., 26, 198
United Nations, 179
United States of America, 5, 10, 76,
    78, 81, 97, 99, 102, 103, 106,
    142, 151
utilitarianism, 174–5

Vallentyne, P., 162
Van den Haag, E., 26
Varese, Federico, 10, 62, 65
Veatch, R., 112
victim, 2, 25, 27, 31, 34, 35, 67, 79,
    82, 83, 85, 120–1, 124–5,
    138–41, 142, 145, 167, 177, 189

victim-oriented (V-O) approach, 67,
    80–6
Vietnam, 128
Vincent, J., 127
violence
    badness, 115–26, 131–2,
        141, 168
    bilateral relationship, 29, 33–4
    cultural violence, 150–1
    and death, 111–14
    defined, 6, 90–1
    as essence of politics, 9
    essentially contested, 29
    as excessive force, 18–21
    Fundamental Principle, 178–9,
        180, 181, 184
    goodness, 168–9
    Intention-Oriented (I-O)
        approach, 7
    justifications, 164–85, *see also*
        Consequentialist Argument;
        Identity Argument
    justified, 9
    and the law, 189, 198
    memories of, 125
    as necessary evil, 173
    by omission, 7
    prima facie wrong, 6, 82, 107, 110,
        124, 131–2,
        140, 145, 181
    romanticized, 172
    social dynamics, 33–8
    social meaning, 113
    syntax, 13
    transformative, 81–2, 85
    trilateral relationship, 29, 34,
        38, 67
    universal concept, 11, 29
    Victim-Oriented (V-O)
        approach, 7
    as violation of integrity, *see*
        integrity
    as violation of rights, 21–3, 64,
        130, 131, 132
    wrong by definition, 6, 107
    wrongness, 122–6, 141, 145

violent, 13–14
vulnerability, 2–3, 117–18, 119,
        123,124–5, 139–41, 142, 143,
        146, 153

Wachbroit, R., 144
Wade, F.C., 26
Waldenfels, B., 27, 42, 47
Walzer, Michael, 4, 68, 99, 101, 109,
        180, 181, 183, 186
war on terror, 178
Warren, K.B., 162
Wasserman, D., 144
Weber, M., 15, 26, 97, 108, 123,
        190–2, 194–5
Weinberg, L., 198
Weinstein, M.A., 27, 28
Wertheimer, A., 17

White, A., 156–7, 160
Williams, B., 41
Wolff, Robert, 21, 27
Wolin, S., 26, 198
Wood, A.W., 153, 162
Worcester, K., 26, 198

Yaish, M., 62, 65
Young, Iris Marion, 10, 143, 163

Zerilli, M.G., 108
Zinn, Howard, 4, 185
Zur, J., 28

9/11/2001, 66–7, 69, 80, 183, 184,
        186
11/12/2002, 67, 69, 80